Living Stones

*The History and Structure
of Catholic Spiritual Life
in the United States*

Second Edition

Joseph P. Chinnici, O.F.M.

ORBIS BOOKS

Maryknoll, New York 10545

The Catholic Foreign Mission Society of America (Maryknoll) recruits and trains people for overseas missionary service. Through Orbis Books, Maryknoll aims to foster the international dialogue that is essential to mission. The books published, however, reflect the opinions of their authors and are not meant to represent the official position of the society.

ORBIS/ISBN 0-57075-092-0

Come to Him, a living stone, rejected by men but
approved nonetheless, and precious in God's eyes.
You too are living stones, built as an edifice of
the Spirit, into a holy priesthood, offering spiritual
sacrifices, acceptable to God through Jesus
Christ.

1 Peter 2:4–5

Contents

Foreword
Christopher J. Kauffman   ix

Preface to the Second Edition   xi

Part I   An Enlightenment Synthesis, 1776-1815   1

    Chapter 1   Religious Pluralism: The Social
               Foundations of Christian Piety   5

    Chapter 2   Nature and Grace: The Personal
               Foundations of Christian Piety   12

    Chapter 3   "Spiritual Matters": The
               Ecclesiological Dimensions of
               Christian Piety   20

    Chapter 4   The Sentiments and Affections of Jesus
               Christ   26

Part II   The Immigrant Vision, 1830–1866   35

    Chapter 5   Christ, the Person, and the Church   37

    Chapter 6   The Triumph of the Purgative Way   52

    Chapter 7   The Immigrant Vision: The Golden
               Chain Binding Heaven and Earth   68

Part III   The Spirituality of Americanism, 1866–1900   **87**

    Chapter 8   Conversion and the Mission of America   91

    Chapter 9   Piety, Asceticism, and Prayer   100

    Chapter 10   The Mystery of the Incarnation   113

    Chapter 11   The Crisis of Americanism and the
                    Structures of Catholic Spiritual Life   119

Part IV   A Fractured Inheritance, 1900–1930   **135**

    Chapter 12   Spirituality and Social Reform   137

    Chapter 13   The Eucharist, Symbol of the Church   146

    Chapter 14   The Cenacle, Soul of Catholic Action   157

Part V   Seedbed of Reform, 1930–1965   **173**

    Chapter 15   Virgil Michel: The Priesthood of the
                    Faithful   177

    Chapter 16   Dorothy Day: The Heroic Ideal   186

    Chapter 17   James Keller: To Light One Candle   194

    Chapter 18   Thomas Merton: Contemplation for All   205

Epilogue   *211*

Notes   *214*

Index   *251*

Foreword

The spiritual life has been portrayed as a journey from ordinary prayer to an intense awareness of Divine Presence. Such an ahistorical treatment presupposes the universality of the human condition and refers to the spiritual life as the pursuit of perfection. Another traditional approach is to focus upon the particular paths of spirituality, such as the Augustinian, Franciscan, Dominican, Ignatian, or those of such periods as the late medieval, the Counter Reformation, or the French baroque. Until recently the study of American spirituality has followed the direction of these European models.

Joseph P. Chinnici, O.F.M., is the first to relate the particular structures of American religious conditions to the distinctive manifestations of Catholic spirituality. Rather than perceive the life of the spirit in terms of the path to perfection, or according to particular schools, Chinnici examines the conditions of separation of church and state, religious liberty, denominational pluralism, nativism, and anti-Catholicism as the bases for the understanding of the salient patterns of spirituality within the context of the American Catholic experience.

As a post–Vatican II historian who has consciously incorporated the recent trends in historiography and the new models of ecclesiology, Chinnici has ground a historical lens through which he views the relationships between anthropology, spirituality, and apologetics. As he implies in his introduction, the profound cultural shift of the late 1950s and 1960s has provided him with the distance with which to sharpen his perspective. The result is an extraordinary vision of the development of American Catholic spiritualities.

Chinnici focuses upon the qualities of the Enlightenment and shows how these were infused into Bishop John Carroll's positive anthropology. Hence the latter's sermons, writings, and exhortations manifested a spirituality in which nature and grace were not locked in the struggles of the traditional world but were tending toward a harmonious convergence. The shift to a negative anthropology that stresses the near irreconcilability of nature and grace was characteristic of an immigrant church besieged by the hostile forces of nativism and anti-Catholicism. Thus the medieval notion of the church as a perfect society provided security to the immigrants. At the same time there was the need for the Americanization of the immigrant community; this negative anthropology led to a separation of faith and culture.

In each period the cultural mix shapes not only the articulations of the prayer life of the people and the ecclesiological models but also the ways in which church leaders articulate religious belief. There is, therefore, a particular apologetic suited to the conditions of a specific historical period. In short, the edifice of the Spirit constructed from the living stones has assumed a variety of architectural designs according to the interactions between religion and culture; there are many historical edifices, just as there are many mansions in the kingdom.

This book is a unique rendering of these edifices of the Spirit on the shifting cultural landscape of America.

Christopher J. Kauffman

Preface
to the Second Edition

Although this book was first published only seven years ago, its origins date from another age, an era thirty years past. I began to research for *Living Stones* in the late 1960s; to write it in the mid 1980s. The celebration of the bicentennial year of the establishment of the Roman Catholic hierarchy in the United States in 1989 seemed like an appropriate occasion to synthesize the various parts of the historical picture which had begun to emerge. The book was the result of a personal quest—the search for a Catholic identity through the retrieval of the past. This overview of the community's history of life-in-the-Spirit was very much shaped by two major realities: the experience of the seemingly vast changes which had occurred in the religious sensibility and expressions of the Catholic community in the 1960s, and the methodologies, research and archival base which had been established in historical work up to that time. Now, in 1996, as we find ourselves in a different era, in the midst of the emergence of a more complex sensibility, I find it is not so much the perspective which has changed as its implications for life and for research. But in this introduction to a work of history, let me reflect primarily on the impetus of the project and some of its approaches.

Living Stones was written from the perspective of a historian who experienced the changes in the community from 1950 to 1970, and who observed, suffered, enjoyed, and asked the questions peculiar to that particular post-World War II generation. If one experience was uppermost, it was that many of the participants in those changes experienced not simply the loss of this or that aspect of Catholic self-identity and practice (e.g. abstinence on Friday, the collapse of particular devotions, an increasing pluralism in the interpretation of the Church's moral norms), but the dissolution of a structure of belief, the collapse of a home constructed out of abstract principles, and a "scholasticism of the heart." Those who lived through the 1950s, 1960s, and 1970s experienced a "before" and "after." In 1960 institutional structures, moral norms, devotional practices, liturgical prayer, ascetical disciplines, and social work formed a single edifice of truth founded on the living stones of Jesus Christ and his representatives on earth. At least that was the dominant self-portrait. By 1970 people realized that a shift by one stone engendered a shift in the whole structure. How else explain the acrimonious debates over clerical attire, the length of a nun's skirt, changing penitential practices, receiving communion in the hand, or the acceptance and/or rejection of the papal teaching on birth control? Certainly, by the 1980s, the plethora of speculations about Christ himself, his involvement in human history and culture, his pain and poverty signaled the fall of the divinely immutable keystone and the collapse of the pre-conciliar self-image of a "perfect society."[1]

For myself, this experience of change revealed an insight into "system," the simple fact that many different dimensions of life were often symbolically if not literally interconnected. The Body of Christ was indeed built of "living stones," and a Catholic's self-identity, experience of society, convictions about the institutional church, devotional life, attitudes toward asceticism, and image of Christ were bound together into a cultural whole. Given this experience, the questions shaping the historical endeavor became: How in fact were these many different dimensions of life interconnected in any given era of history? Had the changing complex of events and people ever occasioned new alignments of these elements in a way similar to the contemporary experience? If the church was built of living stones, how had those stones been alive, working to form an edifice of the Spirit? In short, what in the past had been the structures of Catholic belief and practice, and how had those structures shaped the spiritual lives of previous generations while at the same time being shaped by them? Embedded in these questions themselves was the uniquely historical inclination and hope that the history of change itself could establish continuity in an era of dissolution. Within the experience of transition, my Catholic and scholarly instincts

---

[1]This experience is well described in Charles A. Fracchia, *Second Spring: The Coming of Age of U.S. Catholicism* (San Francisco, 1980), and Garry Wills, *Bare Ruined Choirs: Doubt, and Radical Religion* (Garden City, New York, 1971). The most perceptive historical analyses of the "before" and "after" experiences are Philip Gleason, "In Search of Unity: American Catholic Thought, 1920 1960," *Catholic Historical Review* 65 (April 1972): 185-205, and William M. Halsey, *The Survival of American Innocence: Catholicism in an Era of Disillusionment, 1920-1940* (Notre Dame, Ind., 1980). For the period they examine, see most recently Eugene McCarraher, "American Gothic: Sacramental Radicalism and the Neo-Medievalist Cultural Gospel, 1928-1948," *Records of the American Catholic Historical Society of Philadelphia* 106 (Spring-Summer 1995): 3-24.

turned to tradition. I became enamored of John Henry Newman, and his ideas of growth, development, and permanence indicated a way to approach the history of the Church.[2] The contemporary context of this experience and its very significant impact helped in a considerable way to reveal the many different eras and expressions of religious sensibility which had lived in harmony, succeeded each other, intermingled, and conflicted in the history of the Catholic community.

After ten years of research and in contrast to what had been a static picture presented in church history books, rituals, sermons, catechisms, and theology tomes shaped through the prism of abstract reason, it appeared to me that the spiritual life of the community, even in its short two-hundred-year development in the United States, had undergone considerable change; in fact, a close examination of significant time-frames (oddly enough, the material itself almost broke down automatically into thirty year segments) indicated that different understandings and practices of liturgy, prayer, asceticism, and morality were connected with different political, social, personal, and ecclesiological presuppositions within the community. Even the dominant image of Christ had mutated given the changing experiences of the people. All of this occurred within the context of the shifting dimensions of society, American culture, and Protestant-Catholic relationships. As I saw the history of the Catholic community, the 1960s did not represent so much a drastic break from the past, a "revolutionary moment" as current commentators phrased it, but one more step in the continuing struggle to live contemporary life in a truly Catholic way. What collapsed in the 1960s was not Catholic identity but a form of the community's religious sensibility ("the fractured inheritance") which had developed at the turn of the century and had dominated its self-image. Indeed, it now seemed to me that our history could more accurately be presented, and thus be made available to us, as an interactive drama in which God, Father, Son, and Holy Spirit, worked within a pluralism of understandings and practices struggling with each other to establish direction or equilibrium or peaceful coexistence or some semblance of charitable toleration. Behind this presentation and at its heart lay a statement of faith and the permanency of a vision of Christocentric humanism, which in itself was a statement about "Church." Hence the title and the references at the beginning and at the end to 1 Peter 2:4-5. Given the state of research, the vast amount of sources available, and my own limitations, I tried to present this perspective by selecting significant figures or movements from 1789 to 1960.

---

[2]I mention this influence directly since several reviewers of *Living Stones* wondered about its theological and methodological presuppositions. See, for background, Edward Jeremy Miller, *John Henry Newman on the Idea of the Church* (Shepherdstown 1987); Roderick Strange, *Newman and the Gospel of Christ* (Oxford 1981).

Thus, the first section discussed John Carroll's vision of the Christian life and analyzed the relationship among his commitment to religious liberty, his understanding of nature and grace, his view of the church, his practice of prayer, and his image of Christ. During the initial immigrant period three representative figures were chosen to illustrate how the shifting experiences of society, anthropology, and church affected the understanding and practice of spirituality. The sources also indicated that this immigrant vision coexisted in the community with a "Carrollite" tradition. The third section, examining the controversies surrounding Americanism, sought to compare the outlines of the spiritual life that directed the work of Orestes Brownson, Isaac Hecker, and John Joseph Keane with those of the immigrant church. The last two sections, covering much of the twentieth century and developed to be seen in mutual relationship, were written with a view of understanding the roots of the spiritual crisis of the conciliar era: Why did it seem in the 1960s that we had lost a sense of coherent Catholic identity when, in fact, our identity had been pluriform all along? Could it be that what dissolved was not identity but a "rhetoric of identity," a way of speaking about ourselves as if we were disembodied and ahistorical abstractions? Perhaps if we had seen our past more accurately, the changes of the 1960s would not have been so startling.

This historical project of the retrieval of spiritual pluriformity and its resolution in Christocentric humanism was helped by a number of factors. Within the discipline of history itself, the years from 1969 to 1989 witnessed a considerable growth in methodology and a utilization of sources which encouraged investigation into the relationships among people, events, and social, intellectual and religious structures. Cultural anthropology proceeded from the assumption that the material conditions of life, structures of society, and intellectual and religious convictions of an age often came to focus on the symbolic expressions of language, ritual and devotion. This discipline greatly affected the perception of the historian's task and made possible for the student of American Catholicism an exploration of the interrelationships between inner convictions and social structures.[3] Sociology and psychology also invaded the discipline of history in response to the search for a "history of meaning" (there could be no greater question in the 1960s) that would unite objective and subjective poles of human experience.[4] During the same period, much of the scholarship in

---

[3]See especially the works of Mary Douglas, *Purity and Danger: An Analysis of the Concepts of Pollution and Taboo* (New York, 1966); *Natural Symbols: Explorations in Cosmology* (The Cresset Press, 1970); *Risk and Blame: Essays in Cultural Theory* (New York, 1992).

[4]See in particular William J. Bouwsma, "From History of Ideas to History of Meaning," in *A Usable Past: Essays in European Cultural History* (Berkeley, 1990, first published 1981): 336-347; Bernard Bailyn, "The Challenge of Modern Historiography," *Ameri-*

American Catholic studies also moved away from institutional or biographical preoccupations to more social concerns. Immigrant history especially
applied the methods of sociology, anthropology, and psychology to historical investigation. The history of Catholic theology was also studied.
Finally, within this scholarly context, the history of spirituality began to
develop by using the many different disciplines to analyze the total complex of a person's and of a community's theological or religious attitudes,
their "spirituality" or "vision of the Christian life." Numerous studies began to show how people's self-understanding, educational background,
experience of society, and intellectual convictions related to their experience of God, Christ, and the saints; to their view of the sacraments and
liturgy; and to the role assigned to knowledge and love, evil and sin, virtue and vice.[5]

While using the traditional data furnished by conciliar legislation, private correspondence, and public statements, these many different approaches also revealed new sources with which to examine the spiritual
self-understanding of an epoch: sermons, prayer books, religious journals,
paintings, holy cards, ritual behavior, devotional practices, and theological and apologetic works. For myself, archival depositories housing the
papers of John Carroll, Isaac Hecker, John A. Ryan, Vigil Michel, James
Keller, and others became accessible. The diary of John Neumann, the
writings of Dorothy Day and Thomas Merton, the hitherto unused sermons of Martin Spalding and John Hughes, and the published narratives
of the retreat and eucharistic movements provided fresh perspectives on
vast developments within the community. Disciplines, methods, and
sources thus combined to encourage a new look at the American Catholic
community as an "edifice of the Spirit, built of living stones."

Living Stones tried to enflesh some of the possibilities inherent in these
new approaches to history; it certainly reflected my own research limitations and the orientations of the scholarship in the field up to the mid-
1980s. At that time Jay Dolan (1976, 1978), Robert Orsi (1985), Anne

---

can Historical Review 87(February 1982): 1-24; Peter Stearns with Carol Z. Stearns,
"Emotionology: Clarifying the History of Emotions and Emotional Standards," *American
Historical Review* 90 (October 1985): 813-36; Joseph P. Chinnici, "Broadening the Horizons: The Historian in Search of the Spirit," *U.S. Catholic Historian* 8 (Winter/Spring
1989): 1-13.

[5]See Joseph P. Chinnici, O.F.M., "The History of Spirituality and the Catholic Com-
munity in the United States: An Agenda for the Future," in Nelson H. Minnich, Robert B.
Eno, S.S., and Robert F. Trisco, eds., *Studies in Catholic History in Honor of John Tracy
Ellis* (Wilmington, Del., 1985), pp. 392-416. For use of the term "spirituality," see Walter
Principe, "Toward Defining Spirituality," *Sciences Religieuses/Studies in Religion* 12
(Spring 1983): 137-141. For recent methodological and topical developments see "Fo-
rum: The Decade Ahead in Scholarship, Robert Orsi, David W. Wills, Colleen McDannell,"
in *Religion and American Culture* 3 (Winter 1993): 1-28.

Taves (1986) and myself (1979, 1985) had completed studies on revivalism, immigrant popular religion, and nineteenth-century devotionalism.
Beyond a lengthy article in the *Dictionnaire de Spiritualité* there existed
no comprehensive survey. Most notably, the chapter on Dorothy Day was
the only one to attempt to view the history and experience of the community through the lens of a prominent woman. I had made no trips to the
archives of Elizabeth Seton, Mother Theodore Guerin, Magdalen
Bentivoglio, and Katherine Drexel, to name a few people outstanding for
their holiness and impact on the community. Lack of reflection on the
black and Hispanic experiences also represented the limitations of my research lens. Chapters on the history of contemplative prayer, the development of lay spirituality in the periodical *Integrity* and the Christian Family Movement, and the formative influence of the religious communities
awaited exploration. The "Jansenist" strain in American Catholic life still
needed to see the light of day. The book contained few if any references
to the history of shrines and holy places, the importance of architectural
space, and the commercialization of religious piety.

Fortunately, since the research for this book developed there has been
an explosion of work in the field of American Catholic spirituality. Selections from the spiritual writings of Seton, the Maryland Jesuits, Rose
Hawthorne Lathrop, and the tradition of the Sisters of Mercy have become available through the *Sources of American Spirituality*.[6] Some scholars have looked closely at the Jesuit, Carmelite, and Benedictine traditions; others have detailed the changing history of life-in-the-Spirit among
women religious; one very significant study breaks open the spiritual depths
of Dorothy Day's experience.[7] The Hispanic and black traditions are now

---

[6] Ellin M. Kelly and Anabelle M. Melville, eds., *Elizabeth Seton: Selected Writings*
(New York 1987); Robert Emmett Curran, ed., *American Jesuit Spirituality: The Maryland Tradition 1634-1900* (New York 1988); Diana Culbertson, O.P., ed., *Rose Hawthorne
Lathrop: Selected Writings* (New York 1992); Kathleen Healy, ed., *Sisters of Mercy: Spirituality in America, 1843-1900* (New York 1992).

[7] See for examples Peter McDonough, *Men Astutely Trained: A History of the Jesuits
in the American Century* (Free Press 1994); Joseph P. Tetlow, S.J., "The Most Postmodern
Prayer, American Jesuit Identity and the Examen of Conscience, 1920-1990," *Studies in
the Spirituality of the Jesuits* 26 (January 1994); Constance Fitzgerald, O.C.D., ed., *The
Carmelite Adventure: Clare Joseph Dickinson's Journal of a Trip to America* (Baltimore
1990); Joel Rippinger, O.S.B., *The Benedictine Order in the United States: An Interpre-
tive History* (Collegeville 1990); Mary Lea Schneider, O.S.F., "American Sisters and the
Roots of Change: The 1950s," *U.S. Catholic Historian* 7 (1988): 55-72; Angelyn Dries,
O.S.F., "Living in Ambiguity: A Paradigm Shift Experienced by the Sister Formation
Movement," *Catholic Historical Review* 79 (July 1993): 478-87; Mary DeCock, B.V.M.,
"Turning Points in the Spirituality of an American Congregation: The Sisters of Charity
of the Blessed Virgin Mary," *U.S. Catholic Historian* 10 (1989): 59-69. For general infor-
mation on the development of women's history see the new edition of Mary Jo Weaver,

receiving their due.[8] The origins of twelve-step spirituality, the meaning
of suffering, the darker strains of sacrifice, and a major new study on
"material christianity" indicate the vast perspectives now opening up in
the Church's past.[9] A short general interpretive survey has been written.[10]
Perhaps the way towards a new history is only now developing; the limitations of *Living Stones* are obvious.

The limitations of this book sprang from within my own history; its
possibilities emerged from the generous gifts of numerous people. Archi-
vists, fellow historians, and colleagues at the Franciscan School of Theology, Berkeley, graciously contributed their expertise and support. The
National Conference of Catholic Bishops and the group of historians engaged in the bicentennial project provided "food for the journey" and scholarly perspective. With her technical help, challenging questions, encouragement, and sound research, Kristeen Bruun helped bring the project to
birth. As this second edition is prepared for publication I continue to remain immensely thankful for my good friend, historian, companion, and
"sponsor" in this project, Christopher J. Kauffman. This current edition
would never have been possible without the enthusiastic support of William Burrows of Orbis Books. Once again, I would like to dedicate the
work to a group of people who have demonstrated for me the Franciscan
tradition of Christocentric humanism: my teachers, Valentine Healy,
Benedict McCormick, and Geoffrey Bridges; my confreres and mentors
Kenan Osborne, Lester Mitchell, Godfrey McSweeney, Giles Valcovich,
Louis Vitale, and John Vaughn. Who, in the words of Saint Bonaventure,

---

New Catholic Women: A Contemporary Challenge to Traditional Religious Authority (Indiana 1995) and Brigid O'Shea Merriman, *Searching for Christ: The Spirituality of Dorothy Day* (Notre Dame 1994).

[8]Since the literature is growing rapidly, see for examples, Jay P. Dolan and Allan
Figueroa Deck, S.J., eds., *Hispanic Catholic Culture in the U.S.: Issues and Concerns*
(Notre Dame 1994); Jay P. Dolan and Gilberto M. Hinojosa, eds., *Mexican American
Catholics and the Catholic Church, 1900-1965* (Notre Dame 1994); Michael E. Engh,
S.J., "From Frontera Faith to Roman Rubrics: Altering Hispanic Religious Customs in
Los Angeles, 1855-1880," *U.S. Catholic Historian* 12 (Fall 1994): 85; Thaddeus J. Posey,
O.F.M. Cap., "Praying in the Shadows: The Oblate Sisters of Providence, A Look at Nine-
teenth Century Black Spirituality," *U.S. Catholic Historian* 12 (Winter 1994): 11-30.

[9]See John Samuel Tieman, "The Origins of Twelve-Step Spirituality: Bill W. and Ed-
ward Dowling, S.J.," *U.S. Catholic Historian* 13 (Summer 1995): 121-135; James Terence
Fisher, *The Catholic Counterculture in America, 1933-1962* (Chapel Hill 1989); Robert
A. Orsi, " 'Mildred, is it fun to be a cripple?': The Culture of Suffering in Mid-Twentieth-
Century American Catholicism," *The South Atlantic Quarterly* 93 (Summer 1994): 547-
90; Colleen McDannell, *Material Christianity, Religion and Popular Culture in America*
(New Haven 1995).

[10]John Manuel Lozano, *Grace & Brokenness in God's Country: An Exploration of
American Catholic Spirituality* (New York 1991).

can hope to investigate with wonder, read with unction, speculate with devotion, observe with joy, and work with piety, unless someone teach him? What have we that we have not received?

In conclusion, on the occasion of this second edition, I still believe that *Living Stones* does provide some adequate orientation to a vast field of exploration and experience. It is my hope that it might continue to stimulate further research, which in turn may modify some of its conclusions. This is the nature of scholarship. Also, I hope that it might still provide us with a way of thinking about our past which makes us part of a living tradition. Today, we live in a Church and society grappling with "culture wars" and searching for some stable point of reference. Our past was no stranger to this experience. In fact, the religious history of the Roman Catholic community in the United States indicates that people lived and developed their faith in a dramatic fashion, always in relationship to the changing profiles of family, neighbor, society, and Church. Previous generations also have grappled with pain, sin, change, limitation, conflict, and tension; and they have built within that context and in continuity with what was handed on to them, a living community of faith, a liturgical expression capable of mediating the presence of God to people's experience, an image of Christ that made the Incarnation real, a church structure filled with vitality, and a practice of charity and asceticism rooted in the Gospel. In short, they formed "church," and in continuity with them we too must be built into "an edifice of the Spirit, into a holy priesthood, offering spiritual sacrifices, acceptable to God through Jesus Christ."

October 4, 1996

Living Stones

PART ONE

An Enlightenment Synthesis, 1776–1815

In 1774, a ship docked at Bobby Brent's landing, a Catholic enclave near Richland in northern Virginia. Returning home from Europe, thirty-eight-year-old John Carroll stopped there first to visit his sister Anne, now married to Robert Brent, who had been one of Carroll's childhood schoolfellows. Carroll had left Maryland twenty-five years earlier at the age of thirteen to attend the Jesuit school at Bruges in Belgium run by Jesuits who had fled Britain and relocated there during English persecutions. The school served the children of wealthy Catholics from both Britain and the colonies. Unlike his friends and cousins, John Carroll had stayed in Europe when his schooling was complete. He had entered the Jesuits at the age of eighteen, prepared for ordination, and then gone back to teach at the school where he had once been a pupil. Through the school and through his family's contacts, he had formed many friendships among the English aristocracy: lifelong friend and fellow Jesuit Charles Plowden (1743–1821); Charles-Philippe Stourton, son of Charles, Lord Stourton, with whom Carroll toured Europe in 1771–72; Thomas Weld, in whose Lulworth castle Carroll would be consecrated bishop; and Lord and Lady Arundel. As will be seen, Carroll's contacts with these British recusant Catholics significantly affected his spirituality.

It was in response to the suppression of the Jesuits by Pope Clement XIV in 1773 that John Carroll decided to return home. Upon his return, he lived on his mother's estate Rock Creek in southern Maryland and took up the duties of a colonial priest. He rode circuit among his far-flung parishioners, visiting different homes about every two months. There were as yet no churches, and eucharistic reservation was impossible, yet many people joined a league of prayer in honor of the eucharistic presence of Christ and spent a half hour kneeling in private prayer at a specified time. Devotion to the Sacred Heart, a Jesuit devotion, was also commonly practiced. The Revolutionary War was fought, and Carroll accompanied his cousin Charles Carroll and Benjamin Franklin on the first diplomatic mission to Canada. In 1784 Carroll was named superior of the mission, and in 1790 he was consecrated the first bishop of the church in the United States.

Among the many charges that the papal brief *Ex hac Apostolicae* laid at the feet of John Carroll as the first bishop of Baltimore, the building of a cathedral symbolized most powerfully the young church's spiritual life. "Everything is to be raised, as it were, from its foundation," Carroll told his congregation of Catholics and Protestants on Sunday morning, December 12, 1790. Foremost on the agenda was the foundation of a seminary, the building of a Catholic college, and the construction of numerous churches, but at the heart of the endeavor was the Cathedral of the Assumption, a project that "terrified" the new bishop.

Carroll first mentioned the cathedral in a 1795 letter to his English friend, Charles Plowden. He began the appeal for funds in 1803 and laid the cornerstone in 1806. To design the church, the bishop solicited the services of Benjamin Henry Latrobe, the architect of the nation's capitol. The lay board of trustees, commonly attached to each parish because the law prohibited the church from incorporating and owning property, commissioned a cathedral compatible with the ideals of the Enlightenment: order, harmony, discipline, reason, quiet dignity. The cathedral's central dome, octagonal drum, short choir, and gray-granite exterior blended well with the republican style that dominated the nation's capital. Carroll died before the church could be completed, but his successor as archbishop of Baltimore, Ambrose Maréchal (1764–1828), wrote to the Congregatio de Propaganda Fide in these terms: "Without a doubt its size and grandeur will far surpass that of any temple built up to this time in the United States of America, whether by Protestants or by Catholics. Even the Protestants of Baltimore take pride in it. It is, indeed, the greatest ornament of the city." Today, despite some alterations, the Cathedral Church of the Assumption still stands in Baltimore as a fitting symbol of the spiritual life characteristic of the Catholic community during Carroll's era.[1]

The social reality, intellectual convictions, and religious practices that comprised John Carroll's vision of the Christian life and that he labored to symbolize in the Cathedral of the Assumption will be the subject of the following discussion. Chapter 1 shows how Carroll's understanding was rooted in both the need to accept the equality of all religions in the social sphere and his conviction that religious liberty was a fundamental human right. Of paramount importance for this view was the Enlightenment's acceptance of the close relationship between human aspiration and divine grace. Chapter 2 will examine Carroll's theological anthropology. The bishop's understanding of the church as a Christian community will be analyzed in chapter 3. The section concludes with a description of Carroll's Christocentric piety. As the primary architect of the Catholic community during its formative period from 1776 to 1815, Carroll established in these four key elements a synthesis of his Catholic and American identity that would stand as an ideal for his own and future generations.

CHAPTER
1
Religious Pluralism: The Social Foundations of Christian Piety

*B*e ye ready: because at what hour ye know not, the son of man will come" (Matt. 25:13). With these words the Lord cautioned the disciples to be prepared for the end. He went on to describe for them the separation of the sheep from the goats at the scene of final judgment. Since that time, through artistic and rhetorical imaginings of both the final and particular judgments, theologians, popular preachers, painters, and parents have passed on to generations of the Christian community the values that they consider most important in the living of the Christian life. Presumably, when Christians delineate by what standards they themselves desire to be judged and how they picture their personal reckoning, they then reveal what is closest to their hearts, the focus of their spiritual identity. John Carroll was no exception to this tradition.

In his sermon "The Last Judgment," Carroll imagined the individual coming before the "tribunal of God" for an accounting of his or her life. Left entirely alone before the sovereign majesty, the Christian can only depend on the deeds of a lifetime. Now is the time, Carroll noted, that an individual will become "fully sensible of the advantages of religion" and the "strict adherence to its precepts." What would this entail but humble submission to revealed truths, adherence to the self-restraint imposed by the gospel, practices of charity, exercises of piety, prayers, fastings, and self-denial? Also sig-

5

nificant would be the victories over human respect, parental care of the religion and virtue of children, conjugal fidelity and Christian love, filial duty, compassionate tenderness toward dependents and inferiors, justice in dealings with others, tenderness for a neighbor's reputation, and all the other Christian virtues.

The bishop continued his sermon by picturing the specific examination of the individual, "enlightened by reason & natural law," according to the "evangelical law, the rules of a Xtian & Catholic." The particular judgment, based on these criteria, would reveal every sin; the consequent sentence would be irrevocable. "My dear brethren," Carroll concluded, "let us represent to ourselves that we are now before the tribunal of heaven—& that we hear the judgment on us, *depart* from me etc. But happy we are, that this is yet only a supposition—by changing our lives, we may avoid it."[1]

Carroll's sermon "On the Last Judgment" reveals his fundamental conception of the Christian life. When seen in the context of his other comments on the gospel, and of his references to prayer books and manuals of devotion in use in his time, Carroll's sermon indicates the social, political, and religious convictions of a large portion of the Catholic community. For both the preacher and the congregation, the "last judgment" showed the way in which they integrated their spirituality with their own social and personal circumstances. Given as it was before a crowded assembly of Protestants and Catholics, the sermon indicated how Carroll used his role as preacher, liturgical leader, and administrator of the sacraments to inculcate a communal spiritual life reflecting the compatibility between Catholicism and the value of religious liberty.

In the sermon on the "Last Judgment," Carroll addressed his listeners as "Xtian Brethren," as "Xtian and Catholic," or simply "Christians." This method of address followed his usual custom of referring to "Catholic Christians," "Christian people," or the "Christian Catholic church." Even in a document addressed solely to members of his own communion, the bishop used "Christian" as the substantive term and "Catholic" as the modifier.[2] The usage was decidedly noncontroversial and indicated that in a public forum the focus of Carroll's spiritual vision was not what was distinctively Catholic but what was commonly Christian. The words pointed to the heart of his personal conviction.

In a letter to Charles Plowden, dated October 12, 1791, the bishop recommended one of the popular irenic pamphlets of the era, *An Essay Towards Catholic Communion*, to anyone who wanted to promote unity between the churches. When commenting on the opinions of the English Catholic Joseph Berington (1743–1827), Carroll noted his own desire "to wrest out of the Hand of Fanaticism the rod of Oppression."

He continued in his letter to Berington: "You have expressed on the Subject of Toleration those Sentiments, which I have long wished to see come strongly recommended from eminent writers of our Religion; and which I am well persuaded, are the only sentiments, that can ever establish, by being generally adopted, a reasonable system of universal Forbearance, and charity amongst Christians of every Denomination." This viewpoint easily coincided with Berington's picture of a group of people thinking freely, acting consistently and arguing civilly for the triumph of "genuine, unadorned truth." In such an atmosphere, "Religion with its attendant virtues, would challenge our first belief; and the religion of our choice would necessarily be the Christian."

Carroll could also have adopted with pleasure the position expressed by John Fletcher (1766–1845), a British apologist, in his book *Reflections on the Spirit of Religious Controversy.* "It is my lot," Fletcher wrote, "to move within a small, though respectable, circle of acquaintances, who loudly censure everything controversial." The stream of visitors at Carroll's deathbed testified to his own commitment to take Fletcher's description seriously. In his desire to reach across the institutional and social barriers created in the wake of the Reformation, Carroll viewed religion as a "system of piety and humility: and it is in holy communication with God, by prayer and meditation, that he speaks most plainly to the heart and unfolds the truth and beauty of his law."[3]

John Carroll's irenic vision of Christian life and his desire to create in his sermons an atmosphere of tolerance, mutual respect, and rational argument—in short, a "system of piety and humility" that would be socially constructive—took shape during the Tidewater struggles over religious pluralism between 1776–1800. In 1774, the same year he returned from Europe, the political and religious forces in Maryland began a series of conventions to draft a constitution. The Maryland Constitution, completed in 1776, proclaimed the equality of all Christian denominations before the law. Presbyterians, Episcopalians, Methodists, Baptists, Pietists, Lutherans, Quakers, and Roman Catholics were urged to put aside religious differences, distinguish principles from people, and use only spiritual persuasion in the forum of public discourse. A general atmosphere of tolerance existed between 1776–80.[4]

Carroll's sermons on infidelity reflect his position: a conservative Federalism committed to the acceptance of religious pluralism but conscious of the need for an aristocracy of virtue and an insistence on the institutions of religion. For example, when commenting on the French Revolution the bishop argued for the necessity of Christianity for social order and criticized those who propagated principles "so repugnant to piety, to justice, to humanity, to the peace of individuals & families, to the sanctity of marriage, the inviolability of compacts, the security of political societies, & the tranquility of established governments."[5] In the social and political context of late eighteenth-century Maryland, the bishop knew that if stressed too much, religious differences could jeopardize civil unity; yet if differences were not presented sufficiently, distinct communions could merge into a vague deism. The balance between public amity and private sectarianism may have been tenuous but it was necessary. So Carroll addressed his flock as "Catholic Christians."

The bishop accepted religious pluralism not only out of political necessity but also from personal conviction. Carroll indicated to his friend Charles Plowden that he was pleased with the toleration prevalent in the United States, at one point noting that he had "contracted the language of a Republican." The language Carroll employed revealed his commitment to "every natural right," "rights of conscience," "equal liberty," "the common rights of nature," "civil and religious liberty," "rights legally acquired," and "the great principle of religious liberty." His commitment to religious pluralism flowed from a strong insistence on personal conscience, respect for government by law, and the primacy of rational discourse, not custom or authority, in the quest for religious truth and civil harmony.[6] Because of his unique inheritance of a colonial Maryland boyhood and republican political experience, he was able to accept these qualities as part of his own spiritual life.

John Carroll also inherited three of the more creative continental strains in post-Reformation spirituality. His background reflected the more humanistic elements of the French tradition, the British Catholic tradition of the seventeenth and eighteenth centuries, and the Spanish tradition of Saint Ignatius of Loyola. All of these strengthened his ability to synthesize a Catholic life with religious pluralism.

Bishop Carroll was exposed to his first major spiritual inheritance, the more humanistic elements of the French tradition, during his Jesuit education. In the course of his studies, he was presented with the ideal of the Christian gentleman in the *Introduction to the Devout Life* of Francis de Sales (1567–1622). This seventeenth-century spiritual writer bequeathed to future generations a profound recognition of the role of persuasion, the importance of personal intention, and the centrality of charity in the spiritual life. De Sales was a master of gentility, combining the classical dictum of "nothing human is alien to me" with an insistence on God's transforming grace.[7] If Carroll spoke with the flavor of the "*suaviter in modo* so much recommended by the courtly Chesterfield," de Sales prepared the way.[8] As the

American summarized it: "... considering likewise the language of scripture and tradition, I do not think, that J. Christ ever empowered his church to recur to the means of force and bloodshed, for the preservation of faith against error. My idea, in this, as in every other lawful defense is, *ut fiat cum moderamine inculpatur tutelae;* that the means be proportioned to the attack; persuasion, argument, coercion by spiritual censures, unless force of arms be used against the friends of truth."[9]

The emphasis on free will, conscience, and interiority of French author and archbishop François Fénelon (1651–1715) also profoundly influenced the American churchman. For example, in 1811 Carroll personally approved the publication of a *Catechism on the Foundation of Christian Faith*. The work contained several long extracts from the letters of Fénelon. "What shall I give you," Fénelon prayed:

> I who have received every thing from your hand? O eternal love! You ask but one thing of me, that is the *free wish* of my heart; you have left it to me free, in order that I might consent from my own choice to the immutable subordination with which I might continually hold my heart in your hands; you desire only that I should wish that order which is the happiness of all creation; but in order to make me wish it, you show me without, all its charms to render it amiable to me; and more, you enter by the charms of your grace within my heart to give motion to its springs, and to make me love what is so worthy of being loved.

The extracts from Fénelon went on to argue that God had "placed men together in a society where they ought to love and succour one another as children of the same family who have but one common Father."[10] It would be hard to see how the American could have avoided the intellectual shadow that the French archbishop cast over the eighteenth-century Catholic Enlightenment. Fénelon's integration of the inner and the outer could be discerned in Carroll's acceptance of each person's conscientious quest for religious truth and in the role of amicable conversation in conversion.

The English Catholic tradition of the seventeenth and eighteenth centuries constituted the second major source enabling Carroll to fashion a spirituality suited to the demands of religious pluralism. This was a tradition formed during periods of both persecution and adjustment to the existence of Protestantism. Through his friendships, his education, and his own colonial heritage, Carroll knew the spiritual tradition represented by the British writers John Gother and Richard Challoner.[11]

John Gother (d. 1704), one of the most prominent convert pamphleteers, wrote devotional works known for their emphasis on Scripture, the social mission of Christianity, and the apostolate of the laity. Gother's writings were "ecumenical too, not only in their charity and respect for the consciences of others and prayers for those 'not yet in the church' but also in their avoidance of the miracle-mongering and hyperbolic language (especially as regards to Mary), equally offensive to Catholics and Protestant English readers." Gother's instructions circulated in the colonies. They incorporated in a sober and precise style the riches of the fathers of the church (a source Carroll himself used), Thomas à Kempis, and others. As an indication of Gother's perduring influence, the 1817 *Laity's Directory* included a section from his "Suitable Behavior in Church." Suitable behavior meant "awful strict silence, the most profound exterior respect, and penetrating inward devotion of heart," sentiments that run throughout Carroll's sermons.[12]

Richard Challoner (1691–1781), heavily influenced by Gother, became the most important English Catholic devotional writer in revolutionary America.[13] Challoner's works embodied a dignified piety, strong moralism, the promotion, in contrast to any aristocratic pretense, of mental prayer for everyone, and some knowledge of affective prayer. Carroll's own Ignatian training complemented these characteristics. Most important, Challoner's work evidenced a conviction of the possibility of a direct, personal experience of God. This was important for a community that might not see a priest or any other official representative of the church for months at a time. Many of the spiritual traits that Challoner promoted, as will be seen, emerge in Carroll's sermons and focus on the imitation of Christ. In the context of religious pluralism, they were easier to carry out because they were common to all Christians.[14]

The tradition of Saint Ignatius of Loyola (1491–1556) comprised the third major influence on John Carroll's spirituality that predisposed him to take a more tolerant view of religious pluralism. Although the Jesuits were founded, to some extent, to combat Protestantism and became known as unwavering supporters of Counter Reformation religious politics, the society in its early years had a more humanist leaning, and Carroll naturally gravitated toward this view. For example, he referred in his letters to the "enlarged system of St. Ignatius," and relied on a more liberal interpretation of Ignatius's life. It can also be assumed that Carroll was raised in the interpretation of Ignatian spirituality presented in *The Practice of Christian and Religious Perfection* of Alfonso Rodríguez (1538–1616). Both Rodríguez and Vincent Huby, S. J. (1608–93), whose *Spiritual Retreat* Carroll introduced to the American public in 1795, built their systems on the doctrine of charity and reacted strongly to the more rigoristic and defensive positions of other Jesuit writers. The Ignatian tradition that Carroll accepted correlated well with his French humanistic strain and his English devotional heritage.[15] Each of these traditions emphasized the love of creation and humility in dealing with others. These three strands of post-Reformation spirituality provided the foundation for all of Carroll's piety.

CHAPTER
2
Nature and Grace: The Personal Foundations of Christian Piety

*J*ohn Carroll's theological anthropology—his understanding of the relationship between reason and faith, nature and grace—provided another foundational element for his irenic spirituality. Carroll emphasized the convergence, not the rupture, between the life of grace and human aspirations. In the sermon on the "Last Judgment," the bishop spoke of the individual "enlightened by reason & natural law," according to the "evangelical law." His sermon on the conversion of the Samaritan woman was even more instructive on the relationship between the natural and the evangelical laws. Commenting on Matthew 9:21, "She said within herself, if I shall but touch his garment, I shall be healed," the bishop noted that the confidence of the woman in the Lord's ministrations "was not the effect of blind presumption. In the sincerity of her mind & heart, she had considered the life and wonderful works of J. C., & had formed a most rational conclusion, that his power was etc. The grace of God aided & assisted her disposition; & thus her faith was formed."[1]

Carroll typically noted the subject's disposition, her rational preparation that opened her to the transformation effected by God's grace. Reason and faith were not confused; but neither were they at odds. The situation of the bleeding woman was analogous to the relationship Protestants and Catholics had with the true faith. Conversion, an essential element of the spiritual life, was meant to be gradual, building on the gifts of nature, not obliterating them. For Carroll, the starting point of the life of grace was always reasonable consent and personal integrity.

This transformationist view of the relationship between reason and faith emphasized the eternal law reflected in the natural instincts implanted in each individual.[2] In 1784 Carroll presented a surprisingly moderate interpretation of the phrase *extra ecclesiam nulla est salus.* He distinguished between communion (i.e., participation in faith, sacraments, and government) and membership (possessing a "sincere heart" and "disposition to embrace the truth") and argued that Catholics were obliged to believe that *"out of our communion* salvation may be obtained." Carroll supported his position by citing the Council of Trent's decree on justification, a decree reflecting the optimistic view of the person of the sixteenth-century Catholic reformers.[3]

In the churchman's struggles with the currents of infidelity he consistently argued for the basic truths of "natural religion": the existence of a Supreme Being, an after life, and, because of the "blindness generated by shameful and disorderly lusts and passions," the necessity of revelation. Betraying once again his philosophical inclination toward the integration of nature and grace, Carroll pointed in "Faith and Infidelity" to the experience of the classical Greek philosophers. "Socrates," he wrote, "universally esteemed as the wisest of the heathen world, after having discovered by the acuteness of his mind, and the penetration of his intellectual powers, the existence and many of the perfections of the one, only God, affords us nevertheless a memorable instance of the darkness in which human reason, unassisted by revelation, leaves the mind involved." Although the excesses of the French Revolution led Carroll to focus on the disruptive powers of passion, he still maintained his basic position on the rule of reason in the exercise of true religion. Above all, his was a "reasonable piety."[4]

John Fletcher's *Reflections on the Spirit of Religious Controversy* (1804) described the theological foundation of Carroll's view of nature and grace most succinctly. The effects of religion and grace, it argued,

> do not deprive the will of its liberty, nor take from the heart its inclinations: they do not set upon the soul, as physical, and mechanical forces, like weights, whose effects may be measured by their gravity; or levers, whose powers may be calculated by their length. Acting in harmony, or correspondence with the inclinations of the will, and the dispositions of the heart, while they enlighten the docile and perfect the attentive, they neither withhold the negligent, and the proud from disbelief; nor deprive the dissipated, or the sensual of the unhappy liberty of becoming vicious. Amid the influences of religion, the will continues free; and along with all the energies of grace, liberty subsists entire.[5]

Here was a notable movement away from any type of reliance on external practices, a refusal of mechanistic, deterministic categories. The statement on grace and freedom was phrased in terms of longing, inclinations, dispositions, and their fulfillment in the love of God. As the person was evaluated as possessing rights in the political sphere, so too he/she bore a natural inclination toward religious truth. Together, Catholics and Protestants were Christians. Carroll's argument was similar to that advanced by the *Catechism on the Foundation of Christian Faith*, the book whose publication the archbishop had personally approved in 1811. This work, quoting Fénelon, noted that "God imparts to each man a first germ of an intimate and secret grace which is blended imperceptibly with reason, and which prepares man to pass gradually from reason to faith." These germs of grace were so interconnected with nature that people at first did not discern them. They could be seen in a "confused sense of our impotence," a desire for that which we lack, "an inclination to find about us what we seek for in vain within ourselves," a sadness, an emptiness, a hunger and thirst for truth. Only gradually did these germs develop, to be distinguished from human reason and to come to fruition in the life of faith: "This secret and shapeless germ is the beginning of the new man: *conceptionibus similes*. It is not reason alone, nor nature left to herself; it is a growing grace which hides itself under nature in order to correct it by degrees."[6]

In his sermons Carroll was careful not to argue that nature requires grace (this would have limited the freedom of God), but that in some sense grace refashioned nature without destroying or replacing it. He presented his understanding of the relationship between creation and redemption, the old and new dispensations, in a sermon entitled "Duties of Parents." The bishop considered the language of Ephesians 6:4, "Fathers . . . bring up your children in the discipline and correction of the Lord," to be the language of both nature and religion. Nature, "uncorrupted by passion" and unseduced by false philosophy, suggested to parents the duty of teaching their children their obligations to the "Governor of the Universe." "Religion offers her aid, her more persuasive motives, & all her powerful sanctions to strengthen the dictates of nature." Baptism, he continued, reminded parents that "in consequence of this mystical rite, their children are not merely the children of God, in the course of nature, and by the benefit of creation; but [that] they become has [sic] adopted children in the dispensation of grace." Children were now ordered not only to a state of happiness required by nature but they also became "partakers of the divine nature; and rendered capable of obtaining an inheritance, a co-heirship of eternal glory with Christ himself; a felicity far exceeding our natural appetites, and, in the language of the Apostles, greater than eye has seen, than ear has heard, or it has entered into the heart of man to conceive." A more enticing picture of the Christian life could hardly be presented.[7]

The full significance of this anthropology and its consequences for shaping a spirituality suitable to religious pluralism can be seen clearly in the light of post-Reformation theological developments. In the seventeenth and eighteenth centuries, Jansenist theology refused to acknowledge an internal connection between nature and grace, emphasizing the conquering of passions by grace and the necessity of aids to prevent a person from falling into sin. People following the light of reason or deprived of the authority of the Catholic church were seen as naturally prone to error.

To counteract the Jansenist view many Catholic apologists argued for the existence of a completely natural happiness and piety, one governed simply by reason. However, this position made the action of God a force extrinsic to human social and cultural development and allowed for cooperation among Christians only in an external fashion. In the case of both the Jansenists and the proponents of a theology of pure nature, the link between the covenant of creation and the justifying action of the Holy Spirit was sundered. In contrast, Carroll's intellectual roots went back to the sixteenth-century Catholic reform. This tradition expressed a strong awareness of sin and a rigorous asceticism, but it also emphasized a synthesis between nature and grace and focused on personal experience. Thus Carroll was able to think of faith as an internal dynamic rooted in the personal, cultural, political, and social life of all Christians. Conversion to the true religion, as in the case of the Samaritan woman, could best be accomplished through an attractive and reasonable presentation of the faith.[8]

Speaking and writing in the context of religious pluralism, Carroll emphasized social virtue and the close union between reason and faith. His liturgical life, the symbolic heart of Catholic spiritual expression, also indicated that he fashioned his spirituality in this context. In the sermon on the "Last Judgment" he referred to the gospel of the day read for the people's instruction. This phrase indicated that the sermon was probably preached before a congregation of Catholics and Protestants during a public liturgical event, either during the Mass or at vespers on Sunday afternoon. In either case, the attempt to combine the Catholic Latin liturgy with a gospel read in English and a word addressed by the minister to a congregation of "Christians" represented the way in which Carroll tried to shape the community's spiritual and sacramental experience. He summarized the context that gave birth to this program in a letter to the prefect of the Propaganda Fide in Rome. "The peculiar form of our government," he wrote, the frequent contacts of Catholics with sectaries in the discharge of public duties, the contacts too in private affairs, the need to conform with others whenever it is possible without detriment to faith and the precepts of the Church,———all this postulates uninterrupted care, watchfulness and prudence in the pastor of souls. They must be on guard lest the faithful be gradually infected with the so-called prevailing indifference of this country; but they must likewise take care lest unnecessary withdrawal from non-Catholics alienate them from our doctrine and rites, for, as they outnumber us and are more influential, they may, at some time, be inclined to renew the iniquitous laws against us.[9]

Carroll's desire both to avoid indifference (i.e., to be explicitly Catholic) yet not to alienate Protestants in Catholic "doctrine and rites" could be seen in the bishop's approach to two of the most significant elements in the community's spiritual life, the language of the liturgy and the celebration of the sacrament of matrimony.

Throughout his ministry, Carroll demonstrated a consistent willingness to make the liturgy intelligible to Protestants and to the poor illiterates of his own church. As superior of the American missions, he considered the use of Latin to be "one of the greatest obstacles, with Christians of other denominations, to a thorough union with us; or, at least, to a much more general Diffusion of our Religion, particularly in N. America." Carroll desired a vernacular liturgy, believing that some change in the discipline, which had been enforced at the time of the Reformation, should be "*insisted on,* as essential to the Service of God & Benefit of Mankind." There is evidence that he actively discussed alterations in the liturgy when he went to England for his consecration as bishop in 1790, even though he knew such actions would exceed his ordinary powers. The regulations of the diocesan synod in 1791 made ample provision for the use of the vernacular, when permissible, in the Roman rite. Rumors of Carroll's vernacular changes filtered over to England and caused some anxiety among his friends there. Robert Plowden, the brother of Charles, wrote to Carroll in March, 1799, that "only a few months before I was positively assured by a clergyman of my acquaintance, a man of first rate abilities in point of theological knowledge that yr Ldsp was making alterations in the administration of the Sacraments, contrary to the laws of the Church. . . ." In 1810 the United States bishops passed regulations to limit the use of the vernacular in the administration of the sacraments and to exclude it from the Mass completely.[10]

In 1821 a priest working at Saint Patrick's in Washington testified to the perdurance of these practices. He noted to his archbishop that "Rev. Mr. Matthews, (the pastor) uses for interments, and likewise frequently for baptisms, the English translation of the Roman Ritual instead of the Latin Original, on account of the late Right Revd. Archbishop Carroll's having formerly so stated." Again, in 1829, Francis Patrick Kenrick, sixth archbishop of Baltimore (1796–1863), noted the wide diversity of liturgical practices in the United States, among which were the baptismal interrogations and prayers in the vernacular, the omission when administering extreme unction of the anointing of the feet, "because of the Protestants gathered around," and the recitation of the marriage vows from the English ritual, the Roman rite being added afterward. Joseph Rosati, bishop of Saint Louis from 1827–43, wondered about the same practices: "Can priests use the English language for the administrations of Baptism, Matrimony, Extreme Unction and in the prayers established for burial? Such use exists in some dioceses, a use which certain bishops foster by their own example."[11]

It should be noted that the vernacular changes referred to usually took place at the key rites of passage: baptism, marriage, and burial, or precisely when Catholics and Protestants would most likely be together. There is even some evidence that English was employed during the Mass at those times, the *misereatur* and *indulgentiam*, when the priest addressed the congregation. In 1806 a Sulpician teaching at Saint Mary's Seminary voiced his opposition to the prevailing customs and focused on the heart of the issue in these words:

> Nevertheless, today we see that a pastor of Baltimore and certain other fellow priests of ours, under the eyes of the bishop and with his approval, administer the sacraments and perform ecclesiastical rites (e.g. for burial, etc.) in the English language, which more often than not seems ridiculous and inharmonious. . . .

> So likewise, when we recently attended the funeral of a certain friend together with the bishop and several other priests, we were not only amazed, seeing ourselves associated in a serious and religious ceremony with heretical ministers who had been invited, [unclear] but above all because the priest, old and full of piety, at the introduction of the body into the church before it was taken to the burial place, recited the prayers assigned in the ritual for burial in the English language, and, even though he was surrounded by a large group of priests, no one responded to the versicles because this innovation was displeasing to them.[12]

Catholic spiritual life, founded on sacramental participation, was designed during the Carroll period to demonstrate commitment to the Catholic tradition and yet encourage the community to accept the demands of religious pluralism in a positive way.

An examination of Carroll's legislation and sermons on the sacrament of matrimony furnishes a second example of a liturgical life shaped within the context of religious pluralism and founded on a positive theological anthropology. In this area of the community's expression, the bishop struggled to establish a strong Catholic identity and at the same time to create a communal spiritual life attractive to the outsider. On the one hand, Carroll repeatedly argued against intermarriage between Catholics and Protestants. He believed that the frequency of these unions led the Catholic community into religious indifference. Perhaps at these times he was thinking of his sister Eleanor, who had married a non-Catholic, and of his Protestant nieces and nephews. His request to Propaganda to extend his dispensing powers to the second degree of consanguinity reflected a concern to broaden opportunities for Catholics to marry Catholics in the small and socially restricted Catholic community. The strict regulations of the Synod of 1791 discouraging mixed marriages testified to this preoccupation. The bishop readily acknowledged his reluctance to perform mixed marriages. "Now, to correspond with these designs of Providence," he said, "it is ordained by the Church, that its members should choose for their indissoluble companions through life, only such as are united in the profession of the same faith." This position remained constant throughout his life.[13]

On the other hand, the whole tenor of Carroll's apologetic discourse argued for convergence and peace between Protestants and Catholics. His sermons on the dignity of matrimony followed the lines established by his anthropology. The sacrament of the new dispensation was placed in the context of creation. "The necessary and essential dependence of all creatures on their Creator," he noted, "is sufficient of itself to render every rational being religious by its very nature and constitution." Soon after the creation of Adam, "the Creator made provision for the binding of him in society that he might enjoy its comforts." The true Christian religion, according to Carroll, completed this old dispensation. Marriage was the means by which the wisdom of God "adapts that religion, of which he is the author, and which alone deserves to be dignified by that honourable appelation, to the improvement and perfection of his rational creatures. . . ."[14]

This approach, following the strongest traditions of humanistic theology, allowed Carroll to be exceptionally affirming of natural ties and affections. He ranked "the assistance and consolations derivable from the society of a companion" as the first end of marriage; the love of posterity as the second end; only then "last in order, as well as the lowest in perfection" came marriage as "a defense and resource against the assaults of temptation." In one of the more beautiful passages in his writings, Carroll summarized his view in these words:

> Whoever loves God, and is penetrated with a grateful sense of his manifold blessings and favors, must wish and rejoice, that thousands and tens of thousands of tongues should proclaim his greatness, and sing forth his praises; and whoever are disposed to engage in matrimony, while their minds are under this impression of love for, and gratitude to God, will

refer their intended union not merely to the purpose of having posterity to inherit their own names, but to honor the Creator and Father of mankind; they will resolve to receive the children with which heaven may bless their marriage, as gifts to be rendered worthy of an heavenly reward. . . . Thus their natural birth will be a preparation for their regeneration to God through Jesus Christ, in the waters of baptism. How far above and superior to the vulgar and common estimate of marriage, is this view of it, exhibited by our divine religion? And how much is it to be wished, for the happiness of mankind, that it were always considered in this light.[15]

Carroll's need to address the reality of religious pluralism in a positive way combined with his political and theological anthropology to provide the foundations for a vision of the Christian life that was irenic in tone and Catholic in substance. These convictions also directed the institution of the church to the service of the spiritual development of the person and placed the building of community at the center of Carroll's pastoral program. The bishop's ecclesiological issues will be the subject of the next section.

CHAPTER
3
"Spiritual Matters": The Ecclesiological Dimensions of Christian Piety

*J*ohn Carroll's ecclesiology can be analyzed by examining his use of the term "in spiritual matters" *(in spiritualibus)*. In a letter of April 27, 1778, he described a fellow priest in these words: "James Watton, who has as fine land as any in America, is said to make a bad hand at farming. This you, who know him, will not be surprised at. But if he does not succeed in temporals, he is indefatigable in his spiritual occupations."[1] This use of "spiritual" in juxtaposition to temporal concerns typified Carroll's approach. An understanding of the development of the term *in spiritualibus* will indicate the significance of his position.

In the Middle Ages, the term "in spiritual matters" had come to be defined in the context of a unified church and state. It referred to those realities, both temporal and spiritual, over which the church possessed juridical control. The post-Reformation period continued this usage but added a defensive meaning differentiating the church's sphere of action *"in spiritual matters"* from the state's action *"in temporal matters."* Here "spiritual" came to imply an institutional and juridical understanding of the church focused on her rights, status, power, control, and authority in opposition to the state. Within the church, "in spiritual matters" was linked with the power and authority to govern parishes and dioceses (the church's sphere of control) in temporal as well as spiritual matters.[2]

A different experience formed Carroll's understanding of "spiritual matters." When the Society of Jesus was suppressed in 1773, the former Jesuit missionaries still individually possessed their temporal holdings, but corporately they were without resources. Since their ties to one another were dissolved, "in temporal matters," they were set adrift. Carroll described the situation to Charles Plowden: They were "without father, without mother, oppressed with grief, uncertain of our future destiny."[3] The situation became even more acute when after 1776 the missionaries could no longer accept the episcopal jurisdiction of the vicar apostolic in London without appearing to owe a foreign allegiance. Now, "in spiritual matters" they were also set adrift. Carroll took action to address both situations. Fearing that Rome might claim the former Jesuit estates in Maryland, Virginia, and Pennsylvania, he proposed a Draft Plan of Clergy Organization that insisted *within the church* on the separation of the spiritual and temporal spheres. The plan, eventually adopted in 1784, noted explicitly that "the person invested with Spiritual Jurisdiction in this Country, shall not in that quality have any power over or in the temporal property of the clergy." Second, in 1783, Carroll and the others petitioned Pope Pius VI that some "spiritual jurisdiction" be given to John Lewis, the former Jesuit superior. The common usage of "in spiritual matters" implied teaching authority, the power to confirm and to bless oils, chalices, and altar stones. It did not carry any of the temporal connotations associated with management and administration.[4]

Carroll indicated a similar understanding of "spiritual" when he wrote to Joseph Berington and expressed his desire to ascertain the "Extent and Boundaries of the Spiritual Jurisdiction of the Holy See." After he was made superior of the American mission in 1784, he reiterated this understanding in his battles with the trustees of Saint Peter's Church, New York. While acknowledging the temporal power of the laity, Carroll referred to his own "spiritual" authority to maintain the proper mode of episcopal government and Catholic discipline in preaching, the administration of the sacraments, and other pastoral actions. He maintained this position for the remainder of his life.[5]

In the light of this history, when John Carroll used the term "in spiritual matters" it is clear that he referred to the juridical tradition emphasizing the rights and responsibilities of the hierarchy of the church. This institutional aspect of his ecclesiology cannot be ignored.[6] But more important, given the context of Carroll's life, "in spiritual matters" also took on a radically new meaning. First, since church and state had been separated in the American republic, the need to insist on spiritual rights and power with respect to the state no longer existed. The term *in spiritualibus* could now cease to carry the strong defensive and institutional overtones of previous centuries. Second, because of his Jesuit experience and his battle with lay trusteeism, Carroll also differentiated within the church between spiritual and temporal concerns. This left "spiritual occupations" free of any of the secular connotations of management, control, and administration of church property. Thus, for James Watton, "to be indefatigable in spiritual occupations" meant primarily to be occupied with building up the church through the sacraments and pastoral work. Given Carroll's anthropology, it meant acting with persuasion, creating community in a profoundly "spiritual" sense. Such an understanding enabled Carroll to develop an ecclesiology dominated not by a concern for the institutional lines of authority but by communal spiritual growth and the encouragement of peaceful relationships among persons. How he did this can be seen in the way he defined *church*, in his focus on the ministry of Christ as a model for everyone, and in his description of the priesthood.

In the midst of the controversy with the trustees of Holy Trinity Church, Philadelphia, and despite the need to emphasize structure, jurisdictional authority, and organization, John Carroll described the church as "one indivisible society through the whole world, of which Jesus Christ is the invisible, and, as has been said, the Successor of St. Peter is the visible head." The bishop noted that jurisdictional offices existed for the "souls of men"; even the power of the pope was "ordained for, and directed to the preservation of unity in faith and worship, amongst all true believers." Carroll stressed that the origin of the church was in Jesus' ministry, his "being sent" from the Father. Since this was the case, ministry was essentially both an office and a commission. Quoting the letter to the Ephesians, Carroll referred to his Catholic Christians as "fellow citizens with the Saints, and the domestics of God." Throughout the document the leader of the church in the United States recognized the unity existing between ministers and congregations. As he had put it earlier, in his sermon before the 1791 synod: every Christian is bound to save his own soul and to cooperate in the salvation of others "by example, by persuasion, by influence, and authority." For Carroll, the church, led by duly authorized bishops, was the community of those who believe in Jesus Christ.[7]

In many of his writings the bishop spoke about the ministry of Christ, a ministry that, given the language, had obvious ecclesiological connotations. "The Son of God," Carroll preached,

> Priest forever of a much higher order than Aaron and destined to introduce a far more perfect dispensation of grace and religion, comes down from heaven, and by the wonderful and omnipotent operation of the Holy

Ghost, assumes and is united to a body, formed of the same materials, as our own. During the course of his mortal life, he remains in this tabernacle of his body, inviting us to the practice of virtue by his example, confirming our faith by his miracles, enlightening our ignorance by his doctrine, protecting us by his prayers, and devoting himself daily for our sakes, to humiliations, to suffering, to poverty, to reproach and injuries: and after fulfilling these functions of a Pastor, and prophet, and Legislator, he concludes his life in the office and exercises of a Pontiff, and victim: for our iniquities, he is covered with his own sacred blood.[8]

Carroll described each of the functions of the hierarchical church with reference to the ministry of Christ, thus emphasizing the personal dimensions of the institution. In his sermon on "Charity," he explained this vision of Christian community in detail.

The sermon on "Charity" began with a christological reflection on Mark 8:2, Jesus' feeding of the five thousand. Christ's examples of "relieving the corporal necessities of the multitudes" and instructing them in the doctrines of eternal life "teach us," Carroll said, "in what manner we are to exercise charity on behalf of our fellowmen, by extending our solicitude to lighten their miseries both corporal and spiritual, on one hand to use the means afforded us by Providence to assuage the evils of poverty and disease; on the other to deliver them from the ignorance of God's holy law."

The sermon stressed the identification that should exist between Christ, the Christian, and the church. Despite obstacles of ignorance, incredulity, and discouragement, Christ showed people that "the true spirit of Christianity is a spirit of charity & compassion, that it is an illusion to deem ourselves, the Disciples of Christ, without becoming interested in the necessities of our neighbor, & exacting endeavors to relieve them." In this way, Carroll made identity with Christ the indicator of church membership. Following the example of Jesus, Christians should work for unity, care for the poor, anticipate people's needs, visit the sick and wretched, share the substance of their lives, and instruct the ignorant. "By this, says Christ, *shall men know you are my Disciples, if you love one another.*"

The bishop continued by describing the Eucharist as the sign of Christ's bounty, the power of his resurrection, the reality that should both convict the Christian of sin and challenge him or her to thankfulness and reparation. The last third of the sermon was an exhortation to build Christian family life by practicing mercy in the ordinary affairs of life. Giving responsibility for the spiritual growth of the community to the laity, Carroll argued that intellectual instruction should not be left to "those, who can seldom see your children and servants." Instead, families should gather together in prayers every evening, learn the catechism, and "consecrate to God the actions of each day of our whole life." If some people objected that they were too ignorant to teach others, let them remember, Carroll admonished, that the bishop himself had "always found the children & servants of pious and diligent tho' ignorant and illiterate Xtians, the best instructed in the principles & practices of their religion."[9]

The sermon on charity was remarkable for its blending of the ministry of Jesus, eucharistic theology, and a vision of the church as founded on personal, familial, and communal responsibility. The same orientation permeated Carroll's view of the ministerial priesthood. In his discourses on Holy Orders, perhaps the most personally revealing of all his writings, the bishop described priests as "coadjutors of God," "ministers of Christ," people whose lives existed to cooperate in the work of salvation and to promote the happiness of people. Always, the priesthood was described not in reference to institutional status but in reference to Christ, who called the individual to continue a visible ministry on earth, "subordinate to & associated with him in the performance of the most sacred duties of adoration and religion." For Carroll, there was only one mediator:

> Remember, that in every act of your ministry, you will have him invisibly present, acting through you; that the functions, which you will perform before men, are his functions, and that he will present them to his eternal Fr., as his own: that the doctrines, which you are to teach, are his doctrines; that the reconciliation of sinners, which you will pronounce with your lips, is a reconciliation perfected by him; that the solemn & most awful Sacrifice, which you will offer on his altars here, is the Sacrifice, which he offers on the cross. . . .[10]

The American churchman never described the priesthood in isolation from the community as a "state" or "independent office," nor did he refer to the "dignity of episcopal authority." The letter to the trustees spoke of the "pastoral office," "pastoral charge," "ministerial functions," "duties," "holy function of the pastoral office." The priest, Carroll noted, was "one, who prays officially, who pleads in the name of the whole Church, in the name of the Society of the Just." Many of his sermons testified to the contractual arrangement perceived to exist between priest and people. The congregation witnessed to the call of the priest, added their endeavors to his, and he, in turn, was responsible for their welfare.[11]

Perhaps the distinctiveness of Carroll's vision emerges most clearly when his views are compared with those of a fellow missionary, John Ashton (1742–1815). Ashton delivered the closing sermon at the first diocesan synod in 1791, the same gathering at which Carroll probably described his understanding of the priesthood. Ashton commented on the text: "Be vigilant, labour in all things; do the work of an evangelist;

fulfill the ministry, be sober" (2 Tim. 4:5). The Jesuit set his tone by referring to the evil times, when "error has supplanted sound doctrine, when the fables of pretended philosophy have eclipsed evangelical wisdom and mankind intoxicated with the enthusiasm of liberty, will not submit to the sweet yoke of Xt." In this way, he placed the priesthood in a defensive context, one that defined the minister as guardian and protector. Ashton referred to the priest, not to Christ, as "Way," "Truth," and "Life." *Church* meant hierarchical structure, not the congregation of the faithful. According to this missionary, the duties of the priest were twofold: personal sanctification and sanctification of neighbor. The sermon heightened the distinction between priest and people. The former fed, led by example, and cured the latter. His vision and Carroll's could hardly have been more disparate.[12]

"Indefatigable in spiritual occupations": Carroll had used the phrase to describe the work of a fellow missionary. It implied, for the bishop, a vision of the church as a society existing with distinct offices and duties, yet oriented toward the development of a unified Christian and Catholic communal life. At the center of Catholic life stood the life of Jesus himself and the practical identification of each individual believer, lay or cleric, with Jesus' ministry. The last portion of this exposition of Carroll's spirituality will examine the means to that identification with Jesus, Carroll's view of Christian piety.

CHAPTER
4
The Sentiments and
Affections of Jesus Christ

$\mathcal{O}$n March 1, 1785, John Carroll wrote an exposition on the "State of Religion in the United States" to the prefect of the Propaganda Fide in Rome. Among the many items mentioned, the piety of the native-born Catholics in Maryland and Pennsylvania received considerable attention. The superior of the American missions felt that while the people were faithful to the practices of religion and frequented the sacraments, their piety lacked warmth. "All fervor," he wrote, "is lacking, which usually is developed by constant exhortation to piety since many congregations attend Mass and hear a sermon once a month or every two months." Of the immigrants, very few discharged their Easter duty. For all, a love of dancing and other amusements, a fondness for love stories, and the unavoidable mixing with Protestants often threatened the integrity of soul and body.

In 'this report, Carroll used the term *piety* to encompass the necessary exercises of religion, moral conduct, and interior disposition or fervor. He reported a similar position in his sermon on "Confirmation," a sacrament that he believed should excite "sentiments of a lively faith" and sanctify the soul "by the Spirit of piety—prayer: Sacraments: Keeping the day of the Lord—exercises of works of mercy, spiritl. & corporal. Devon. to the Bd. Virgin Mary." An examination of these areas of the duties of religion, moral conduct, and fervor will indicate the basic components of his piety.[1]

In trying to create a strong Catholic community in the United States, Carroll focused his attention on the Liturgy of the Eucharist and the following of the church's calendar. The Synod of 1791 described in elaborate fashion the arrangement for services and the observance of feasts in the city, "where there are many clerics, or where the laity have been suitably instructed in singing, and the other ministrations at the altar." The *missa cantata*, preceded by the Litany of Loretto and solemn asperges, provided an occasion to announce the observance of fast and feast days and to instruct the faithful in the correction of their faults and the perfection of their Christian lives. Afternoon vespers was followed by the singing of the antiphons to the Blessed Virgin, benediction, and catechism. In outlying districts, where there was only one priest, the priest heard confession, recited the Litany of Loretto or the Most Holy Name of Jesus, performed the asperges, and then began the Mass. The whole was followed by the recitation in the vernacular of the Our Father, Hail Mary, Apostles' Creed, acts of faith, hope, and charity, and then catechism for the uninstructed.

Carroll noted in one of his sermons that proper observance of the Sabbath, presumably in this way, enabled people to withdraw their attention and affection from cares and to meditate on the truth of religion, their dependence on God, the importance of a virtuous life, and the precautions necessary to grow in Christian holiness. In addition to Sundays, in 1801 the following feasts were significant holy days: Circumcision, Epiphany, Annunciation, Easter Monday, Ascension, Pentecost Monday, Corpus Christi, Assumption, All Saints, and Christmas. There also existed particular "days of devotion" celebrated by prayers, litanies, and hymns.[2]

Carroll tried to inculcate in the community a genuinely liturgical spirituality. His desire to encourage the vernacular and lay participation has already been noted. The English Catholic tradition of John Gother's *Instructions* and Richard Challoner's *Garden of the Soul* supported this focus on the liturgy as the primary component of piety. Numerous other works encouraged liturgical music, often in the vernacular. In addition, Carroll was anxious to promote good preaching during all the services. He saw the Divine Office playing a prominent role in the life of the laity. For example, *The Office of the Holy Week, according to the Roman Missal and Breviary*, published in 1810 and found in Carroll's library, contained the whole liturgy in Latin and English. In this way, while the pious Christian "unites his voice with that of the priest, and of the choir, in the various parts of the Divine Office, he may penetrate also the sense of those holy prayers, and sanction by the fervor of his heart, what he promises with his tongue." Many others shared these views.[3]

An important part of the liturgy was the hearing of the gospel. Carroll wished to foster in the community a lively awareness of the

Scriptures. In January, 1789, he began negotiations with Mathew Carey, the publisher, about the issuing of the Rheims-Douay Version. The bishop was familiar with the Scripture scholarship of his day, but he felt that the Rheims-Douay Version had "the long established credit of faithfulness." He worked hard to gather subscriptions for the Bible, which eventually came out on December 1, 1790. The English Catholic tradition to which Carroll was heir had avoided the Counter Reformation's divorce of tradition from Scripture. The prayer books of the time translated the Epistles and the Gospels to make them available to the people. Carroll's sermons and writings manifested an assiduous reading of the Word of God.[4]

The sacraments of penance and the Eucharist were central to this type of piety. Following the Jesuit tradition of focus on the Eucharist, the Synod of 1791 encouraged priests to arouse the faithful "more and more to the greatest devotion towards this immense pledge of divine mercy." Before receiving first communion, which was not to be delayed too long nor given immediately upon the age of reason, candidates were instructed to make a general confession, "after a careful examination of conscience, and with great contrition of heart." The synod also insisted on the observance of the Paschal duty of receiving confession and Communion during Lent or Eastertime. Both the 1791 decrees and the 1810 bishops' meeting encouraged benediction of the Blessed Sacrament. The centrality of penance and the Eucharist emerged clearly throughout Carroll's sermons.[5] They provided, along with the observance of Sunday, the cycle of feasts, and the use of Scripture, the essential structure of his Catholic Christian piety.

A strong emphasis on morality permeated Carroll's writings and comprised the second major element in his piety. This orientation derived from the focus on clear and reasonable ideas in his philosophical training and his reaction to the forces of infidelity, which he understood to be rooted in "the blindness generated by shameful and disorderly lusts and passions." The bishop's understanding of the vagaries of the human heart balanced his optimistic interpretation of the relationship between nature and grace. Reason, insufficient of itself to control "boisterous and tumultuous desires," needed revelation to impose a regime of self-control, moderation, humility, and obedience. The sermon on "Penance" presented a clear picture of this dimension of the Christian life. People could fix the inconstancy of their hearts and achieve peace by observing the laws of God, "with docility of mind and humble obedience"; frequent inspection into the state of the soul and noticing every relaxation; "subduing your passion"; "seeking a remedy for sin in the Sacrament of reconciliation, & a preservative of virtue in the Sacrament, the holy & [ador]able

Sacrament of Christs body and blood"; "exercising in a spirit of humility, the works of corporal and [spiritu]al mercy."

The bishop's Lenten pastoral of February 1792, was uncompromising in its demand that temperance, self-denial, fasting, voluntary mortification; discipline, meditation, reading, and works of charity receive the attention of serious Christians. When commenting on the justice of the Scribes and Pharisees, Carroll noted: "The Son of God contents not himself with repressing the most criminal transports of outward violence, but inculcates in us the necessity of keeping our turbulent and fretful passions under continual restraint." In the context of morality, the sacraments were perceived as remedies for sin. To support this asceticism the bishop encouraged meditation on both the finality and the uncertain hour of death, a practice typical for the period. "Behold the holy & watchful God descend from heaven," he preached. "He pronounces the terrible sentence against the delaying sinner: cut down the tree, & cast it into unexhaustible flames."[6]

Despite its severe tone, Carroll's moralism avoided the extremes of rigorism. For example, correspondence between the bishop and Stephen Badin (1768–1853), a French priest on the Kentucky frontier, indicates how much the Baltimore prelate followed the moderate asceticism associated with Francis de Sales and Alfonso Rodríguez. Badin preached consistently against dancing, so much so that the people got the impression that it was a sin. He had heard, on the other hand, that Carroll actually tolerated "spectacles during Lent." The frontier priest also practiced delayed absolution for sins, exacted public penances for public offenses, imposed fasts before granting dispensations, and withheld the Eucharist from some.[7] "If all my Penitents are not admitted to the Sacred Table," he wrote, "I can assign no other reason than that for which the number of goats at the last day shall be far greater than that of sheep." Thomas Wilson, a Dominican priest working on the frontier, complained to Carroll about the constant neglect of the sacraments in Badin's congregation.

> Young people are not admitted without a solemn promise of not dancing *on any occasion whatever*, which few will promise & fewer still can keep. All priests that allow of any dancing are publicly condemned to Hell. People taught to believe that every Kiss lip to lip between married persons is a mortal sin. Old men not allowed the marriage act more than once a week. People publicly warned on our arrival, that there are all sorts of Priests good & bad etc. etc. Women refused absolution for their husbands permitting a decent dance in their house, not to mention a thousand things far more ridiculously severe.[8]

The bishop questioned all of these practices and considered Badin a rigorist. Raised in a tradition that integrated nature and grace, Carroll focused his piety on fidelity to duty in small things, purity of intention, and habitual conformity to the will of God. Carroll's sketch of his secretary was a direct reflection of his own piety: "Of an open and frank disposition, he pursued the path of rectitude without affectation or a gloomy severity, incompatible with the precepts and example of the Divine Model of all good Shepherds. He loved innocent and virtuous society, never forgetting the decencies of his profession, nor yet excluding such relaxations, as were consistent with the most rigid morality."[9]

The third characteristic of piety that Carroll referred to in his 1785 report was fervor. This element served to modify his moralism and accounted for the surprising warmth of many of his sermons. *Fervor* meant interiority, a piety centered in the will and its dispositions. It signified, above all, as Carroll noted in his sermon on charity, "transforming into our hearts the sentiments and affections of Jesus Christ."[10] Alfonso Rodríguez described this tradition of prayer when he wrote that the masters of the spiritual life

> would not have us employ all the time of prayer, in running over the points of meditation, but that we should particularly apply ourselves to the inflaming our will by motions of affection, which being first produced in the heart, have afterwards their effect in all our actions. And it is to this, say they, we ought particularly apply ourselves in prayer. As he who digs in the earth, whether it be to find water, or to find a treasure, leaves off digging, as soon as he finds what he sought after; so in like manner, when by profound meditation, we have found the treasure of charity, and the love of God, that fountain of living water we sought after, it is not necessary any longer to busy ourselves in digging, but we must think of enriching ourselves with those treasures of grace we have found; and of refreshing ourselves by copious draughts, from this fountain of eternal life, and entertaining ourselves with those affectionate motions wherewith we shall find ourselves touched. This is the end of prayer; this is the fruit we ought to reap from it; and it is this all the meditations, and all the reflections of our understanding ought to aim at.[11]

That Carroll followed this advice is best illustrated through his devotion to the Sacred Heart and his understanding of meditation.

Carroll's Jesuit training at Saint-Omer, Liège, and Bruges, in the mid-eighteenth century, emphasized devotion to the Sacred Heart. While visiting Rome in 1773, the young priest noted that the Jansenist faction repeatedly attacked the devotion so closely associated with the Jesuits. It had been practiced for many years in the American missions. In 1793 Carroll requested Propaganda to permit the Mass and Office of the Sacred Heart on the Friday after the octave of Corpus Christi, a request that he repeated in 1802. A good idea of what the devotion meant can be gathered from the prayer book compiled by the Jesuits at Georgetown in 1793, *The Pious Guide to Prayer and Devotion.* Carroll ordered 100 copies.[12]

The *Pious Guide*, designed in part to refute the Jansenist criticism that Sacred Heart devotions were excessively materialistic, indicated that "heart" was the symbol for the whole humanity of Christ. It celebrated the sanctification of the human by the divine. "Whatever belongs to the adorable person of Jesus Christ," the *Guide* read,

> claims all our veneration in an infinite degree; the least part of his sacred body, a drop of his blood, a hair of his head deserves the utmost adoration. Every thing that has but touched his sacred body, becomes thereby, venerable, as the cross, the nails, the lance, the thorns.

In practicing this devotion, Christians modeled their hearts on the divine original. They encouraged their own gradual transformation, penetrated into the most august sanctuary, gained confidence in the mercy of Christ, and received unspeakable delights and comforts.[13]

The Sacred Heart, according to the *Pious Guide*, could be considered under two aspects: it was, on the one hand, a heart full of love and breathing nothing but the salvation of mankind. On the other, it was "a Heart that is offended, insulted and [despised] by unthinking man, by sinners void of all sense of gratitude and unaffected by his Love." The purpose of the devotion was to honor Jesus, share in his grief, and make amends. The advantage was that anyone could practice it. "It is not confined thereby to some select and privileged souls, more versed in spiritual matters, and more enlightened than the common. No, it lies within the reach of all degrees of people, the unlearned as well as the most learned." The point was that all had a heart to give to God; all were challenged to throw themselves into that "burning furnace," "repair into that sacred asylum," drink from that "spring of living water."[14]

The devotion focused attention away from needless external practices and toward an identification with Jesus in the ordinary activities of life. The ultimate goal was to "perform all our daily actions, in union with the Sacred Heart; so that, when we pray, we pray with it; when we love, we love with it; when we act, we act with and in it; when we suffer we suffer in and for it." Such an identification could be fostered by prayers to the Sacred Heart: acts of reparation, adoration, thanksgiving, love, atonement, and petition.[15]

Devotion to the Sacred Heart was one of the chief means by which Carroll came to appreciate the humanity of Christ. The other means was his exposure to the practice of affective meditation in the Ignatian tradition. An eight-day retreat based on the *Exercises* was mandatory for the scholastics at the schools in Belgium. In addition they were encouraged to make three days of recollection at the beginning of the year. Although very little is known of Carroll's personal practices during his years as bishop, he did write an introduction to the American edition of Père Vincent Huby's *Spiritual Retreat*. Carroll recommended Huby's directed meditations to all "those sincere Christians who study to know themselves, and to serve the maker, with constancy and fidelity in spirit and truth." Carroll encouraged people to take a few days of retirement to devote themselves to prayer and watchfulness and give serious consideration to the extent of their religious duties. "An inflamed love of God," he wrote, was the "prevailing and permanent affection" of Father Huby's soul. Through this book, he "endeavours to transfuse into others the glowing sentiment of his own heart. Every religious truth, every subject on which he treats, leads him to, and is concluded with, fervent acts of love and adoration of God, and of compunction for having offended him."[16]

Carroll's encomium of Vincent Huby's meditations provides a significant clue to his understanding of the word *fervor*. Huby emphasized docility to the Holy Spirit and self-reflection. He tried to present the Ignatian method to a wide public of priests, magistrates, artisans, merchants, and scholars, to popularize a strong interior life through purification of the heart. The meditations were very theocentric, beginning with the love of God and concentrating on this love manifested in the Creation, the Incarnation, and the Redemption. The following was a representative example:

> How liberal, how unbounded, is the love of God for man. It is this love, that has drawn him out of nothing, that preserves him, and that, by the ministry of creatures, abundantly provides, not only for his necessities, but even for his conveniences and gratifications.
>
> It was this love, which preserved Adam not only from the miseries naturally annexed to his condition, such as diseases and death, the darkness of ignorance, and the rebellion of concupiscence, but which moreover dignified and ennobled the first instant of his existence, by enlightening his mind with the splendor of celestial brightness, and sanctifying his heart by the intuition of supernatural grace. All these inestimable blessings were bestowed on us in the person of our first parent: and, had not his disobedience perverted the order which the divine goodness had established, they would have been all transmitted to his most distant posterity. . . .
>
> All this is truly great and wonderful; but what is a still more astonishing and incomprehensible prodigy of love, is, that God, as St. John says, should have so loved the world, as, for it, to deliver up his only son to the ignominious death of the cross.[17]

According to Huby, it was only in the light of this great love that one could begin to understand sin and the necessity of penance.

As Carroll had noted, each meditation begun in this way ended with acts of adoration and compunction. This was very similar to the method adopted by de Sales in his *Introduction to the Devout Life* and similar to the method mentioned by Rodríguez in his chapter on "Holy Communion." The approach followed Ignatius and consisted of three parts:

1. giving thanks to God for the gift received
2. accusing oneself for not having made such good use of it
3. begging grace to make better use of it in the future

This style of meditation provided a structure for many of Carroll's sermons and for numerous other short reflections in his writings. Given the importance of devotion to Mary in the bishop's life, his sermon on the Assumption can serve to illustrate the method. Beginning with the Scripture passage, "he who is mighty hath done great things to me, & holy is his name," Carroll immediately drew his listener into the action of God and Mary's response.

> On this day we solemnise the remembrance of the glorious rewards; on this day, we are meet together to celebrate the solemn festival of the assumption of the glorious V.M; that is, of her being removed from this world, this vale of tears, to everlasting glory in heaven.

The bishop then stressed the identification existing between Mary and the believer:

> Above all, let us constantly bear in mind the holy & virtuous examples left us by her in this life, if we wish to enjoy a share of her happiness in the next.

Two points for reflection were added so that people might begin to realize their failure in the light of their greatest calling:

> that the dignity wch. Mary derived from the sanctifying grace bestowed on her at the moment of her conception, in consideration of her future dignity of M[othe]r of God, discovers to us the great excellency of the grace of adoption & reconciliation bestowed on us thro the means of the Scmts. of baptism, & pennance [sic]:
>
> & 2ly. that the fidelity of Mary to that first grace teaches us our indispensable obligation of using our earnest endeavor to preserve the grace of justification conferred on us in either of the above mentioned Sacraments.[18]

Although this particular sermon remained incomplete, the custom would have been to conclude with a prayer for grace, point three of the schema. Carroll followed a similar method in sermons on "Charity," "John the Apostle," and "An Appeal for School Funds."[19]

Several features of this method of meditation should be noted. First, the approach was designed to move the congregation, to excite their hearts, to instill in them "the sentiments and affections" of the example given. This purpose correlated well with Carroll's commitment to persuasion as the best means for creating harmony. Second, the method focused on the person's experience of grace, drawing him or her into self-reflection on human dignity. This self-reflection placed the person from the beginning of creation in the light of God's life. In this way, the meditation supported Carroll's basic position on the close relationship between nature and grace. Third, reflection on grace led to a recognition of the need for human repentance in the context of the church. The bishop significantly allied the action of God with the sacraments of baptism and penance. Fourth, the preacher encouraged a close relationship between the Gospel example, the priest, and the people. Here was the meditative corollary of the church as the "congregation of those who believed." Last, the whole meditation represented in the early days of the American republic a popularization of affective prayer, a style of contemplation open to everyone.

In conclusion, John Carroll's vision of the Christian life was profoundly incarnational. Inheritor of three of the more creative strands of post-Reformation Catholic spirituality, Carroll fashioned a synthesis open to the demands of his own social setting. The social realities of religious pluralism and the need to create civil harmony encouraged him to emphasize the rules of a "Catholic Christian." He attempted in his ecclesiology to recognize the demands for hierarchical structure and the need of each person to offer "reasonable service." His life of piety, with its liturgical orientation, strict moralism, and affective prayer correlated well with his basic understanding of the person and the church. Challenged to be an example to all, John Carroll fashioned a spirituality that was Catholic, Christian, and American. It was well-suited to a small Catholic minority in the eastern United States during the early nineteenth century. The next three chapters will examine how new leaders came to shape a vision of the Christian life for their own times, responding to the needs of the growing Catholic church in the years 1830–1866.

PART TWO

The Immigrant Vision, 1830–1866

You will all rejoice, Venerable and Beloved Brethren, in these evidences
of the vitality and diffusion of our Holy Faith, in the midst of the difficulties and evils that surround us. We depend on your fidelity to its sacred
teachings, and your zealous co-operation, to give effect to our labors in
your behalf, that so, all that has been planned and done by us, may be
to the Glory of God, the Exaltation of His Holy Church, and the Salvation
of Souls for which Christ died.[1]

With these words the Catholic bishops assembled at the Second
Plenary Council in Baltimore in 1866 concluded their pastoral letter
to the people. Their image of Christ as one who died for souls, their
vision of the "exaltation of the Church," and their call for the fidelity
and cooperation of the people reflected an approach to the Christian
life that had been developed in the community since the beginnings
of nativism and the First Provincial Council in 1829. In the 1866
council documents, Titles I and II, on "the Orthodox Faith" and "the
Hierarchy and Government of the Church," set the doctrinal and ecclesiological boundaries of Catholic life within a Counter Reformation
framework; other sections presented images of conduct and piety for
the bishops, priests, religious, and laity; still others governed the style
of Catholic life in indulgences, benediction of the Blessed Sacrament,
vespers, daily prayer, confraternities, catechism classes, virtues to be
encouraged in Catholic schools, and the content of prayer books. Seen
as a whole, the council's decrees and its pastoral letter presented the

immigrant church's "mystique of salvation," its "system of religion," its vision of the spiritual life.

It is the purpose of the next three chapters to examine the social, intellectual, and personal foundations for this vision of the Christian life. Using the experience of a representative leader from the American, Irish, and German communities as foundational guides, three significant areas of the immigrant vision will be examined: the images of Christ, the person, and the church; the view of asceticism and prayer; the expressions of devotionalism. In the course of the discussion it will become apparent how much the mid-nineteenth century experience of religious bigotry and poverty shaped an ecclesiology and anthropology significantly different from that of John Carroll. Although the post–Civil War period will be referred to, especially in the area of devotionalism, concentration will be given to the pre–Civil War era, since that is the time during which the major lines of immigrant religion emerged.

CHAPTER
5
Christ, the Person, and the Church

ᓚᕤᕿᓓᓂ

A native of the Kentucky region and inheritor of the American colonial tradition, Martin John Spalding (1810–1872) was baptized by the Belgian frontier priest, Father Charles Nerinckx. He received his early education in the spiritual life from Bishops Benedict Joseph Flaget (1763–1850) and John Baptist David (1761–1841) at Saint Joseph's Seminary, Bardstown. Spalding studied at the Urban College of the Propaganda in Rome, where he received his doctorate, and returned to Louisville four years later. While engaging in pastoral work in and around Bardstown, the young priest quickly became known as the leading Catholic apologist of the era. Spalding was consecrated coadjutor to Bishop Flaget in 1848. He served as bishop of Louisville from 1850 to 1864 and then as archbishop of Baltimore until his death in 1872.[1] Through his writings, legislation, and pastoral leadership, the Kentuckian exercised a formative influence on the Catholic community. He knew at first hand the conditions of the church in the United States and experienced the poverty and discrimination suffered by the Irish and German Catholic immigrants. It was in the context of this experience that he came to form his vision of the Christian life. Spalding wrote the following description in 1845:

> To take an enlarged and adequate view of Christianity, we must stand at the foot of the cross, with the blessed Mother of the Crucified, and look abroad from the lofty eminence of Calvary. A new and brilliant prospect will then open before us, and a new light will burst upon our eyes. Then we will be able to view the Christian system in all its length

and breadth, in all the wondrous harmony of its parts, and in all its
divine adaptation to the wants of man.[2]

A beautiful image of the church gathered with the Blessed Mother at
the foot of the crucified. But what did it mean? How was it interpreted? In what ways was it helpful to the community and expressive
of its deepest faith?

In what follows, these questions will be addressed by examining
Martin Spalding's apologetic writings during the years when the immigrant church was born, between 1830 and 1866. This examination
will indicate the social and intellectual foundations of Spalding's vision of the Christian life and how it functioned in the community.
His vision was composed of four distinct but interconnected elements:
a belief in the corporate and hierarchical nature of social reality; a
biblical interpretation of the immigrant experience; an understanding
of the atonement framed within the American context; and an image
of the suffering Christ.

MARTIN JOHN SPALDING: THE SERPENT ENTERS THE GARDEN

A sense of the corporate and hierarchical nature of social reality, gal-
vanized by personal experience and education, was the first major
characteristic of Martin Spalding's spiritual vision. To some extent
his youth on a Kentucky farm and the close-knit kinship bonds of the
Spalding clan seem to have given the young man a feeling for a corporate, family identity with strong patrilineal lines.[3] This personal
experience coalesced well with his Roman education in ecclesiology.

During his thesis defense in 1834 Spalding accepted Robert Bellarmine's definition of the church as a unified, hierarchical society.
Most of his propositions focused on the juridical relationship existing
between pope, bishops, and priests, and indicated a preoccupation
with the European ecclesiological debates of the seventeenth and
eighteenth centuries. The laity entered into this schema only inasmuch
as they were obedient subjects of the ruler. As Spalding later wrote,
"While on earth, Christ gathered together a body of disciples; He organized them into a regular society, by selecting from them officers
composed of two distinct orders—the twelve apostles and the seventy-
two disciples."[4] Spalding's Roman education on the relationship between church and state served to strengthen this viewpoint. Since he
saw the state as a perfect society embodied in the ruler, the priest
insisted on the church as a publicly constituted body possessing juridical rights of its own. Indicating little awareness of John Carroll's
understanding of religious liberty and separation of church and state,

Spalding wrote: "Christian princes ought to defend the Church, not rule it; for they are the children of the Church not its fathers or pastors." Although he would modify this position somewhat in his later writings, Spalding's emphasis on the corporate and hierarchical nature of social reality perdured through the Second Plenary Council of 1866.[5]

This tendency to view both church and state as corporate entities was further encouraged by Spalding's experience when he returned to the United States. With respect to the church, the struggle of Bishops Flaget and Guy Ignatius Chabrat to establish a uniform church polity on the frontier exposed Spalding to the difficulties of lay trusteeism and the consequent decision to enforce strong episcopal centralization. Shortly after Spalding arrived in Kentucky, Chabrat published *General Regulations* governing the congregations of the diocese. The regulations strengthened the role of the bishop in establishing new congregations, excluded any private homes or stations from serving as churches, and assigned the ownership of all property in trust to the bishop. The church, in the context of the debate over trusteeism, was primarily a legal corporation with its temporal goods vested in the moral person of the bishop.[6] Viewing the church through this corporate lens also enabled the apologist to deal more effectively with a growing Protestant militancy. "The greatest deficiency in religious matters in this country," Spalding wrote to Bishop John Baptist Purcell of Cincinnati,

> is the want of a thorough *organization carried out with efficiency in every Diocese*. The Methodists and other sects have this: with the machinery of a vast book concern, tract Societies and an admirable system of itinerancy, they exert a powerful influence from one end of the Union to the other. You find them everywhere and in such out of the way places, as you would expect to find nobody. We are comparatively inactive. The chief reason of it is that we do not have sufficient organization.[7]

The native-born American summarized much of this anti-Protestant polemic in his 1847 book, *Evidences of Catholicity*.[8]

With respect to the state, Spalding reflected the constitutional debates over slavery and the European reaction to the French Revolution when he argued that the civil contract should imply some restraint on civil liberty. "The compact," he stated, "express or implied, between the governor and the governed, necessarily supposed some sacrifice of personal freedom on the part of the latter for the general good of the body politic." Like his spiritual mentors Flaget and David, Spalding possessed such a strong sense of the passions governing people that he believed they could not "be kept together in society without a restraining influence and authority to which all must bow, and be-

fore the decisions of which all private interests and passions must
give way." This position, in contrast to the Enlightenment's interpretation of contract, was implied in the pastoral letter issued at the
Second Plenary Council in 1866. Throughout his writings, Spalding
emphasized corporate, not personal rights.[9]

A final influence on Spalding's corporate view could be discerned
in the central place that original sin played in his theological polemic.
Although he admitted that the Fall had not destroyed the understanding, memory, and will, he emphasized the fact that "error and
vice had overspread the earth, and had rendered its habitation dark-
some, its very atmosphere pestilent."[10]

The apologist followed the restorationist presentation of Bruno
Franz Liebermann (1759–1844), whose *Institutiones Theologicae* attacked the Enlightenment's confidence in both the reason of the philosophers and the common sense of the people. This focus on the Fall
structured Spalding's thought in such a way that he concentrated on
solidarity in sin; the remedy, then, could only be solidarity in a divine
religion, the integrity, purity, and unity of which recaptured the original state of justice. "Perhaps the most beautiful feature in the Catholic
religion," Spalding wrote, "and, at the same time, one of the most
striking evidences of its divine origin, is the wonderful harmony which
pervades its entire system of faith, worship, and morals."[11] In contrast
to John Carroll, who distinguished between the essentials and accidentals of faith, Spalding concerned himself with organic unity. Religion, for him, was primarily "system." In all of these ways, through
his personal experience, education, and apologetic conflicts, the native
American was led to emphasize the corporate nature of social reality,
whether it be in the family, the church, the state, or the solidarity of
all in sin and grace. As will be seen, this perspective had a profound
impact on the immigrant church's view of holiness.

Spalding indicated how the social reality of immigration and nativism contributed to his spiritual vision in his interpretation of the
Catholic experience during the Philadelphia riots of 1844. During that
year a rumor spread that Catholics intended to exclude the Bible from
common schools. The leaders of the American Protestant Association
bonded together and agitated for the formation of the Native American
Party. The "Bible was paraded in processions," and preachers fo-
mented popular riots against the Catholics of the city. In a matter of
months, two churches were burned, a seminary and retreat house
"consumed by the torches of an incendiary mob," forty houses ruined,
and numerous people killed or wounded. In an apologetic response,
Spalding railed against the injustice suffered by the Catholic community and reviewed the history of the nativist current sweeping the
United States.[12] Most significantly, he interpreted the events in Phil-

adelphia by making an extended analogy with the Genesis story of Creation and Fall. "Time was," he wrote,

> when everything bade fair to make this a glorious republic, *in deed* as it was *in name*. Time was, when the United States promised to be the peaceful home and happy resting place of the oppressed of every nation, of the exile from every country. Time was, when our young republic presented to the forlorn of every clime the idea of an earthly paradise, in which all were to meet and commingle, and be happy, on terms of perfect equality; where the voice of contention and strife should not be heard, and where all that were sheltered under the American flag should be as free, as the air which stirred its ample folds.
>
> But, alas! this beautiful vision was soon dissipated, and the poor stranger was awakened to a sense of the sad reality! The serpent of religious bigotry soon entered into this fair paradise, marring its beauty, infecting its hitherto virgin atmosphere with its poisonous breath, and breaking the spell of its sanctuary quietude with horrible hissings. The charm was broken; the stranger *felt* that, instead of being in an earthly paradise, he had been cast out, like his first parents, into a frightful wilderness; that instead of being at home, he was in a *strange* country where he was branded as an alien and an enemy.[13]

Spalding's use of this biblical motif of Creation and Fall to interpret the religious significance of nativism revealed two major characteristics of his understanding of the Catholic community's spiritual journey at mid-century: a particular sense of the interplay between justice and injustice in history; and the feeling of emotional exile and the need for a home.

The Genesis story enabled Spalding to describe the interplay between justice and injustice in history as parallel to the relationship between Catholicism and Protestantism in the United States. On the one hand, he used the story to defend the integrity and purity of a Catholic body unjustly exiled from the paradise of religious liberty. The apologist carefully described the true American character, "wise, moderate, liberal, and expansive," as founded on the "solid *strata* of sounder sense and better feeling."[14]

Catholics themselves had contributed to this foundation. In the person of Lord Baltimore, they had first defended every person as "free to worship God according to the dictates of his conscience." In many of his essays Spalding argued that civil liberty was born in the Middle Ages and that the *Magna Carta* had Catholic origins.[15] He believed there was a strong convergence between the American republic and the doctrine and constitution of the Catholic church. In an essay on the "Influence of Catholicity on Civil Liberty," the apologist argued that by identifying everyone as "children of wrath," church doctrine equalized rich and poor, causing them to kneel side by side in her most stately temples, "all reduced to the same level of humble suppliants for mercy!" Also, since the church possessed a spiritual constitution, she could not be incompatible with any government. In fact, as an elective monarchy, an aristocracy of merit in which people earned their advancements, and a democracy in which deliberative assemblies (chapters, synods, councils) made the decisions, the church possessed a constitution akin to that of the United States. The Pope himself, he noted, "usually decides nothing without consulting his counselors, the college of cardinals, and seldom determines anything against their advice."[16] Spalding's whole apologetic was designed to make the church the true bearer of the American heritage and thus the defender of Edenic justice in a world gone astray.

On the other hand, Spalding's interpretation of Genesis branded the Protestants as the true aliens. It is they who had sinned by denying the birthright of religious liberty to others. As he put it, the serpent of religious bigotry, first spawned in the betrayal and disobedience of the Reformation, had now entered the once fair garden of republicanism. Protestants were depriving Catholics of their "just and equitable *right*."[17] The advantages of Spalding's argument were that it gave the church some degree of righteousness in the midst of the nativist onslaught, it allowed for the rapid and natural americanization of Catholics, and it brought some of their deepest religious resources to bear upon their assimilation. Its understanding of the interplay between justice and injustice would play a significant role in the apologetic explanation of the holiness of the church as a reflection of the "spotless Lamb of God."

Spalding's use of the Genesis story also allowed him to address from a religious perspective the immigrant's various feelings of exile. The emotive language of the description should be carefully noted. Victimized by religious bigotry, the American Catholic was a *sad, poor stranger* in an *alien* land. The serpent of prejudice destroyed by its "horrible hissings" and "poisonous breath" the *beauty, virginity*, and *sanctuarial* charm of paradise. The consequence, as Spalding pictured it, was emotional: the "charm was broken"; the stranger "*felt* he had been cast out"; he or she lived in a "frightful wilderness," a "strange country"; the alien was "branded."[18] Elsewhere Spalding argued that the world after the first sin, "a dreary dark and frightful waste," corresponded to the contemporary "cold and dreary land of Protestantism," dominated by a "caviling piety, which seems always uneasy and trembling, lest it should be transported too far." In such a "cold" place, Catholicism offered to the sinner a "religion of the heart," a home for "tender and thrilling emotions."[19]

This dislocation that the immigrant felt was not only social and emotional but also temporal. The American principles of openness, straightforwardness, and liberality had once existed ("Time was . . ."); now, they were no more. Dominated by nostalgia, Spalding looked backward in his attempt to reclaim both Christendom and the early days of the republic.[20] This feeling of alienation and homesickness was also inherent in the Irish immigrant. From Spalding's perspective only the mythic story of paradise and Fall could carry the emotional freight of the experience. In pre–Civil War nativist America, the Catholic was truly an alien condemned to wander in a "dreary, frightful wasteland." Any vision of the spiritual life would need to address this experience.[21]

Eight months after writing this political interpretation of Genesis, Spalding presented an entirely different commentary, one that indicated another major way in which his vision of the Christian life was influenced by his intellectual and social context. This time he was responding not to social nativism but to the theological accusation that Catholic practices such as celibacy, penitential austerities, and corporal afflictions were examples of the Catholic doctrine of "salvation by works." After stressing the organic unity of Catholicism, its corporate and systemic character, the apologist attempted to give an explanation of how it accounted for both grace and free will. He began with the Fall: "Man created originally to the image and likeness of his God, and constituted in a state of innocence and sanctification, became, by his fall, a victim of cruel wounds and of deeply seated hereditary infirmities, both of soul and body." Because of this reality at the heart of human existence, religion necessarily took on a medicinal character. To right the original injustice, the Savior came to offer his sacrificial and expiatory spirit; the atonement, the cross of Christ, thus became the centerpiece of human history.[22]

Spalding then went on to emphasize not only Christ's work but also man's free cooperation in the atoning sacrifice. "God, who created us without consent or aid," he wrote, "will not save us without our cooperation." The merits of the atonement, he argued, could be applied only to those who strive, do violence to themselves, practice self-denial, mortify their members, and "imitate the example of Christ." The saints had done this very thing. The native American was very careful to note that these sacrifices were efficacious only when united to the cross of Christ, but he also emphasized human action.[23] He concluded his essay on "Satisfaction" with this telling paragraph:

> With how many blessings has not this doctrine [of the atonement] strewn the earth! How many splendid temples, how many magnificent hospitals for the sick, how many asylums for the afflicted of every class, has it not erected! Visit the noble institutions of the middle ages, still existing all over Europe; ask the history of their foundation; and some old record

will inform you that they were reared, in many cases, by opulent penitents—*ad expianda peccata,* for the expiation of sins committed in their
past life! Let the innovators produce monuments like these.[24]

In the context of the mid-nineteenth-century United States, this emphasis on the unity between God's action and their own *will* and *work*
freed Catholic immigrants to claim their true American identity, to
participate in society, to build the institutional church. In a paradoxical way, Spalding's interpretations of the atonement to deal with
human weakness and the original injustice actually concluded by fo-
cusing on human action. This view was the mirror image of his previous interpretation of the church as the true bearer of the American
Eden. Spalding's vision of the Christian life would flow from this position.

One other significant feature emerged in Spalding's interpretation
of the atonement. He knew that the vast majority of the immigrants
were poor, plagued by poverty, disease, persecution, and death. How
was a person to account for this? Spalding argued that the betrayal
of Eden entered into the very stuff of human history: "Sickness, all
the ills of life, and death itself,—what are they but the wages of that
fatal sin, by which our first parents disobeyed the command of God
in the garden of paradise." Theologically, he noted, even after the
"guilt and eternal punishment of grievous sin have been remitted by
God," there remained a portion of temporal punishment to be exacted.
The apologist presented several examples of this divine principle in
action: Moses and Aaron, though pardoned, died "in sight of the
promised land, without being allowed to enter it"; even after Moses
prayed, 23,000 Israelites were slain because they had worshiped the
golden calf; despite the Lord's forgiveness, the chosen people wandered in the desert for forty years; David "sinned grievously," "re-
pented sincerely," yet lost his child; even though Jesus "expiated the
fault by the death on the cross, yet is the temporal penalty still sternly
exacted *to this very day,* and it will be exacted to the end of time."
These examples matched the social and political experiences of the
Catholic community at mid-century. Life exacted a tremendous cost,
even for one baptized into the ark of salvation.[25]

In summary, Martin John Spalding's vision of the Christian life
was founded on three distinct but interconnected elements: a belief
in the corporate and hierarchical nature of social reality; a biblical
interpretation of the immigrant experience that was sensitive both
to the demands of civil justice and the feelings of alienation; an understanding of the atonement that gave a large role to human action
and yet accounted for the prevalence of poverty and disease. These
beliefs developed out of the complex interaction of Spalding's personal

experience, his education, his Kentucky pastorate, the social ills accompanying immigration, the intolerant forces of nativism, and the apologetic challenge of Protestantism. The apologist's vision was designed to further the assimilation process through an emphasis on Catholicism as the bearer of true American values and on the importance of voluntary sacrifice and work in the Catholic schema of justification. The apologetic strength of Spalding's position was that in all cases the realities of the immigrant experience could be understood and met only within the confines of the church, a corporate institution representing truth, justice, beauty, and grace in the world.

THE IMAGE OF CHRIST

Given this background of the immigrant experience and its interpretation, it is now possible to examine Spalding's image of Christ. His apologetic works were laced through with the following images of Jesus, exiled, crucified, and victorious: Jesus "neglected the rich and mingled freely with the poor"; he suffered at the hands of an angry mob; immaculate, he "vouchsafed to clothe Himself with man's nature, and to become Sponsor to His Father! Jesus suffered, Jesus died, in the midst of agony unspeakable, in the consequence of the fall of Adam, and of the accumulated guilt of his tainted descendants"; his arms, "extended on the cross embraced all mankind without exception: His heart loved all, and his heart's blood was bounteously poured out for all." "In spite of all the watchfulness and persecution of his enemies, in spite of Pharisaic spies and Roman guards, He rose again, as He had clearly predicted, on the third day; He arose to die no more; His triumph was permanent and eternal. In Him truth triumphed most signally over error, innocence over slander, virtue over persecution."[26]

Spalding particularly recommended the following images of Jesus as shepherd to his people that he had received from one of his spiritual mentors, John Baptist David: Jesus embracing poverty; Jesus obeying his Father; Jesus laboring for God's glory; Jesus praying. He challenged Catholics to imitate the conduct of Jesus: "His continual mortification—He renounces, He crucifies Himself in all things; His life is a course of fasts, of watchings."[27] Loving us as much as he does,

> it was just and necessary that He should humble Himself as much as He has done. First. As man; because fallen human nature, even united to the Divinity, is still nothing before God, if considered in itself. "My substance," says He by the prophet, "is as nothing before Thee." Hence in the Man-God, the baseness of the humanity hides, and, in some measure, eclipses the grandeur of the divinity. Secondly. As Redeemer of men;

because in that quality He becomes their substitute. He takes their sins on Himself; and in that character, He deserves all the shame, humiliation and punishment due to sin. Thirdly. As the Model of men; because in this quality He must give them an example, which may afford a remedy proportionate to their greatest evil, which is pride. Man had lost himself by endeavouring to become like God, his Creator. He must now save himself by endeavoring to become like God, his Redeemer.[28]

Clearly, this was the course of Jesus on earth: Exiled, poor, struggling, and unjustly persecuted, he took the life of the immigrant community upon himself and substituted for its iniquities. Jesus also promised victory when he entered heaven to prepare a place for us. "What are the sorrows and sufferings of this fleeting life," Spalding asked, "compared with the cumulative glory, the abounding happiness, and the eternal bliss which await us in heaven! I will bear all the ills of life with cheerfulness and love, buoyed up by this blessed hope!"[29]

Spalding communicated this image of Christ through public lectures, private retreats, missions, and publications. It was the central image in one of the most popular prayer books of his era, *True Piety*, and other leaders, such as John Hughes of New York and John Neumann of Philadelphia, shared this vision.[30] The Kentucky pastor hoped that the immigrant community would perceive this Christ, so much an icon of their own identity, when they worshiped at the sacrifice of the Mass, gazed on the Mother kneeling at the foot of the cross, or received ministrations from the Sisters of Loretto, whose habit pictured the open heart of the crucified.[31]

By placing this image of the exiled, crucified, and victorious Christ at the center of his vision, Spalding was proclaiming the Savior's availability to American Catholics. The image functioned in two ways. First, it obviously promoted a strong identification between the individual and Christ. Victimized by religious persecution, the immigrant could take consolation in the image of Jesus before Pilate listening to the jeers of the crowd: "Crucify him." Reflecting on the history of religious persecution, the immigrant could realize "that still darker clouds have often hung over the pathway of our Catholic ancestors, and yet they despaired not, and those clouds have passed away."[32] Guilty of sin and struggling with personal passions, he or she could turn to a Savior who willed to suffer for all. This identification between the individual and Christ occurred in the events of daily life, a practical reliving of the paschal mystery and opportunity for penance and the practice of virtues. The point was that every experience and every Catholic belief could be interpreted in the light of the exiled and crucified Christ and marshaled for his imitation. The church tells us, Spalding argued, what John told the Jews on the banks of the Jordan: "Bring forth, therefore *fruit worthy of penance;*" and what Christ said, speaking of John: "The kingdom of heaven *suffereth violence and the violent bear it away.*" She tells, us, that those only are foreknown by God and predestinated to life eternal, who *"are made conformable to the image of His Son:"* that we must *"suffer* with Christ, if we would reign with him."[33]

In this way, the Catholic immigrant could suffer for the truth of religious liberty, practice self-denial, build churches, and hope for a better life, in imitation of the great atoning sacrifice. "The yoke of Christ is indeed sweet," Spalding wrote, "and His burden light; but it is still a *yoke* and a *burden*, and the yoke is sweet and the burden light, only to those who bear them willingly and with love, for the sake of Christ, and in union with Christ."[34]

This identification between Christ and the immigrant could be encouraged in different ways. The Mass especially educated the person into Christ's sacrificial spirit; its action, Spalding wrote, "brings the Catholic daily and hourly to the summit of Calvary, where his devotion receives a new impulse, and his soul kindles with a new fervor."[35] Meditation, a tradition that Spalding inherited from Benedict Joseph Flaget and John Baptist David, enabled the person to *"feel* He is the way." Involving an active exertion of the mind and heart, this personal prayer in the "school of the crucified" gave succor to the immigrant "in his hour of conflict, and by throwing around his struggling infirmity the panoply of His omnipotent strength, completed the work, and giveth to him the victory."[36] Although the meditations Spalding encouraged focused on the reality of sin, his point was that the recognition of our pain, our sin, and our weakness was what attracted Christ to us. Bishop David's reflection on Jesus delivering himself up on the cross typified the balance:

> Sweet captivity! Glorious bondage, which makes you a child of God, an heir of heaven, and leads you to the possession of His kingdom. Accept of it; thank your Jesus for His love, and ask Him pardon for your sins. Beg him to break your bonds asunder. Beseech Him to make you a captive of His love. Put on these glorious chains, and never lay them aside.[37]

Spalding himself labored to exemplify this image of Christ in his own life and to encourage it in his priests.[38] Laity, bishop, priests—all were to gather with the mother at the foot of the crucified, there to embrace Christ who first embraced them.

The image of Christ also functioned in Spalding's vision in a significant ecclesiological way. Christ was the type of his body, the church, in its exile, sufferings, and victory. Through its institutional concern for the poor, the church imitated Jesus' mercy. Modeled on his life of exile, the perfect society could "expect to be slandered, to be persecuted, to be nailed to the cross with her blessed Founder and Spouse." Bearing all these insults with meekness and patience, the corporate body could also expect to "rise again with renewed life and vigor, from the tomb to which her enemies had thought in the folly of their hearts, that they had forever consigned her."[39]

Last, as his body, the church represented Christ's divinity. Just as Jesus had journeyed with sinners, hypocrites, and traitors and still remained sinless, so the church's sanctity was not incompatible with sinners in her midst. As Son of God, Jesus had established a divine religion composed of clear doctrinal truths, sublime moral principles, and complete external institutions. This religion, addressing the maladies of the human condition, was related to the church as soul to body, so much so that the church was marked by precisely the same qualities as the religion it contained, "as the casket does the precious jewels."[40] Ultimately, it was only in this church that the immigrant could find a home and receive the saving balm of Christ.

In summary, two significant features of Spalding's image of Christ and its function in the Catholic community should be noted. First, in his apologetic works, retreats, and preaching, the Kentucky prelate succeeded in proclaiming Christ to the pre–Civil War Catholic community. His proclamation, in turn, provided the community with a strong personal identity and a spiritual vision to support it. Appealing as it did to intellect, will, and emotion, the vision elicited loyalty precisely because of its personal and social significance. The image was a mystique of salvation, functioning to mediate an experience of God in the only language people could understand. Second, within its cultural context, the image of Christ carried important overtones of Americanization. Jesus' sacrificial work, far from inducing passivity and guilt, freed the immigrant to participate in society at large, to build its institutions, and create its fortunes. In turn the church, imitating Christ on the cross, became both the home of the immigrant and the Lamb whose wool, dyed white in the blood of persecution, represented the truest values of the American Revolution: religious liberty, equality, and government by law. United with this Christ, the immigrant could be a good American, a child of the church, and an image of God.

Spalding's image of the close unity between Christ, the immigrant, and the church dominated the pre–Civil War era.[41] It is important, then, to note that the image contained within itself not only life but death. Precisely because it was so well suited to the poor, struggling, and persecuted Catholic of the pre–Civil War era, and so dependent on a corporate and juridical understanding of church, the image could not adequately reflect a community no longer profiled by those realities. As the social context would change, so also would history's Lord need to be proclaimed anew.

The heart of the historical issue was the way in which Spalding related the humanity and divinity of Christ to the history and holiness of the church. The bishop associated the divinity of Christ with his miracles, his teaching, his victory over persecution, sin, and death, and his complete fulfillment at the right hand of the Father. The institutional church, Christ's corporate body on earth, mirrored this glory in its divine constitution, its immutable teaching, its grace-giving sacraments, its beautiful liturgy, and its consoling communion of saints. Spalding drew the following analogy to explain this reality:

> Man is composed of two distinct parts blended into one individual—body and soul; and the Church of Jesus Christ, to be fully adapted to his wants, must likewise necessarily consist of two distinct corresponding elements, intimately united and harmonizing with each other—the external and the spiritual. The RELIGION of Christ is the soul, the CHURCH is the body united with this soul. On the day of Pentecost, Christ infused into the body of His Church, already organized, the Holy Spirit, and "it was thus made into a living soul." Destroy either of these essential elements, and you destroy the individuality of the Church, just as the individuality of man would be destroyed by the removal or destruction of either the body or the soul.[42]

Because of this identification between divine religion and institutional structure, the church as the body of corporate holiness could move through history without being subject to history's changes.

In contrast, Spalding usually associated the humanity of Christ with the immigrant's personal history of exile, struggle, labor, and suffering. Jesus' obedience to the Father exemplified the relationship the individual should have to the official representatives of the church, the external signs of Christ's divinity. Spalding, following John Baptist David, asked the individual to meditate on the humility of Jesus with this comment: "Fallen human nature [read the "immigrant"] is still nothing before God [read the "church"] if considered in itself. 'My substance,' says He by the prophets, 'is as nothing before Thee.' Hence in the Man-God, the baseness of the humanity hides, and, in some measure, eclipses the grandeur of the Divinity."[43] The bishop would never have applied these words to the corporate church, divided as it was into those who taught and those with the "duty of hearing, of being taught, and of obeying."[44] Entering the church, the individual was still shackled with a human history; clinging to the church as to Christ, he or she had some measure of divinity.

Spalding's synthesis of the corporate church's divinity and the immigrant's humanity created in his mind the identity or individuality of the pre–Civil War Catholic community. Bonded by the forces of history, together the immigrant and the church could image the Lord of their history, reflecting in their social and spiritual interdependence the incarnation, death, and resurrection of Christ.

This image of Christ, the person, and the church continued into the post–Civil War period. Devotional writers like Thomas Scott Preston (1824–91), Otto Zardetti (1847–1903), and Thomas F. Hopkins (1841–1904), pictured the corporate church as immutable, triumphant in its holiness and beauty; the individual Catholic, as struggling in this vale of tears; the mediating image of Christ, as the Sacred Heart.[45] The sermon that John Hennessy, the bishop of Dubuque, preached before the Third Plenary Council in 1884 summarized the approach. The bishop noted that Christ loved the church in her sanctity that was manifested in holy things (churches, altars, chalices); doctrines, sacraments, and laws; and individual members. He defined the church as a "supernatural society instituted and organized by Christ," and compared it to the Incarnation in these telling words:

> As the human will of Christ, though free, was so controlled by the divine nature that it could neither sin nor be for an instant out of harmony with the divine will; so the Church, the Body of Christ, though composed of those whose wills are free, and intellects weak, and passions strong, is so governed, directed and influenced by her divine Head, that she can never for an instant betray the truth confided to her by God for the sake of his people, or lose the charity with which the Holy Ghost filled her on the glorious feast of Pentecost. The divine nature of Christ so filled His humanity with heavenly gifts through their mysterious union, that there is between both an interchange of attributes, so that God is man and man is God. So true is this of the elements of the Church, of the Church and her Head, that the Apostle calls the Church Christ, and that they who hear the Church hear Christ and they who persecute the Church persecute Christ.[46]

In the bishop's mind, it was precisely the perfection of the church, in her constitution, doctrine, and practice, that made her like unto Christ. Holiness in the individual, in turn, meant "the infusion of sanctifying grace and supernatural virtues" through the ministrations of the church.

Spalding's identification between divine religion and institutional structure had thus come to full expression by the Third Plenary Council in 1884. Pictured together were a Savior whose divine nature controlled his human will; a supernatural society whose divinity overshadowed the humanity of its institutions, its teachings, and practice; and a sinful humanity in need of the church's ministrations. But what would happen if experience and images changed? If Christ's humanity in its poverty and humility became the focal point of reflection? If the doctrines and practices of the church became subject to development? If humanity became free and intelligent? It was precisely in those areas that the battle over Americanism would be fought, and a different model of holiness would emerge.

CHAPTER
6
The Triumph of the Purgative Way

On June 14, 1858, the archbishop of New York wrote a circular letter to some selected Catholics soliciting donations of $1,000 each. "We propose," he noted, "for the glory of Almighty God, for the honor of the Blessed and Immaculate Virgin, for the exaltation of Holy Mother Church, for the dignity of our ancient and glorious Catholic name, to erect a cathedral in the city of New York. . . ." Within two months John Hughes had collected $103,000 and 100,000 people gathered on Fifth Avenue to watch the Irish immigrant lay the cornerstone of the new Saint Patrick's. In his sermon of that day, Hughes thanked the people for their great generosity and offered "honor and tender reverence from every Christian heart" to Mary, the Immaculate Virgin, and to Pius IX, "the supreme head of the Catholic Church." He placed the cathedral under the patronage of the Virgin and Saint Patrick. The archbishop also viewed the building as symbolic of "the great and glorious Catholic Church, which embraces the whole human race as one family." He referred to the project as a great work for the poor, providing employment in a time of depression and standing as a "head-fountain, sending out its living waters of faith and charity on all sides, and as a great nursery for cultivating the principle of charity among generations that are to succeed us."[1]

John Hughes's reference to the pope, his appeal to Saint Patrick, and his economic justification for the building of the church spoke volumes about the ecclesiological, social, and intellectual changes occurring in the Catholic community in the first half of the nineteenth century. The changes would necessarily structure the Catholic's understanding and practice of the Christian life. Using the experience and reflection of John Hughes as somewhat representative, this chapter will examine the immigrant church's vision of prayer and asceticism.

JOHN HUGHES: POWER AND POVERTY IN THE IMMIGRANT COMMUNITY

Born in County Tyrone, Ireland, John Hughes (1797–1864) was one of the many poor, exiled immigrants who constituted the bulk of the nineteenth-century Catholic community. He knew at first hand both the English penal laws that severely restricted the social and political life of Irish Catholics, and a family's struggle to live off the unyielding rocky soil. In 1817, "friendless and with but a few guineas in his purse," he followed his father to the United States, where he lived as a gardener and quarry worker in Pennsylvania. At the behest of Mother Elizabeth Seton (1774–1821), John Dubois (1764–1842), the French Sulpician who administered Mount Saint Mary's College, Emmitsburg, Maryland, received the young exile into the seminary. Hughes studied there from 1820 until his ordination in 1826. He spent his early ministry in Philadelphia and established himself as a pugnacious controversialist who confronted both Catholic lay trustees and Protestant polemicists. The Irishman was consecrated a bishop in 1838 and served from then until his death the diocese of New York, first as coadjutor, then as bishop (1842), and finally as archbishop (1850). Through his polemical writings, which spanned almost four decades, his continuous struggles with trustees, and his efforts to establish an independent Catholic school system in the 1840s, Hughes imprinted his own style of leadership and vision of the Christian life on the young immigrant church.[2]

At Hughes's memorial service, Bishop John Loughlin of Brooklyn challenged the congregation to remember their deceased prelate in words that captured the heart of his episcopacy:

> One of the great thoughts of his great mind, the desire of his heart, was that his children in the Faith should not be socially or civilly inferior to their fellow citizens. He knew to what dignity their Faith raised them. He knew they had a correct understanding of their moral obligations, and the duty of defending their civil and their social rights he never lost sight of. Remember your Prelate who has spoken to you the Word of God. Follow the great principles of his and your Faith.[3]

Hughes pursued this course of giving the Catholic social, religious, and civil identity in two distinct phases. His earliest controversial writings during his Philadelphia period (1827–1838) mirrored the specifically theological preoccupations of the emerging nativist current in the United States. A second phase surfaced after 1838, when Hughes first assumed episcopal duties in New York and began to respond in a pastoral way to the needs of the Catholic immigrants. During both periods, the apologist attempted to differentiate Catholicism from Protestantism, to establish a cohesive and unified church, and to encourage immigrant assimilation into American life. This vision of Catholic life and the theological and social forces that shaped it can be seen in Hughes's defense of the Catholic religion in theological debates, his arguments over lay trusteeism, and his reaction to the forces of immigration and free-market capitalism.

From his earliest years, John Hughes's view of the Catholic religion was shaped within a polemical context. Right after his ordination, he published a small pamphlet answering nine theological objections to Catholicism. In opposition to his Protestant opponent, the young priest emphasized Christ's creation of a visible, hierarchical church, the existence of tradition, the doctrine of meritorious works, the seven sacraments, transsubstantiation, Latin liturgy, purgatory, and the importance of the use of images and relics, prayer to Mary and the saints, and the efficacy of indulgences.

The debates with the Presbyterian John Breckinridge in 1833 and 1835 also reflected this theological inheritance, mediated to Hughes through his Gallican teachers, John Dubois and Simon Gabriel Bruté (1779–1839). Although the Irish American rejected Robert Bellarmine's view of the temporal power of the papacy, he emphasized in Counter Reformation fashion the supremacy of the pope and the infallibility of the church, and equated the Catholic rule of faith with a "visible society of Christians, composed of the people, who are taught, and the Pastors who *teach*, by virtue of a certain divine commission."[4] Throughout his writings Hughes made Catholicism the mirror image of Protestantism, contrasting the former's unity in doctrine and polity with the latter's diversity. He contrasted Catholicism's infallibility with Protestantism's opinion; its subordination to authority with private judgment; its visibility with the rejection of external worship; and its reliance on tradition with *sola Scriptura*.[5] Given this theological context of controversy, any vision of the Christian life that Hughes presented would necessarily look like a resurgent Counter Reformation Catholicism.

The tendency to equate the Catholic religion with the perpetuity and immutability of its doctrine, moral teaching, and sacramental and institutional structure received further definition during Hughes's battle with lay trusteeism. He arrived in Philadelphia in 1827 during the years when the acrimonious debates between Bishop Henry Conwell (1745–1842) and the trustees of Saint Mary's Cathedral were at their height. In later years the bishop would associate these trustees with "scenes of strife," riot, and bloodshed.[6] Both as a deacon for Conwell and as a resident priest, he found himself now supported, now rejected by the fickle and irascible governing board. In a letter to his mentor Bruté, he described public opinion as "credulous, it concludes according to its premises, and when it is ill informed its conclusions are rash, and often times wrong. It has had to acknowledge this a thousand times, but in every new case its decisions are as dogmatical as before. It is an idiot—because it has no *memory*, and of course cannot learn wisdom by experience."[7] Hughes considered the populace to be dominated by "extravagant notions of liberty." In contrast, "Religion," he wrote, "must stand on its own divine authority, this is the critical juncture for making its basis permanent and solid—By crushing in the bud the factious efforts of those who would wish to change its foundations."[8]

After Hughes became a bishop in New York, his pastoral activities focused on several issues explicitly touching the life of the laity. In his 1842 pastoral he commented on the diocesan synodal regulations that recently had forbidden the administration of baptism in private homes, the practice of hasty marriages, unions between Catholics and others contracted without a promise to raise the children in the Catholic faith, and membership in "secret societies." The bishop also presented the rationale for his approach to lay trusteeism. He rejected the imitation of "the secular or sectarian examples by which we are surrounded" and rooted the strifes and contentions associated with trusteeism in the system itself. Trustees, he argued, contracted debts too readily because they knew their limited tenure in office removed them from the final responsibility; they lacked the confidence of the people who formed a "natural repugnance to contribute charities to laymen for such purposes"; last, in an effort to attract people and to raise money, trustees often made eloquence and not piety, zeal, or learning the criterion for the parish's acceptance of the priest. In all cases, Hughes felt, the faithful paid the price for the institution of this "uncatholic system."[9]

To counteract the evils of trusteeism, Hughes's pastoral reserved to the pastor, under episcopal direction, the hiring and firing of church employees, the expenditures of monies, the contraction of debts, and the general management of church property. If possible, all property should be vested in the bishop's name. "Our object," Hughes concluded "is to fulfill the duties of our station, not only by preserving as far as in us lies, the purity of faith and morals over which we are appointed to watch, but also of preserving whatever the piety of the faithful has consecrated to the service of Almighty God, and for the support of religion."[10]

Hughes was immediately attacked by the representatives of several other faiths who linked together the regulations on mixed marriages, secret societies, and lay trusteeism. All of the decrees, they argued, encroached on "the rights and freedom of the Catholic body." In response, the bishop argued for the uniqueness of the Catholic system, its distinctive polity, and the moral character of its obligations. At the heart of the issue for Hughes lay the acceptance of the Savior's divine commission, and no one, "no minister of theirs—no bishop— nor Pope—nor all together—have any power to alter one iota of that sacred deposit, which Christ bequeathed to his followers." Appealing to the American principle of separation of church and state and religious liberty, Hughes noted that Catholics should be free to maintain their own internal beliefs, structures, and policies. He consistently presented a similar defense of his position throughout the following years.[11]

Several significant features of Hughes's view of the "Catholic religion" emerged in the course of these trustee debates. First, the controversial context led the bishop to emphasize the distinctive and unified nature of Catholicism. Hierarchy, immutable doctrine, and a single discipline were all part of one system of religion. The parts could not be distinguished from the whole. The controversial context thus linked the regulations on mixed marriages, secret societies, and lay trusteeism. The result was the formation of a Catholic identity characterized by strong social boundaries and internal role distinction between clergy and laity. Hughes was well aware that this approach marked a departure from the course set by John Carroll, but the bishop's argument with the Public School Society in 1840 and his response to the anti-Catholic demonstrations associated with the visit of the papal representative Gaetano Bedini in 1853–54 only confirmed him in this need for a militant and hierarchical Catholicism. The Episcopalian *Church Review* commented on this change in Catholic self-understanding in 1863:

> We have among us, therefore, what it is important that we should always recognize, two very different types of Romanism. Though Romanism is bad enough, in any form, let us do justice to the *Carrolites*, and to the memory of Carrol [sic] and Cheverus. Amiable and temperate, and, we doubt not, sincere, this class of Romans are tolerant, and in their way, disposed to be moral and religious. But those of the Bedinian [New York] school are politicians; worldly in their ideas and wholly unscrupulous in their practices.[12]

Second, Hughes's objections to the trustee system revolved as much around the vices of slander, strife, and divisiveness as around the hierarchical nature of authority. This indicated that one of the primary features of Catholicism in Hughes's viewpoint was its communal nature, its fostering of strong, supportive relationships among its members. During Carroll's period, the consistent problem had been charity among Christians; in Hughes's time, disputes among Catholics themselves became equally significant. This relational need established a significant social base for a vision of the Christian life emphasizing the unifying role of authority, the communion of saints, the practice of charity, and the need for penance.

Third, Hughes's defense of a distinctive Catholic doctrine and polity appealed to the American principles of the separation of church and state and religious liberty. During Carroll's period, these principles had been used to support the spirituality of a "Christian and a Catholic"; now, thirty years later, separation of church and state meant the civil right of the church to define its own constitution. There could hardly have been a more startling reversal of interpretation and practice. The one consistent element was the desire to link the Catholic religion and the American proposition, a policy that became even more evident in Hughes's approach to the issues of immigration and free-market capitalism.

When John Hughes became bishop of New York, the diocese constituted all of the state and 50 percent of New Jersey, over 55,000 square miles. Out of 2.7 million people, Hughes estimated 200,000 Catholics and placed the debt at $300,000. The diocese could boast of only one community of sisters. In an 1840 report to a Viennese aid society, the bishop noted the great need to build churches, a seminary, and houses of religious education if the poor Catholic was not to be overwhelmed by the society at large. "The wealth, the manners, sometimes the language," he wrote, "and generally the more elevated condition in society of the people by whom he is surrounded, remind him constantly that he is not in the land of his father, nor among the companions of his youth."[13]

In the next twenty years the situation only became more pressing. Between 1840 and 1860 New York saw 3 million immigrants enter the United States, the vast majority of them poor Irish and Germans. In New York City alone, the German Catholic community increased from 18,000 to 50,000. They were occupationally more skilled than the Irish, who arrived, as Hughes estimated, at the rate of one to two thousand a day after the 1847 famine. In an 1858 memoir the archbishop complained that the better class of immigrants often moved on, and described his flock as the "disabled, the broken down, the very aged, and the very young, I had about added the depraved of all nations."[14] In such a situation Hughes struggled with difficulty to give the church a solid institutional and financial base. His 1841 Church Debt Association failed, as did his proposal for an *Emprunt catholique de New York* to the businessmen of Belgium. In 1852, noting that he could still not furnish sufficient places for worship, he proposed to unite the faithful of the city into an Auxiliary Church Building Association. The plan was well received but collapsed as "the archbishop could never persuade one congregation to help another for any length of time."[15] James Parton, a Protestant who described the Catholic community in the pages of *Atlantic Monthly* in 1868, captured the tone of life during Hughes's episcopacy in these words:

> If in this city of New York, there is any such thing as realized, working Christianity, it may be seen in one of its poor, densely peopled Catholic parishes, where all is dreary, dismal desolation, excepting alone the sacred enclosure around the church, where a bright interior cheers the leisure hours; where pictures, music, and stately ceremonial exalt the poor above their lot; and where a friend and father can ever be found.[16]

The poverty of New York's Catholic community was directly related to the rise of free-market capitalism. Although it caused havoc for Bishop John Dubois, the 1837 depression for many was followed by an era of great commercial expansion in railroads, canals, and the shipping industry. In his 1840 report Hughes noted the commercial character of New York, and many others recognized that speculation in stocks and bonds, a mania for capital, and an increasing division of society into rich and poor characterized the following decade. An ideology of self-interest went hand in hand with this intensification of the market discipline. "In point of fact," one of the more astute Catholic observers of the day wrote,

> the demonic love of gain, the immoderate desire of becoming rich at once and without delay, were already becoming the predominant passion of a large class of men; and there was no knowing where it would stop, as soon as many gigantic enterprises which soon after occupied the thoughts of the public would be planned and forthwith executed.[17]

Catholics found themselves excluded from most public offices, and Protestants controled the schools, poor houses, and hospitals. When they were not accused of causing the poverty, "who could be surprised under these circumstances that the Catholics brooded over their wrongs, and were dissatisfied with the partiality shown to Protestants."[18] The bishop himself pictured the age as typified in "the splendid edifice of a joint stock or banking company in the public square, and in the background a simple structure for a Christian church."[19] As a leader of the Catholic community, Hughes responded to this situation in two ways: first, he wrote a critique of the emerging economic order; second, he presented the Catholic faith as possessing an alternate political economy.

Hughes presented his critique of the emerging social order in a series of writings in 1843 and 1844.[20] He noted the insatiable greed for money and success dominating public affairs. Using England as an example, the bishop described the division of society into three classes: the wealthy who could afford to be socially independent; the middle group, who lived by their labor but managed some degree of self-rule; the poor, those dependent exclusively on their own labor. The masters of the current political economy, he argued, proceeded from the vicious principle of self-interest. They viewed the person simply as a producer and consumer without intellectual, moral, or religious value. As a result, the "social machine had lost its equilibrium of right motion."[21]

The bishop traced this dominance of self-interest in society to the Protestant Reformation. He argued that up to the sixteenth century the profession of the same religion had established a certain uniformity in the exercise of charity, provisions for the poor, and the proper relationship between leisure and work. After the breakup of Christendom, he noted, people discovered that public law, not faith, could be the only regulator of help for the poor. Unfortunately, the public was trained to allow the individual to be the final arbiter in moral and religious matters (the Protestant principle of private judgment). Society thus accepted an individualist and selfish basis for their political economy. Referring to the example of Ireland's poverty, Hughes argued that the current economic conditions created by this free market could not be adequately addressed by "restrictions on commerce," or by a "decrease in population," or by some of the socialist schemes being proposed.[22] As a solution to the problem, the bishop proposed a true Christian (i.e., Catholic) political economy as an alternative. He presented three areas in which his political, economic, and religious vision met the needs of the Catholic immigrant: the theory of justification, a recognition of the inherent selfishness of human nature, and the understanding of the role of the church in society.

The Catholic doctrine of justification, which Hughes outlined at the same time he critiqued free-market capitalism, was the first area in which a Christian political economy converged with the social and economic needs of the immigrant. The bishop rejected the principle of a self-interest based on pleasure that he found prevalent in the social proposals of the Transcendentalists and others. He agreed that society was an "aggregate of human mind and feeling" but insisted that the moral sympathies that should bind people together could only be found in the "presence and action of a religion which can infuse into the masses the warmth and vitality of the Christian virtues reduced into daily practice."[23] He argued that the universities, hospitals, asylums, and saints of Catholicism exemplified this religion. Its base was the doctrine of justification. Contrasting his views with Calvin's notions of election, predestination, and reprobation, Hughes described the Catholic doctrine as an interior application of the justice of Christ, in which guilt was destroyed, pardon bestowed, and the soul was replenished with the grace and charity of the Holy Spirit.

The significant point was that this view recognized grace as a "pure *gift*" but allowed for God's additional grace to enable the soul to cooperate and progress in holiness. Hughes cited the example of a man giving capital for trade to a number of persons, thus placing them in the sphere of commerce. The measure of their increased capital depended both on the benefactor's generosity and their own activity. "The grace of Christ, which is His gift," Hughes wrote, "is the capital renovating the power of the soul, and enabling her to enter into the commerce of charity, which has *God* and the neighbor for its objects, and by which 'treasures,' in the language of Scripture, may be laid up in heaven." This Christian commerce was carried on from the beginning in the apostles, martyrs, virgins, missionaries, teachers, friends of the poor, buriers of the dead, and all those who embraced voluntarily the mortification of the cross. Surely, the bishop concluded, only this Catholic doctrine could establish a sound basis for healing social, moral, physical, and religious wounds.[24]

While Hughes recognized the moral sympathies that bound people together and their intrinsic renovation effected by grace, he also knew another side to human nature: its weakness and inherent selfishness. As with many other people who grew up in the wake of the revolutionary struggles that convulsed Europe after 1789, he consistently filled his writings with references to "poor fallen nature," the "fallen world of ours," "natural ferocity," "self-interest," and "human passion."[25] Hughes's experiences with trusteeism and the Public School Society confirmed the impression that an evil principle clung tenaciously to human nature so that grace often remained ineffective even after justification.[26] But here too, the bishop believed, a Christian political economy provided a solution. Instead of rejecting self-interest, it placed the thirst for power and possession at the service of the spiritual life. People would discover that within the Christian political economy,

> man's interest would be graduated on a scale proportioned to the whole of his nature, combining the spiritual with the corporeal; and the whole of his destiny, extending to eternity as well as time. Then, indeed, self-interest thus understood would constitute a principle sufficiently high and sufficiently ample to combine the acquisition of wealth, with the sacred regard for the rights and privileges of human beings.[27]

Throughout his essay in 1844, the bishop accepted the notion that self-interest was the governing principle of human nature. Christianity did not destroy this but directed it outwards; charitable works were meant to accrue to the benefit of the practitioner. For example, when a rich man gave to the needy, he acted according to the "principle of Christian interest," or, when he entered religious life, "he understood perfectly well, what he was about—comprehended the advantage of the step."[28] Although this argument was not a dominant strain in Hughes's writings, it indicated the extent to which free-market capitalism and the problems of immigrant poverty could shape his vision of the Christian life.

A knowledge of the lust for power and possession prevalent in capitalism and the consequent oppression of the poor led Bishop Hughes to argue for a third way in which a Christian political economy could meet the needs of the immigrant. Sin had so entered the human heart, he noted, that a regime of self-control could be established only by an external power capable of "extending the obligation of *duties*, in exact proportion with the extension of rights."[29] "Humanity cannot elevate itself, it requires a lever," he preached on the eve of the Civil War.[30] This "external power" or "lever" was the Christian faith embodied in the Catholic church, an institution divinely constituted by Christ to infuse into the heart the love of God and neighbor. In the civil order, the church could support society by arbitrating the free market for the common good; in the personal order, through its preaching and ascetical practices of self-accusation and examination, it promoted the virtues without which a human society would be impossible: discipline, order, obedience, respect for authority. The church, Hughes wrote:

> has, indeed, been reproached with the tendency to abridge the rights of men. But the explanation of this is to be found in the fact, that the inherent selfishness of fallen humanity prompts them to claim injurious immunities; while, as she conceived, her office was to apportion *duties* according to the means which providence furnished for the discharge of them. Men are prompt to assert their rights; but prone to forget that every right is accompanied with a corresponding duty. To every class and condition she assigned its own particular range of Christian obligations.[31]

In Hughes's mind, the doctrine and authority of the church thus provided a solution to the social problem: it restrained passion, arbitrated for the common good, and provided the means by which the human heart could be justified and ennobled.

In 1854 the archbishop argued in a sermon that religion was not a sentiment but a power that governed the whole of life. In an age of the wildness of speculation, people now possessed knowledge of whence they came and why they existed; religion attached them to God through a communication of the knowledge of God. Marked with a reason perverted by passion, people could turn to religion for a true morality and a motive for performing their duty; religion attached people to each other. Confronted with their own weakness, they could be grateful for the sacramental institutions that ennobled them; religion united them to the merits of Christ. Religion, in Hughes's mind, meant "to bind, or rebind, to reattach."

> And what is the meaning of this? That by religion God has given us a bond of union to Himself by which He elevates us towards Him; by which it is in our power, by His grace, to imitate Him as far as we can. He is all merciful; He is all just, and makes justice a part of man's duty. He is all truth, and He tells us that falsehood offends. This is the communication of religion. It binds us fast to God.[32]

Hughes's vision of the Christian life bound the Catholic in all directions: to God, to Christ, to neighbor, to society, to the land of citizenship, and, most important, to the church. The vision differed in most respects from John Carroll's, and yet it provided a foundation in a new age for what Carroll wanted most, an American and Catholic identity.

THE PURGATIVE WAY

The context of Hughes's polemic and his need to enunciate a Catholic political economy enabled him to forge the strongest possible links between the social situation, the immigrant, and the Catholic church. The bishop's presentation of justification bound the person closely to the structures, authority, institutions, and doctrines of the church, yet freed that person to take an active role in society. The focus on self-interest united the needy immigrant to the sacramental ministrations of the church and also baptized emergence into a capitalist economy. The moral values Hughes encouraged—obedience to authority, discipline, self-examination—serving the individual Catholic, the church, and society, were designed to further the process of assimilation. Five major areas of Catholic prayer and asceticism can be used to illustrate how these developments both reflected and influenced the Catholic spiritual life of the period: an understanding of liturgical prayer as a symbol of the church's juridical authority; an emphasis on methodical meditation; the concept of prayer as a contractual arrangement between the believer and God; the proliferation of prayer books and varieties of devotion; and the loss of contemplation.

John Hughes argued that the principles of his Christian political economy came together in the "economy of religious festivals." He noted that the natural rhythm of Sundays and holy days that the church had enforced had limited overproduction. As a result, labor had remained valuable, and the price of bread, low. In his mind, the abolition of rest redounded to the benefit of capitalists. The way to stabilize the economic system was to practice the calendar of feasts and accept the liturgical law of the church. In the church, he argued, "the lawgiver, the landlord, the capitalist, and the laborer—all men of all classes—were required to stand at least once a year in *judgment upon themselves*, in the presence of God and his minister."[33] Through the celebration of its liturgical year and the enforcement of Sundays and holy days, the church could insist on the benefits of spiritual self-interest and counteract the selfishness prevalent in society.

In the argument of John Hughes, Sundays and holy days became symbolic of the relationship between the church and society. The cycle of Catholic worship was analyzed as the primary instance of the church's moral authority in the social fabric. By reasoning in this way, Hughes appeared to critique the economic culture of his time; actually, he baptized it. In his Christian political economy, days of rest represented redeeming acts of justice for the rest of the week's activity. This view corresponded well with the emphasis on the mass as a sacrifice and the Eucharist as an act of the virtue of religion, a constituent element of justice. Prayer books, articles, and provincial councils reinforced the interpretation throughout the century. For example, at the Third Plenary Council of Baltimore in 1884, Bishop Stephen Ryan of Buffalo described religious festivals as "green refreshing oases in the desert of our dreary, plodding life." The observance of Sunday gave testimony "to the authority and tradition of the Church of God." Worship, he argued, presented God with true divine homage, fulfilled the ends of sacrifice, enabled people to discharge their religious obligations, and became a source of blessing and heavenly grace to the Christian world.[34] In a paradoxical way, by heightening the significance of Sunday, apologists thus came to reinforce the economic practice of the workweek.

The capitalist system and values of the mid-nineteenth century also influenced the language and understanding of meditation in Catholic prayer life. When John Hughes emphasized the church's encouragement of a "rigid process of self-examination and self-accusation," he argued for the social usefulness of a particular style of prayer. This style very much reflected the economy's concentration on personal initiative, rational calculation, and renunciation for the sake of some future gain. *A Manual of Catholic Devotions* explicitly made the connection in its treatment of meditation. The application of the three intellectual powers—memory, will, understanding—to the affairs of life, the *Manual* argued, was universally practiced. All people, "from the highest to the lowest, have some object in view; some scheme to accomplish; some business to pursue: and there is no one, if he wish to avoid being rash or foolish, who does not frequently reflect on and adopt the means most likely to insure success." The *Manual* distinguished the saint from the "worldling" not in terms of the style or method of meditation, but in its object. Thus, the merchant, the tradesman, the farmer, and the ordinary Catholic engaged in an exercise of "stock taking designed to awaken hopes of success and knowledge of personal failures." "What then can prevent you," the prayer book asked,

> from reflecting or meditating on the momentous business of your salvation? Why can you not meditate on what may conduce to, or be an obstacle to the attainment of eternal felicity? Why can you not examine the state of your soul—its dispositions and inclinations,—and consider what you ought to pursue or avoid? The whole secret is to think of *eternity* as often, at least, as worldlings do of *time*,—to feel as much interest for our *souls*, as worldlings do for their *bodies*,—and to be as willing to encounter difficulties and overcome obstacles for *immortal treasures*, as worldlings are for *perishable goods*.[35]

Obviously, methodical meditation was not the invention of the nineteenth century. The *Manual* reiterated a style that had been developing since the Reformation.[36] Still, the emphasis on rationality, calculated effects, and conscientious reflection took on new meaning in a culture with a market economy and in a community trying to prove its social respectability. In response to the complaints of "greedy economists," an article in *Brownson's Quarterly Review* noted that prayer instilled the habit of philosophizing. It cultivated a knowledge of principles, suggested consequences for practical morality, and developed polished manners. In the light of this, the author argued, the practice of daily and weekly prayer could hardly be viewed as "money thrown away, time lost for nothing."[37]

Other forms of Catholic prayer in the nineteenth century emphasized, as Hughes did, an "economy of salvation" focused on the contractual arrangement existing between the devout person and God. Particular devotions, the use of sacramentals, prayer before the Blessed Sacrament, novenas, and litanies concentrated on petitionary prayer and good works as prerequisites for the reception of spiritual and material favors. Prayer and charity opened the treasury of Christ and the saints to all believers.[38] Within the context of social poverty and the rise of capitalism, popular prayer forms made the church into a "temple of interest" accessible to all peoples. "Princes, and lords, and capitalists," John Hughes wrote of the social edifice built by capitalism, are indeed well provided for, beneath its glittering arches—a few others still may find protection within its vestibule; but as for you, oh ye millions of the poor and laboring classes, who are called and compelled to worship at its shrine, ye are strewn around its outer porches; and instead of its sheltering you from the storm and the rains of adversity, you are even drenched with the waters that descend from its roof. Go back among the ruins of former things, you may still find and trace out the deep foundations of the better edifice you destroyed. And, if there be no other hope for you, co-operate with Divine Religion in rearing up its stately walls, and its capacious dome, beneath which, even as regards your temporal condition, you, or at least the heirs of your condition, your children, may yet find shelter and protection.[39]

While encouraging a "Gospel of acceptance," a contractual approach to prayer thus helped to provide the spiritual framework for the Catholic adoption of the "ethic of success" in the latter portion of the nineteenth century.[40] It would eventually pave the way for books like E. J. Remler's *Supernatural Merit: Your Treasure in Heaven*, published and revised four times between 1914 and 1922. "What the general terms *pay* and *salary* are to employees," Remler wrote, "heaven is to Christians."[41]

Still another way in which the market economy influenced the Catholic practice of prayer was through the proliferation of devotional guides. At mid-century almost any prayer book could be purchased for under a dollar and the numbers of books available had increased dramatically. Francis Patrick Kenrick, the archbishop of Baltimore, noted that in such an atmosphere of popularity publishers tended to print more and more elaborate books, "gratifying their patrons by every variety of devotion, which is their duty as well as interest, in all those matters which the ecclesiastical authority sanctions, or leaves free." Kenrick preferred shorter works with authorized devotions. Meager as they seemed, they at least left the readers free to occupy their minds in reflection instead of rendering them unconscious of meaning while reciting all of the possible forms.[42] Praying, especially at mass, had entered the mass market.

A final result of this approach to prayer should be noted. The understanding of prayer as a symbol of ecclesiastical hegemony in a secular world; the emphasis on methodical meditation, usefulness, and prayer as contractual agreement; and the multiplication of forms for the sake of popular appeal—all of these results contributed to the loss of contemplative prayer, the quiet presence of the spirit to God and the world in a union of love. Contemplative prayer could hardly flourish in an atmosphere that emphasized rational calculation, verifiable results, and the acquisition of merit. *Prayer the Key of Salvation*, a guidebook of the period, argued in just this way against affective

prayer, one of the traditional steps to contemplation. "Devout affections of the heart," it read, will not produce the rich gifts of God
because affections "do not contain the least petition for any particular
grace." The author used the analogy of the relationship between the
poor and the rich:

> If a beggar were to say to a millionaire: "Oh, how magnificent is your
> house; how splendid your furniture; how elegant your grounds; how vast
> your wealth," it would hardly excite the rich man to almsgiving. But
> should he say: "My good sire, be kind enough to assist me in my poverty;
> please give me some money, some clothes, some provisions," &c., then
> the man of wealth, if charitably disposed, would hardly fail to give him
> what he asked for.[43]

The guidebook went on to recommend prayers of petition and explicitly attacked the language of mystical union. Economics and contemplation simply did not mix.

Another instance of the disparagement of contemplation occurred
in Martin John Spalding's "Introduction" to John Baptist David's *A
Spiritual Retreat*. Spalding used as one of his sourcebooks a popular
commentary on the *Exercises* of Ignatius of Loyola. The source focused
attention on the incarnate Jesus. Quoting Saint Paul's words that
"Jesus Christ loved me, and gave Himself for me," it continued:

> Yes, for *me* as if I was the only sinner among men; yes, for me, not less
> than for all. Would the sun light me more if I were the only one to receive
> his rays? So, if I had been the only sinner in the universe the Divine Sun
> of justice would not have shed upon me less light or less warmth from
> His bosom. When I receive Jesus Christ at the holy table with a multitude
> of other faithful, do I not receive Jesus Christ as entirely as if I were the
> only one in all the universe admitted to communion? So, in the manger;
> on the cross, where He consummated His sacrifice; on the altar, where
> he remains night and day,—Jesus Christ is my whole salvation and my
> life. . . .[44]

According to the author, this act of contemplation, involving the application of the senses and composition of place, moved beyond self-
examination and meditation. In contrast, although he himself was
familiar with a tradition of unitive prayer, Spalding hardly mentioned
the contemplative act, stressing instead rigid self-examination, reformation of life, resolutions of the will. Such an attitude toward prayer
coincided with his focus on the "sacrificial spirit," thus forming a
spiritual life centered on fidelity to duty, mortifications, and penance.[45] A similar approach characterized the Redemptorist and Jesuit
mission preachers.[46] It was well suited to the formation of the immigrant Catholic community.

The life and writings of John Hughes illustrates how the social forces of poverty, immigration, and free-market capitalism combined with a profound experience of the weakness of human nature and a Counter Reformation ecclesiology to encourage a certain style of prayer and asceticism. This approach supported both a policy of Americanization and a strong sense of internal identity; it would dominate the Catholic community for generations to come. As this view affected the spiritual life it could be best labeled as "the triumph of the purgative way." But what would happen if americanized Catholics no longer engaged in polemical wars with Protestants but mixed freely in society; if the church came to be defined more as an "association" or "communion" than as an institution; if self-interest gave way to "religious aspirations" as the dominant principle in human nature? Ironically, while Hughes and others promoted Americanization, the very success of their efforts would insure a future struggle for a new American and Catholic spiritual identity.

CHAPTER
7
The Immigrant Vision: The Golden Chain Binding Heaven and Earth

*A*s the flames are here burning without consuming or even injuring the writings, so shall I pour out My grace in the Blessed Sacrament without prejudice to My honor. Fear not profanation, therefore; hesitate no longer to carry out your designs for My glory." John Nepomucene Neumann (1811–1860) heard these words in his heart as he knelt in his study to give thanks for a sign from God confirming his desire to introduce forty hours devotion to his people. It was 1853, and although devotion to the Blessed Sacrament had been a part of Catholic piety since colonial times, eucharistic exposition and adoration had not yet become truly popular. Neumann quickly published a pamphlet explaining the devotion, composed prayers and rules for the celebration, and ordered all parishes in the diocese of Philadelphia to begin services. The German and Irish faithful flocked to the event. By 1856 forty hours took place almost uninterruptedly throughout the diocese. During the same period, the bishop established the Archconfraternity of the Blessed Sacrament. This pious society gathered on Sundays and holy days after the recitation of vespers to make reparation for insults given to Christ in the Eucharist. The members listened to sermons, said their indulgenced prayers to the Five Sacred Wounds, and concluded the service with benediction. By 1884, due in some measure to the efforts of Neumann, eucharistic devotions had become staple elements in Catholic spiritual life, and national, provincial, and diocesan legislation would insure that they would remain a structural part of Catholic piety for generations to come.

Neumann's fostering of eucharistic devotions and their consequent popularity may be taken as symbolic of the close link that emerged in the mid-nineteenth century between immigrant religion and devotional expressions. It is the purpose of this chapter to examine this link, first by describing the life and experience of an exemplar of Catholic piety, and then by offering some general explanation of the functions of devotionalism in the Catholic community. Just as the American Martin Spalding reflected the transformation taking place in the Catholic tradition, and the Irishman John Hughes became the standard bearer of immigrant identity, so Neumann, an immigrant from Bohemia, embodied the personal, social, and religious reasons for devotionalism.[1]

JOHN NEPOMUCENE NEUMANN: THE EXEMPLAR

A contemporary of John Hughes and Martin John Spalding, John Nepomucene Neumann has been accepted by later generations as the embodiment of Catholic sanctity during the formative period of immigrant Catholicism. Born in 1811 in Prachatitz, Bohemia, of a German father and a Bohemian mother, John manifested from his youth a personal sense of the closeness of God to everyday life. In his autobiographical memoir he noted that his mother never missed hearing daily mass and gave her faith pious expression in frequent recitations of the rosary, stations of the cross, fasting, and morning and evening prayers. "I had, of course," he reflected over three decades later, "a little altar made of lead, and served Mass almost every day."

In November 1831, Neumann began his studies for the priesthood in the small diocesan school at Budweis and continued from 1833 to 1835 in the archdiocesan seminary associated with the theological faculty at Prague. Reading the letters of Saint Paul, especially 2 Corinthians 11, and inspired by the descriptions of the life of Frederic Baraga (1797–1868) among the Ottawa and Chippewa Indians, Neumann decided to devote his life to mission work in the United States. He arrived in New York in May 1836, was ordained by Bishop John Dubois in June, and began pastoral work among the smaller German congregations in upstate New York. Overwhelmed by the needs of the German immigrants, the young priest never fulfilled his dream to minister to the native American. He was greatly inspired by the strong devotional fervor fostered by the Redemptorists at Saint Joseph's Church, Rochester, and, in 1840, desiring to live "where I would

not have to be exposed alone to the thousand dangers of the world,"
he applied for admittance into that order. After a one-year novitiate,
Neumann took his religious vows on January 16, 1842, and subse-
quently served the German communities in the Baltimore and Pittsburgh regions. In 1847 Neumann became superior of the Redemptorists in the United States, a position he used to encourage the regular
observance of the rule, missions, and the development of a parochial
life characterized by well-ordered church services, confessional work,
preaching, schools, and confraternities. Sponsored by his predecessor
and mentor, Francis Patrick Kenrick, Neumann was consecrated
bishop of Philadelphia on March 28, 1852. He served that diocese as
a model pastor until his early death eight years later on January 5,
1860.[2]

John Neumann's vision of the Christian life can be seen as com-
plementary to that of the Irishman John Hughes and the American
Martin John Spalding. As nativism had shaped the vision of his fellow
bishops, so also it encouraged in Neumann a focus on those elements
in Catholicism that differentiated it from Protestantism. Neumann's
biographer notes that in response to the growth of anti-Catholic societies such as the Red Men, Odd Fellows, and Freemasons, the bishop
emphasized the social cohesion created by orderly and devout participation in church services, frequent reception of the sacraments,
pious practices, and membership in confraternities. As had been the
case with Hughes and Spalding, struggles against lay trusteeism encouraged in Neumann, who inherited the difficulties long associated
with Holy Trinity Church, Philadelphia, a corporate and hierarchical
view of the church. Like his contemporaries, the bishop was burdened
with debt and labored to build an institutional church responsive to
the needs of the immigrants in educational programs, charitable institutions, and parish churches. All three men shared a vision of the
Christian life formed within the structures so clearly articulated at
the First Plenary Council of Baltimore in 1852 and brought to completion by Spalding at the Second Plenary Council, 1866.[3] Together,
the prelates reflected the remarkable coherence of vision characteristic
of the Irish, American, and German Catholic community during the
period.

For the historian of spirituality, Neumann's life becomes significant not for the presuppositions that he shared with his contemporaries, nor for his pastoral work, which was characteristic of the period,
but for the intensity and clarity with which the bishop expressed the
pursuit of sanctity in the pre–Civil War period. Neumann has left a
spiritual journal covering the years from 1834 to 1839 and an autobiography written on the eve of his episcopal consecration in 1852.
His work as a catechist, correspondence with Francis Patrick Kenrick,

and the collection by his nephew Johann Berger of contemporary testimony to his holiness provide an insight into the personal dimensions of religious experience not to be found in the writings of Hughes and Spalding. A brief examination of Neumann's training in Counter Reformation spirituality and his reflection on his own religious experience will offer a final and more personal perspective from which to view the foundations of the vision of Christian life dominant during the immigrant period.[4]

Where his contemporaries Hughes and Spalding gave evidence of how the Gallican and Roman traditions of Counter Reformation theology and practice influenced the development of Catholic life in the United States, John Neumann exhibited more directly the spiritual dimensions of this perspective and its nineteenth-century transformation. Neumann clearly inherited from his mother the Catholic devotional life that had been forged in the heat of religious wars and had perdured in Bohemia since the seventeenth century. Hermann Dichtl, Neumann's spiritual father at Budweis, combined this tradition with an ultramontane ecclesiology in reaction to the eighteenth-century Enlightenment. While studying theology at Prague, the young seminarian came under the influence of the restorationist current represented by Dean Anton Rost (1798–1879), and the professor of moral theology, Stephan Teplotz (1795–1877). Neumann listened to selections from the writings of Charles Borromeo (1538–1584) and from Friedrich Stolberg's *History of the Religion of Jesus Christ*, one of the representative romantic interpretations of Christian history. He read extensively in the Jesuit Counter Reformation theologians Peter Canisius (1521–1597) and Robert Bellarmine (1542–1621), and referred to the following writers and works in his diary: Thomas à Kempis's *The Imitation of Christ*, Louis of Granada's *Guide for Sinners*, Lorenzo Scupoli's *Spiritual Combat*, Teresa of Avila's *Confessions*, Francis de Sales's *Introduction to the Devout Life*, Alphonsus Liguori's *Homo Apostolicus* and *Visits with Jesus in the Most Holy Sacrament of the Altar*, and Anne Catherine Emmerich's *Passion of Our Lord Jesus Christ*.[5]

It is important to note that Neumann's *Journals* mention Ignatius of Loyola and Anne Catherine Emmerich (1774–1824), Teresa of Avila (1515–82), and Alphonsus Liguori (1696–1787), Francis de Sales, and Louis Bourdaloue (1632–1704). Loyola, Teresa, and de Sales represented the humanistic reform tradition that had so strongly influenced John Carroll; the others reflected the transformation of this tradition in baroque, Counter Reformation Catholicism. It was the latter viewpoint that prevailed in Neumann's vision of the Christian life. For example, while Neumann read extensively in Teresa of Avila, he avoided the mystical elements in her experience and instead called on her intercession to help him find a spiritual director; he wished to imitate her virtue, not her prayer. He read de Sales's *Introduction* but noted only that "haste in the performance of the works of devotion is reprehensible." The seminarian quoted Fénelon not on the inner life but to the effect that "when one is a Christian, he cannot afford to be lax." He cited Lorenzo Scupoli not to argue for the cultivation of interior virtue in response to externalism but to strengthen him in his battle against apathy and his predominant passions. Neumann appealed not to Ignatius of Loyola, the spiritual reformer, but to his French descendant Jean Croiset (1656–1738), who emphasized moral rectitude, asceticism, opposition to the spirit of the world, and meditation on the great truths of death and hell to evoke a change of life.[6] The religious experience that supported such an interpretation was typical of nineteenth-century piety, including that of Spalding and Hughes, and consisted of four central elements: a strong sense of personal sin joined with a desire for perfection and a sense of God's presence; an exacting program of self-discipline; a close dependence on Jesus, Mary, and the saints; and a reliance on the sacramental ministrations of the church.

On December 1, 1834, John Neumann meditated on the similarities between himself and Bartimaeus, the blind man in the Gospel of Mark (10: 46–52). What struck the seminarian most was the plea for mercy and the Savior's compassionate response. "I am even worse off than he," Neumann wrote. "What should I do? By my sins, I have lost the glow and vigor of my soul. That man was born blind. You have given me all I needed to reach my goal, my eternal salvation. Have pity on me, O Son of David. . . ." Such consciousness of his own weakness and sin was not unusual for Neumann. He possessed a delicate conscience, and filled his *Journal* with unremitting references to his predominant passions, refusal of grace, vainglory, coldness of devotion, indifference, aridity, insincere dispositions, self-love, anxieties, pride, impurity, and discouragement. He was afflicted with despair, feared his eternal damnation, and, at one time, was tempted by suicide. His confessions became intense revelations of the smallest offenses.[7]

Neumann's sense of personal sin existed in conjunction with an overwhelming desire for perfection and knowledge of God's presence to his soul. He longed to emulate the saints and was acutely aware of his good dispositions and movements of grace. In a fashion typical of the age, his *Journal* recognized not only despair but beauty, not only the loss of God's love but also the availability of grace. For example, after pleading for the graces of perfect humility, fervor, and recollection, Neumann wrote the following meditation on God's care:

O my soul, what exactly were we twenty-four years ago? Where were you then? No one in the whole world knew beforehand he would eventually be created in the image of God. Though all the stars in the sky had passed away or had reached their heavenly goal, you could not have caused yourself to be. Where were you in the beginning? You were not in heaven, nor in hell. You could not create yourself for you did not exist. As a matter of fact, the one who created you is your God who had existed through all eternity and who is all-powerful. Were you able to ask Him to bring you into being? Oh my soul, you were nothing, less than a drop of water or a grain of sand. Had God made you a leaf, a plant, a worm, or a bird, you would have glorified Him accordingly for the brief duration of your existence. You would have contributed thereby to His glory and then disappeared from the world—you would have been turned back into nothing which is just what you were at first.

Thus, my soul, here you are, with a mind to address your Creator. Because you do actually exist, you can turn to your God and give Him glory. You can give him glory for ever because you will exist forever.[8]

Such a passage could have been taken from Vincent Huby's *Spiritual Exercises* and would have appealed to Fénelon or John Carroll. It was part of the tradition of Ignatius of Loyola and Francis de Sales. What Neumann brought to it, and what differentiated his experience from those of the others, was a feeling of interior tenuousness, a conjunction of sin and grace in his experience, a more profound sense of the weakness of human reason and effort, and a conviction that passion unsupported by the aid of religion would eventually lead to sin. This was a position that emerged in John Carroll only after the French Revolution. By Neumann's time the Enlightenment air of confidence in the relationship between nature and grace, reason and faith, had passed into a more romantic, tentative sensibility.

Neumann combined this sensibility with a strong sense of personal responsibility expressed in self-discipline and the assiduous performance of religious duties. He took a vow to fast on any day on which he told a lie, resolved constantly to improve himself, looked for a spiritual guide, prayed continuously for help, meditated on death, hell, and the mystery of the Incarnation, practiced frequent Communion, read from the Scriptures and lives of the saints, and struggled to remain faithful to the duties of his clerical state: daily prayer, the recitation of the breviary, and presence at mass. If Neumann did not attain the mystical heights to which Teresa of Avila beckoned, he strove to imitate her virtues within the limits that history had imposed upon him. This constant desire for improvement and focus on purgation received final expression in his life as a religious, characterized by frequent examination of conscience, visits to the Blessed Sacrament, observance of the rule, obedience to superiors, and the exacting performance of pastoral responsibilities.[9]

In his life of purgation, Neumann experienced a strong bond between himself, God, Christ, Mary, and the saints. He constantly addressed the Trinity as intimate companions of his spiritual journey: "Beloved Father, infinitely good, how I wish I could pattern my life after your law"; "Holy Spirit, see how helplessly I stand before your divine majesty. Receive my prayer despite its imperfection. Grant me what I so much desire: a will that is holy, pure and disposed to obey God's law." Neumann turned for comfort especially to the suffering Jesus: "Dear Jesus, you have died for me. Let it not happen that your blood was shed in vain for me"; "Forgive me, my Savior Jesus Christ. I would gladly bathe myself in your divine blood shed for all mankind on the cross"; "Sweetest Jesus, I would gladly offer You my heart but it is so filthy I fear to betray you anew, for I am still so sinful, more so than my companions. Take my heart, O Holy Spirit, my Sanctifier, my Lord and God. Make it holy, cleanse it tomorrow with the blood of the Innocent Lamb"; "Oh, my Savior, dearer to me than anything in the world, come Yourself into my heart"; "Dear God, your arms open on the cross invite me to return to You; I can see from your half-opened lips that You want to tell me that You are always ready to welcome me just as You promised."[10] Given this strong personal relationship, it was no wonder that Neumann took as his episcopal motto the phrase from the *Anima Christi* which he had learned as a child: "Anima Christi, sanctifica me." He strove to suffuse all of his daily activity with this mercy and charity of Christ.

Neumann also filled his *Journal* with invocations to Mary, "Mother of Grace," his guardian angel, and the saints. "Help me, Queen of Angels and Heaven!" he wrote.

> I shall always pray to You since You are all powerful with my Lord. I shall turn to You today and every day of my life until I die.
> St. Francis Xavier, how I yearn to be like you! Teach me the virtue you recommended to your confreres. I promise to be a conscientious pupil. And you, my holy patron, help me to learn to be truthful, for I still lack this virtue. My Guardian Angel, help me. Make me pay attention to what I say, do and think. My own inclination, my bad habits entice me to sin. O Lord, give me the grace I need to overcome the dangers that surround me.[11]

His personal world was one of communion and interdependence, balancing the strong institutional role that he played in the church.

Neumann's sense of sin and grace, the need for discipline, the spiritual interdependence of people, and their unity in Christ expressed itself in a strong belief in the church as the ark of salvation. He worried about the lack of priests and the people deprived of "the consolations of our holy religion." "Dear God," he wrote, "You established your holy Roman Church to save Your creatures who wandered from You in their sins."[12] In Neumann's view, the church offered certainty in the face of doubt, forgiveness in the experience of sin, sacramental aid for the support of human weakness, and comfort and protection in the midst of persecution and loneliness. This conviction about the church as a spiritual reality and his general understanding of the Christian life directed Neumann's work as bishop of Philadelphia. Knowing God's incarnate mercy to an extraordinary degree, his spiritual life spent itself in ecclesiastical charity. Parochial schools, catechism classes, the building of churches, pastoral visitations, confessional work, preaching, missions, forty hours devotions, the establishment of confraternities, Lenten devotions, and the encouragement of religious life—all of those expressions so common during the period, became the substance of Neumann's imitation of Christ.[13] When Pope Benedict XV commented on John Neumann's life in 1921, over sixty years after his death, he noted that the norm of heroic virtue was the "faithful, perpetual and constant carrying out of the duties and obligations of one's proper state."[14]

Canonized on June 19, 1977, John Neumann embodied the understanding of sanctity dominant in the immigrant church. If Hughes and Spalding graphically represented the social and theological structures of the building, Neumann focused on its personal spirit. After the bishop's death, his nephew recalled the esteem with which the immigrant flock venerated their leader. One superior of a sisterhood remarked: "Aside from his special acts of heroic virtue, his every action, his every word, his whole demeanor, even the tone of his voice, bore the unmistakable character of sanctity. Whenever he came to any of our convents, his first visit was to his dear Lord in the Blessed Sacrament; and whilst before the altar, his whole soul was so absorbed in God that he appeared to be no longer of this world."[15] In this way John Neumann became an icon of the immigrant community's own aspirations. In no area was this more evident than in that of devotionalism, in some senses the heart and soul of immigrant religion.

THE GOLDEN CHAIN BINDING HEAVEN AND EARTH

John Neumann promoted forty hours, benediction of the Blessed Sacrament, Marian devotions, parish missions, confraternities, lenten sermons, prayers to the saints, and numerous other expressions of popular religious sentiment. Those elements in his experience and reflection that provided the foundations for this devotionalism were not unique to the Bohemian immigrant. As previous chapters have argued, a Counter Reformation theological inheritance, a strong sense of personal weakness and sin, an emphasis on sacrifice and self-discipline, reliance on the church as the "ark of salvation," and a feeling for corporate relationships also characterized the experience of Martin John Spalding and John Hughes. Taken together the three leaders of the Catholic community provided strong witness both to the reasons for the growth of devotions in the American, Irish, and German sectors of the community, and also to the important functions that devotional piety performed.

It is not the purpose of this discussion to describe the proliferation of these devotional practices in mid-nineteenth century Catholicism nor to examine the multitude of ethnic variations. Instead, using the experience of the most prominent churchmen as guides, devotionalism will be examined for its significance in the overall "system of religion" adopted by the immigrant church. Rooted in a feeling for the interconnection of all of life, popular practices focused on Jesus (the Sacred Heart, Five Wounds, Litany of the Holy Name, stations of the cross), Mary (rosary, May devotions, miraculous medals), and the saints (celebrations of feast days, novenas, various litanies); the mysteries of the faith (Blessed Sacrament, Christmas crib) not only served as symbols of the community's identity but also took their place within the much larger complex of an American and Catholic vision of the spiritual life. Any understanding of devotionalism must first recognize how it functioned to bind together those elements that were so closely aligned in a total spiritual vision: the immigrant experience and the church as community.

The immigrant experience, as testified to by Hughes, Spalding, and Neumann, seems to have effected the rise of a devotional spirituality in two distinct ways. First, just as a European Counter Reformation romantic theological inheritance shaped the leaders of the community, so the piety of the immigrants developed within the context of the mid-nineteenth century continental religious revival. In Ireland, the experience of the famine midwifed a new religious style emphasizing austerity, the authority and sacramental ministrations of the church, and an aggressive fusion of Catholicism and ethnic identity. A similar process of modernization occurred in Germany, both in Prussian Westphalia and Catholic Bavaria. Confronted with poor harvests, urban migration, and industrial development, people fashioned a religious life opposed to the individualistic and anticlerical forces of the Enlightenment. In both cases, what emerged was a system of religious expression characterized by tighter bonds between clergy and laity within a hierarchical church; moral reformation, especially in the area of sexual expression; popular gatherings in missions, processions, and pilgrimages; new forms of religious sodalities and mutual aid societies; and popular devotions.[16] Hughes, Spalding, and

Neumann were religious leaders in their respective communities precisely because their experience was in some way representative, and they fashioned from it a religious style that was available to all. When the majority of Irish and Germans immigrated after 1865, they naturally accepted the basic structures of piety that the three churchmen and their communities had evolved in the 1840s and 1850s.

Second, just as the leaders testified to the experience of rootlessness and evolved their religious self-understanding within that context, so the German and Irish immigrants and the indigenous American Catholics, confronted with social dislocation, poverty, and religious persecution, developed their vision of the Christian life. For the Catholics of this period, right action, obedience, and discipline became significant supports for a strong internal ecclesiastical identity and a combative social stance.[17] But this "immigrant Puritanism" was systematically balanced by the "beauty" of Catholic life: the lights, candles, and incense of ritual; the personal contact between pastor and people so well witnessed by Hughes, Spalding, and Neumann; the spontaneity expressed in religious revivalism; and the relationships present through the communion of saints. Hughes brought the two elements of discipline and feeling together when he noted that ecclesiastical ministers were sent to "convert the heart; to subdue the natural ferocity of men; to make them love each other." For the archbishop of New York the primary features of civilization, which he equated with Catholic Christianity, were warmth, poetry of feeling, enthusiasm, and effective united counsel.[18] Spalding was known for his rigoristic opposition to dancing, his support of ecclesiastical discipline, and his insistence that the priesthood meant hardship and self-sacrifice. Yet his warm marian devotional piety was also legendary; he encouraged his priests in this way:

> Our blessed Lord came to send fire on the earth, and what does he will more than that it be kindled in the hearts of all men? In order that we may be able to scatter this heavenly fire over the earth, we must take care to keep it always burning in our own hearts; for if we be cold ourselves, how shall we be able to warm others? Happy shall we be if, by a constant and living union with Jesus Christ, the Source, of the divine fire, we maintain ourselves in the fervor of the holy priesthood, and thus become, like St. John the Baptist, burning and shining lights in God's sanctuary.[19]

"Give me warm devotional feeling," Spalding wrote, "even if it sometimes appears to become exaggerated, rather than that cold, caviling piety, which seems always uneasy and trembling, lest it should be transported too far, and be led to say or do too much."[20] A similar combination of self-denial and personalism characterized Neumann.[21] Popular prayer books of the period such as *True Piety* and the *Ursuline*

Manual combined extensive passages on the examination of conscience with heartfelt affections upon receiving communion.[22]

Frederick William Faber, an English Oratorian and spiritual writer whose works were very popular in the United States, illustrated this connection between alienation, social identity, moralism, and devotional feelings in his book *The Blessed Sacrament*. For him, the sacramental presence of the Lord in the Eucharist addressed the experience of rootlessness. "Indeed," Faber noted, "in all things our very safety consists in being afraid, in a sense of inferiority, in a conviction that we are no match either for our own poor selves or for evils from without." In such a world, real contact with the Savior provided motives for action, forgiveness, an opportunity to give one's whole self to "deep childlike joy in a mystery which is the triumph of faith over sight, of spirit over matter, of grace over nature, and of the Church over the world."

This presence was also distinctive to the Catholic religion, providing it with social identity in a Protestant world. Last, a spiritual life centered in the Eucharist could not be divorced from an "inveterate attachment" to the church's ceremonial observances; love of God and love of Rome were inseparable.[23] Faber's explication of the Eucharist was representative of the immigrant vision of the Christian life. The same people who worked as laborers and competed in the marketplace also built the churches and admired the Gothic cathedrals. Devotionalism was the affective counterpart of the "triumph of the purgative way." If the latter established definition and social status, the former provided the spark of life.

Devotions also helped make the church a community that could unite the rich and the poor, the person and the institution, the male and the female, the Irish, the American, and the German, time and eternity. Some of the foundations for this community building function have already been indicated; here it should be noted that the leader's commitment to unity received confirmation in the practices of the faithful. The importance of devotional expressions in the immigrant experience of community rested on three basic principles: devotions grew from a base of social cooperation; they became the symbolic meeting ground of doctrine, institution, and life; they provided for both institutional cohesion and ethnic diversity.

The Irish and German Catholic immigrants brought to the United States a tendency to form associations for political, social, and religious purposes. Once here, the climate of political voluntarism and a need born of poverty and oppression encouraged cooperation and organization, especially in the area of devotional societies. Religious confraternities honoring the Immaculate Heart, the Sacred Passion, the Holy Family, and various saints developed the community base connected with the establishment of parishes and schools. For example, the Sodality of the Blessed Virgin was established at Saint Peter's Church in New York on December 8, 1856. Composed of young women educated at the parish school, it met on the first Sunday of the month to receive instructions, sing hymns, recite prayers, and organize for the decoration of the altar and relief of the poor. Although numbering only 135 members by 1866, it joined the Living Rosary Society (300 members), the Sodality of Saint Aloysius (70 members), the Sodality of the Holy Angels (87 members), and the Sodality for the Holy Infancy (105 members) in a total parish complex that cared for the needs of all the people. The German and Irish immigrants established similar associations in most urban parishes.[24]

The formation of devotional confraternities increased rapidly after the Civil War as the number of immigrants grew and people became increasingly conscious of the importance of building community on the local level. In contrast to Protestantism, Catholicism had emerged from the war united in faith and organization. Observing these developments in New York, John Talbot Smith argued that the war had weakened Puritanism as a social force; parades, grand religious ceremonies, gigantic bazaars, and public debates now became occasions when Catholics could manifest their strength, numbers, and social power to themselves and their neighbors.[25] A growth in communal expressions of faith in honor of the Sacred Heart and the Blessed Mother reflected this newfound awareness in the community of its spiritual resources. One historian estimates that 60 percent of all parish societies founded between 1860 and 1900 were devotional.[26] *Ave Maria*, a periodical dedicated to popular piety, captured the mood of the times when it editorialized:

> There seems, just now, to pervade the whole country, a general tendency towards the formation of "unions" of every kind. Indeed, the hour is favorable to such notions. It is not then out of place to propose the union of sodalities. This, if accomplished, will not only afford pleasure and benefit to themselves, but be, besides, a means under God, of extending and strengthening the influence of "Holy Church." But in order to bring about an actual union, as it were, of bands, it will be necessary to bring about a union of hearts, of sympathies, of souls. They must become aware of each other's existence, whereabouts, aims, hopes, and condition.[27]

A similar sentiment on a smaller scale had animated the work of Spalding, Hughes, and Neumann; the post–Civil War church capitalized on structures that had been established earlier.[28]

These devotional confraternities embodied the immigrants' experience of the church in several ways. Essentially lay, they were organized in connection with the parish and gave a prominent place to clerical direction. They helped form the Catholic body into a "well arranged army," one that could establish bonds of loyalty as a protection against nativist attack. On a practical level, to join a confraternity meant the acceptance of a corporate definition of the spiritual life. Whereas the individual might fall prey to the ravages of the world, the flesh, and the devil,

> in these holy confraternities, the ability of the one is so knit with the ability of the rest, and the good works of all are so common to every one in particular, that they are all fortified and enabled, not only by their own forces, but each other's strength and assistance; insomuch, that partly by the benefit which every one doth reap from his own private endeavors, and partly by the great benefits which arise from the communion of merits, persons do ordinarily, in those devout congregations, make so great a progress in virtue, in a short time, that they become not only invincible, but also formidable to their infernal enemies, and are known to abound with many celestial graces and benedictions.[29]

Second, within the context of a corporate whole and an asceticism that emphasized obedience and sacrifice, confraternities enabled people to form close-knit, smaller units, based on personal contact. They provided the communal base for what John Hughes called the "union of minds and hearts." Gathered into a society at prayer and work, each member could be made "participant of the prayers, sacrifices, fastings, alms, mortifications, and generally of all the good works and meritorious actions of all the other members; from which common affinity, and communications without a doubt many great benefits do accrue."[30]

Last, the associations demonstrated on a popular level what Hughes and Spalding argued theoretically: the compatibility of Catholicism with American democratic values. Membership was voluntary, and men, women, boys, and girls all organized their own societies. Women often played a prominent role. For example, from 1865 to 1888 tabernacle societies grew up in Philadelphia, Washington, New York, and Saint Paul. Of these, the Arch-Association of Perpetual Adoration of the Blessed Sacrament and the Work for Poor Churches was perhaps the most significant. Its major purpose was to "make Jesus Christ in the Blessed Sacrament known, loved, and perpetually adored." Controlled by women, the society met every first Friday, recited the liturgical office of the Blessed Sacrament during an all-day exposition, and came together for monthly business, benediction, and instruction. The Arch-Association distributed to the poorer churches and missions altar cloths, corporals, albs, surplices, vestments, stoles, chalices, and other items for ceremonial use. By 1896 the associations in Philadelphia boasted four thousand contributors and an enrollment of 1,776 persons in sixty-three parishes. Similar societies existed in Boston, Wilmington, Baltimore, Cincinnati, Dayton, Saint Louis, and San Francisco.³¹ Without challenging the cultural confinement of females to the domestic sphere, the association gave women a mission that extended beyond the confines of home and parish.³² Within the structures of the institutional church, confraternities embodied communal and participative values.

Devotions also united the Catholic community by serving as the symbolic meeting ground of doctrine, institution, and immigrant life. This subject has already been partially examined in regard to devotion to the Blessed Sacrament; to further the discussion, the immigrant emphasis on the communion of saints needs to be considered. Many prayer books of the day included novenas to such saints as Joseph, Patrick, John the Baptist, Angela, Augustine, Aloysius, Ursula, and Christopher. The shrines in the homes of the Irish and German immigrants, the statues and pictures in the schools, and the stained-glass windows in the churches made the saints, what they stood for and how they lived, the spiritual link between the major structures of the immigrant church.³³ "The communion of saints," Spalding wrote,

> how sublime the idea it unfolds! How it annihilates time, annihilates distance, and causes the hearts of all the friends of Christ and favorites of heaven to beat in a unison of hallowed feelings! How it reaches, like a golden chain, from earth to heaven, and binds both together in indissoluble love and unity! How it makes us, poor exiles on earth, already "fellow citizens of the saints, and the domestics of God!" How it makes the strong succor the weak, the rich succor the poor, those who abound in merits succor those who are needy, and those who are in glory succor those who are in tribulation!³⁴

On August 22, 1853, John Hughes preached on this doctrine of the Catholic faith, extolling the church as the communion of those bound together by "faith, hope, divine love, and charity."³⁵ The pages of John Neumann's *Journal* were filled with a similar sense of the closeness and power of divine intercessors.³⁶

The doctrine of the communion of saints, commemorated by the church in a continual round of festivals and anniversaries, communicated to all the possibilities inherent in Catholic life. On the doctrinal level, the saints were living examples, in word and deed, of the practical importance of the Catholic teaching on justification. As the apologists asked, could the Protestants boast of a Francis de Sales, Thomas à Kempis, or Fénelon? Could they put forth anyone who demonstrated a concern for the poor, the blind, the lame, the uneducated, in the same way as Francis Xavier, Aloysius Gonzaga, or Charles Borromeo? Could they demonstrate the generosity of soul that had animated the great religious leaders who had embraced poverty,

chastity, and obedience to follow Christ?[37] *Ave Maria* summarized
much of this sentiment when it printed this eulogy of Vincent de Paul:

> O Blessed Father! sent by God,
> His mercy to dispense,
> Thy hand is out o'er all the earth,
> Like God's own providence.
>
> Dear Saint! not in the wilderness
> Thy fragrant virtues bloom,
> But in the city's crowded haunts,
> The alley's cheerless gloom.
> For Charity anointed thee
> O'er want, and woe, and pain;
> And she has crowned thee emperor
> Of all her wide domain.[38]

Surely such a living example witnessed to the close unity between
faith and works, the truth of the Catholic faith, and the social importance of Christianity?

In an even more significant way, the saints not only demonstrated
the practical truth of Catholicism; by their sufferings, the humanity
of their lives, and their intercession, they made that integrity available
to all. Hughes believed that Scripture recorded "the incidental biography of those upon the tablets of whose hearts God, with the pencil
of his love, had engraved those living truths" of injustices suffered
and opponents overcome. Neumann, as has been indicated, became
a living icon, the embodiment to the immigrants of the unity between
Christ, the church, and the person; through him, sanctity became accessible. Spalding listed the following advantages of the Catholic position on the communion of saints: It kept before the eyes of all the
importance of heroic virtue and struggle; it stimulated people to resist
temptation and imitate the example of others; it cheered people on
"their dreary earthly pilgrimage"; it appealed to the noblest feelings
of nature; and it consoled in time of tribulations.[39]

Last, the saints, transformed in glory, presented to the immigrants
triumph over death, continuity in relationships, and the promise of
eternal glory. As Spalding noted, the Catholic religion gave people a
"kind of angel guardian," binding them "into one society knit by a
thousand associations and ties." Abstracting them from the earth,
this religion made people feel but pilgrims and strangers here below.
Death could not end, in Hughes's mind, "that universal and eternal
union subsisting between Christ and the members of His Church." In
short, the doctrine of the communion of saints recognized suffering,
encouraged sacrifice and work for others (the imitation of Christ),

and drew people forward into greater life. This devotional eschatology that permeated the *Journal* of John Neumann functioned within the immigrant experience to stimulate action for the future.[40]

In the vision of the immigrant church the focus on the communion of saints culminated in devotion to the Blessed Virgin Mary. The prayer books contained explanations of the rosary and numerous Marian litanies; prayers honoring the Sacred Heart of Mary and the Seven Dolors; hymns such as "Salve Regina," "Ave Regina Coelorum," and "Regina Coeli Laetare" associated with the liturgical year; and the Little Office of the Blessed Virgin Mary. The people practiced May devotions, joined Marian confraternities, wore miraculous medals, enthroned the Virgin Mother in their homes, and celebrated the feasts of precept honoring Mary. Hughes, Spalding, and Neumann encouraged these devotions through preaching, apologetic works, and legislation. Perhaps the most significant Marian devotion of the era was that honoring her Immaculate Conception. The Sixth Provincial Council of Baltimore in 1846 proclaimed this feast the patronal feast of the church in the United States. Three years later, the seventh council presented a report to the Holy See on the status of the devotion in the country and petitioned the pope to proclaim it an article of faith. Neumann, in his diocesan synod of 1853, asked that the petition, "Queen, conceived without original sin, pray for us," be added to the Litany of Loretto that was to be sung before the principal masses on Sundays and holy days. Among others, the bishop of Philadelphia and John Hughes participated in the preliminary meetings that led to the solemn proclamation of the Immaculate Conception as a dogma of faith in 1854. After that time, numerous pastorals made an effort to relate the devotion to the practical faith of the people. Clearly, Mary, the Immaculate Mother of God, stood at the center of immigrant devotional life.[41]

Devotion to Mary embodied several key dimensions of the immigrant vision of the spiritual life. Praying to Mary symbolized both the weakness and strength present in the immigrant experience. Burdened with sin, subject to passion, and beset by persecution, people could still cooperate in their salvation. William Henry Elder, bishop of Natchez, summarized this experience when he wrote:

> We all know too well that, of ourselves, we are but weakness and misery; that the devil, like a roaring lion, goes about seeking to devour our souls, and that our own sinful passions would, every day, lead us into evil, if we trusted only to our own watchfulness and fortitude, and did not seek for help. But seeking for help, dearly beloved, does not mean simply asking aid from God; it always includes making use of the means which God has put in our reach. If a good Christian finds his house in danger of

> burning, he will not only offer prayers to God for its protection, but he
> will likewise pray his neighbors to come to his assistance.[42]

One of the "neighbors" available to the Catholic was Mary, who, as
Spalding put it, was not a "passive instrument in this great work of
redemption. She was an intelligent instrument; she was a moral agent,
and could have refused her consent. But she was obedient; she as-
sented, and became the mother of her Saviour-God."[43] Community,
in this vision of the spiritual life—whether it be the relationship between people and priest, sinner and saint, the immigrant and the
"mother of the poor"—was born out of the need for help, the willingness to ask for it, and the faith that it would be provided.

In praying to Mary, a person also recognized the difference between
the Mother of God and the sinful individual. She was the greatest of
all God's creatures, "the one on whom he has lavished the largest
treasures of His wisdom and goodness."[44] "Purer than Heaven's purest
Angel," Neumann wrote, "brighter than its brightest Seraph; Mary,
after her Creator, God—who made and gave her all, is the most perfect
of beings; the Masterpiece of Infinite Wisdom, Almighty Power and
Eternal Love."[45] In this role, as powerful intercessor and woman
without spot, Mary represented the corporate body of Christ, the
church: "As the Church has been established by God, both for our
assistance and for His glory, so, also, our devotion to the Blessed Virgin
Mary rests at the same time on our weakness and on God's designs
for the advancement of his honour."[46]

Finally, Mary could not be considered apart from Christ. Quoting
Saint Augustine, Neumann related Jesus and Mary most directly in
his 1854 pastoral on the Immaculate Conception: "Wherever the most
enlightened piety exists, there also, hardly a moment's hesitation on
this subject will be entertained. *'Caro Jesu! Caro Mariae!'* 'The flesh
of Jesus is the flesh of Mary!' " Any devotion to Mary, Elder noted,
meant devotion to "Jesus in His Childhood; to Jesus on the Cross; to
His Sacred Heart; to His Most Precious Blood; to His Five Wounds;
the Way of the Cross; the Visiting of the Blessed Sacrament; the Forty
Hours Adoration." On his deathbed, Spalding appealed to Jesus and
Mary together.[47] Mary, as the greatest link in the "golden chain binding heaven and earth," thus represented the interdependence among
the elements at the heart of the immigrant vision of the Christian
life: the guilt of sin and the possibility of action; Christ, the Son of
God, "born of a woman, born under the law"; the church, instrument
of Christ on earth; and the saints, "those upon the tablets of whose
hearts God, with the pencil of His love, had engraved these living
truths."

Devotional practices functioned in one other way to support the structures of the immigrant vision of the Christian life. By representing on a popular symbolic level the basic social, institutional, and theological convictions of immigrant experience, they helped to provide cohesiveness in the community. Within the confines of this commonly accepted language and meaning about Jesus, Mary, and the saints, both Irish and German Catholics could express their diversity. Spalding, Hughes, and Neumann, despite their different backgrounds and national identities, presented a surprisingly unified vision of the Christian life coupled with a tolerance of different customs, ceremonies, and piety within the community.[48]

This structure of diversity within unity, based on the common experience of poverty and nativism; the common conviction of a corporate church; the common asceticism of the triumph of the purgative way; and the common symbolic language of Jesus, Mary, and the saints continued to be developed in the post–Civil War community. Institutionally, the forces of diversity came to fruition in the ethnic parish. As that happened, more and more emphasis came to be placed upon the elements of unity as fundamental to the Catholic vision of the Christian life. In this way, the devotions focused on Jesus, Mary, and the saints, proceeding from the common base that Hughes, Spalding, and Neumann had both experienced and articulated, enabled the immigrant church to assimilate the forces of pluralism into its vision of the Christian life, its spiritual identity.[49]

When viewed from the perspective of Hughes, Spalding, and Neumann, the "golden chain binding heaven and earth" and the structures that it promoted contributed to the program of Americanization. Devotionalism incorporated the values of unity and pluralism, fostered voluntarism, represented some accommodation to communal institutions, and provided the spark of life and eschatology that fueled the purgative way. Devotionalism also developed within the context of a Counter Reformation polemic, a unique experience of the relationship between nature and grace, and an emphasis on institutional authority and obedience. It symbolically represented a universe far removed from the experience and vision of John Carroll, yet it accomplished for the immigrant generation precisely what John Carroll had wanted: an American and Catholic identity.

The unity of this vision would not go unchallenged. A different experience of society, the person, and the church would engender the search for another approach and another spirituality. It is the origins, development, and progress of that "Americanist" vision of the Christian life that must now be examined.

PART THREE

The Spirituality of Americanism, 1866–1900

In the summer of 1856, John Hughes and Orestes Brownson (1803–1876) both attended the commencement exercises of Saint John's College (Fordham), New York. It was a momentous occasion. Since 1846, when Hughes had transferred Saint John's to a community of French Jesuits from Kentucky, the institution had developed many of the qualities characteristic of the piety of the immigrant church. Designed to duplicate the isolation of a seminary, the college worked hard to avoid the moral and physical pollution associated with the surrounding city. Visits home were limited; mail was censored; the daily schedule was designed around a regime of religious exercises; the virtue of obedience was stressed. The students gathered in sodalities and heard discourses about particular sins, the heroic struggles of the saints, and the devotions necessary to win the struggle for virtue. In this context, Brownson, who had moved to New York the previous year, issued a rousing call for a new vision of the relationship between Catholicism and American civilization, one that directly challenged the view formulated by Hughes, Spalding, and Neumann.[1]

Summarizing much of his talk in an article in October 1856, Brownson referred to the conception prevalent in the larger culture that Catholic immigrants possessed "habits, manners, sentiments, affections, and traditions different from those of the great body of the American people." Although speaking in the face of nativist attacks, he lamented the Catholic isolation and growing lack of confidence in American institutions. The convert and political reformer argued that the American people had never really rejected Catholicism, never cast off the authority of the church, but that nativists feared the Catholic church's potential for political strength. The country needed a demonstration of Catholic allegiance to the "great current of American nationality." The church, he wrote,

> has no fear of strong men, resolute men, independent, self-reliant men, born to command, or to make their way in the world against every obstacle. The active, energetic, self-reliant American character she regards with no unfriendly eye, for she knows that, once purified, elevated, and directed by grace, it is a character from which she has everything to hope. Grace does not destroy nature, nor change the national type of character. It purifies and elevates nature, and brings out whatever is good, noble, and strong in the national type. No national character stands more in need of Catholicity than the American, and never since her going forth from that "upper room" in Jerusalem, has the church found a national character so well fitted to give to true civilization its highest and noblest expression.[2]

"O, for the love of God and of man," Brownson concluded with an appeal to youth, "do not discourage them, allow them to be mute and inactive, or suffer them, in the name of Catholicity, to separate themselves in their affections from the country and her glorious mission." When Brownson finished, the archbishop of New York, never one to pass up a challenge, denied any particular advantages offered to Catholics by the laws of the country and told the students to prepare for a future of persecution. Commencement was ended, but the battle over Americanization, its meaning and the structures that could best support it, had only begun.[3]

The vision that Brownson proposed in August and October 1856 would come to be expanded and clarified into an alternate vision of the Christian life during the next forty years. Brownson himself shared these particular ideas with his fellow convert of the 1840s, Isaac Thomas Hecker (1819–88). Hecker at times associated with a group of clerics in New York City who promoted a rapprochement between Catholicism and American society. Founding the Missionary Society of Saint Paul (Paulists) in 1858, Hecker would also influence John Joseph Keane (1839–1918), bishop of Richmond and first rector of the Catholic University of America, as well as numerous first- and second-generation Paulists, the most prominent being Walter Elliott (1842–1928). The latter's *Life of Father Hecker*, published in 1891 and translated into French in 1897, would furnish the occasion for the publication in 1899 of Leo XIII's encyclical *Testem Benevolentiae*, condemning "certain opinions which are introduced concerning the manner of leading a Christian life." The development and struggle surrounding these people, ideas, and events, would come to be known as the "crisis of Americanism."[4]

Emerging from the context of the vision of Christian life dominant in the immigrant church, Americanism is a significant episode in the history of Catholic spirituality. Concentrating on the works of Brownson, Hecker, Keane, and Elliott, the following pages will examine three different elements in their Americanist religious vision: their understanding of conversion and the "mission of America"; their approach to asceticism and prayer; and their image of Christ, the person, and the church.

CHAPTER
8
Conversion and the Mission of America

$\mathcal{T}$he relationship that Isaac Hecker and Orestes Brownson suggested between Catholicism, conversion, and the "mission of America" developed from the same context of poverty and free-market capitalism that had given birth to the vision of John Hughes. From 1834, when Brownson's support of the Workingman's Movement as a tool of economic reform first caught his attention, Hecker became committed to the tenets of radical Jacksonianism. He joined a small reform party in New York, the Locofocos, which combined an evangelical belief in the divine destiny and special mission of America with a support of individual rights to life, liberty, and property through constitutionalism. After the Depression of 1837, Hecker continued his electoral reform efforts but also turned to more radical efforts of social change for an answer to economic ills.[1]

Hecker met Orestes Brownson in 1841 when the latter was lecturing on the close link between religion and politics. On the advice of the New England philosopher, Hecker traveled to the utopian community of Brook Farm in April 1843. Although greatly influenced by the intuitive and interior religion of George Ripley, Amos Bronson Alcott, and Ralph Waldo Emerson, the "earnest seeker" quickly recognized that the philosophy of Transcendentalism could not satisfy him. "As there is an appetite in the human heart," he wrote years later, "which not all the treasures, honors, joys of nature can satisfy, so there is a void in the mind which all the truth within reach of the unaided natural faculties leaves unfilled."[2] Eventually, Hecker came

91

to believe in the church as the one institution that could answer his quest for social reform, the longings of his heart for communion, and his intellect for certainty. He wrote to Brownson in October 1843 of the importance of the "Church reform," and summarized in his diary of the same month this unique combination of Jacksonian politics, social reform, interior and personal religion, the search for community, and understanding of the church:

> The Church is the centre, the soul of all reform, all progress. The formula of the personal reformer is the denial of self; purity and chastity of life; holiness and oneness with God; love. The second, universal brotherhood; equality in society, in rewards of labor, etc. The third, equality before the state, representative of the whole reciprocity of intercourse. The centre, union of the fragmentary parts of the Church. Catholicity, universal inspiration, universal development, harmonic progress, etc.[3]

After considering and rejecting both Methodism and Lutheranism, Hecker was conditionally baptized in the Roman Catholic church in August 1844. The complex of beliefs that he had formed during the 1830s and 1840s would characterize his thinking for the rest of his life. He took many of these beliefs from his friend Orestes Brownson; thus, a brief review of the latter's positions is necessary before proceeding.

In April 1844, just three months after John Hughes's essay on the "Christian Basis for the Science of Political Economy," and four months before Hecker's conversion to Catholicism, Orestes Brownson published an article outlining his views on the relationship between the church and society. Like Hughes, the New England social reformer severely criticized the class divisions and pauperization encouraged by free-market capitalism. In "No Church, No Reform," an essay that strongly influenced Hecker, Brownson reviewed the various steps through which he had moved to reach his present solution to the economic problem. At one time, he noted, he had acknowledged that perhaps the principle of selfishness, itself the basis of the system, could provide the solution through the harmonization of interests. But this simply would not work: "A community organized on selfish principles, can be nothing but a community of inherently repellant and antagonistic forces, and its only bond of union must needs be the principle of absolute and universal dominion."[4]

What was needed was some doctrine of communion. Brownson next reflected on the principles of Charles Fourier, the French utopian socialist, and argued that men and women should be formed into economic and social cooperatives in which the capital was held in common and profits were shared by all. However, no association could be formed unless people could be governed by disinterested motives;

no reform could occur without the presence and activity of benevolence and sacrifice. A nonselfish order of sentiments was needed. In his search, Brownson turned to William Ellery Channing (1780–1842), the Christian universalist who emphasized the dignity of human nature and its likeness to God. Channing showed Brownson that the gospel embodied that nonselfish order of sentiments for which he longed: excellence of character in love, charity, and fraternity.

When Brownson began to read the gospel, he realized that what people needed was not to be told to do their duty but to "be made to do it; not to know that they *ought* to love, but to be actually induced to love." The only power that could call forth this disinterested love, the basis of social reform, was the presence of Christ himself. He took the Christian into his body, and through the indwelling Spirit constituted him or her a son or daughter of God. Analyzing his own experience, Brownson thus concluded: Man cannot carry himself above himself. He is active, and "active from within; but only in conjunction with another activity, not himself but meeting him *ab extra* [from outside]." This activity *ab extra* that transformed a person from within was the activity of Christ, available to the person through the ministrations of the church. So through communion with the church, the individual could be reformed, and through the individual, society. Brownson was received into the Roman Catholic church in October 1844.[5]

The position that later came to be identified as "Americanist" stemmed in large measure from the conversion experiences of Brownson and Hecker. Although the two men did not always concur, four significant ideas united them. First, both men in the 1830s and 1840s came to subordinate social reform to personal reform. They believed that all institutions, whether church or state, existed to protect and foster the life of the individual. Second, this individual possessed both natural rights and an inclination to associate with others for social, economic, and religious purposes. Third, the church, "the highest and paramount association," was founded by Christ and embodied his presence. It was commissioned by him to impart an interior, personal, and transforming power to the individual, a power that would at the same time fulfill the instinct for truth and justice, overcome selfishness, and instill disinterested love. Last, properly directed by the church, people could change society either through the power of their personal conversion (Hecker) or through groupings for industrial and social reform (Brownson).

Given these common commitments, it is clear that although Brownson and Hecker addressed the same concerns that preoccupied Hughes, Spalding, and Neumann, the converts diverged sharply from the prelates in their understanding and approach to Christian conversion and Catholic life. The two converts, albeit with different emphases, drew the closest possible links between nature and grace, between personal longings for life and truth and the fulfillment of these in revealed religion and the life of communion. In contrast, the prelates recognized a natural order of unifying sentiments but were more concerned with the disastrous effects of selfishness and power on the community; they drew a sharper distinction between nature and grace. Brownson and Hecker, proceeding from experience with democratic politics, viewed corporate reality as primarily an association of free and intelligent people, a communion of those pursuing conversion. The bishops, whose apologetic was shaped more by the restorationist reaction to the French Revolution, viewed corporate reality in its juridical and institutional aspects. Brownson and Hecker, middle class in background and status, saw the church as operating from within society for the purpose of social leadership; the bishops, pastoral leaders of persecuted immigrants, saw the church as protecting and guiding its members in a hostile society.

As a result of these differences, the avenues of thought that the two groups would pursue would be decidedly distinct. The converts emphasized a single identity or the fulfillment of American values in and through the church; the bishops, presupposing a separate identity, promoted areas of compatibility and adjustment between church and society. It is ironic that although both sides agreed that Roman Catholicism, with its teaching on justification, the institutional church, and the communion of saints, was the church "outside of which no salvation could be found," their personal experiences, responsibilities, and philosophies would set them on a collision course over the next forty years. It was in the twenty years between 1855 and 1875 that Hecker fully articulated this new vision, and the Americanist understanding of conversion and the "mission of America" came to be formulated.

After his entrance into the Catholic church and subsequent ordination to the priesthood as a member of the Redemptorist Order, Isaac Hecker's vision of the relationship between the church and society underwent two distinct phases: from 1855 to the First Vatican Council in 1870, and from 1870 until his death in 1888. During both periods he pursued his lifelong vocation, first on the national and then on the international level of society. Reflecting on the course of his own religious life, he explained his vocation in these terms:

> It seemed to me in looking back on my career before becoming a Catholic, that Divine Providence had led me as it were by the hand, through the different ways of error, and made me personally acquainted with the different classes of people (and their wants) of which the people of the United States are composed, in order that having made known to me the

truth, He might better employ me to point out to them the way to His Church. That therefore, my vocation was to labor for the conversion of my non-Catholic fellow countrymen.

In 1858, having left the Redemptorists, Hecker founded the Missionary Society of Saint Paul, later known as the Paulists, to promote this vocational vision. For Hecker, his conversion to Catholicism and his mission to America were inseparable.[6]

In 1855, while still giving parish missions, following the pattern set for the Redemptorists, Hecker published *Questions of the Soul*. This apologetic work departed dramatically from the "purgative way" model promoted in the missions. Two years later he wrote *Aspirations of Nature* and a long article for the Italian journal *Civiltà Cattolica*.[7] Written in the wake of the nativist Know-Nothing campaigns and the Louisville riots so graphically described by Martin John Spalding, these three works clarified still further the major issues that divided Hecker from Hughes and Spalding. Instead of interpreting the nativist campaign as a sign of American intolerance, Hecker viewed it as a providential development showing the harmony between Catholicism and American political institutions and principles. He noted that the immigrant Catholics in the United States, having achieved citizenship, for the most part had entered the Democratic party. It followed that the opposite party, the Know-Nothings, would become anti-Catholic. They were, in turn, divided into two factions: those who opposed Catholicism for political reasons; and those who feared that if the church was given the full religious liberty that the republic granted by law, then the church would triumph in society. The latter faction of the party, composed of the most ardent and fanatical Protestants, wanted to restrict freedom of religion, reinterpret the Constitution, and interfere in the administration of church property.

The Know-Nothing campaign, according to Hecker, backfired. The Democratic leaders, in order to defeat their opponents, had also to defend the church, read its journals, and learn from its adherents. "A strange thing," wrote Hecker, "to see the great portion of the people of the United States interested in studying the Catholic truth and defending the rights and the religion of the Catholics, their fellow citizens." While the Protestant ministers had been shown to support anti-American principles, the Catholic priests and bishops had proven their commitment to the country's institutions. In the course of the struggle, Hecker concluded, Americans also perceived that the Catholic religion promoted the perfection of their civil institutions and grounded them more fully in the gospel. In Catholicism, the learned and the ignorant believed the same articles of faith; at the foot of the altar all social distinction was obliterated; Catholic priests did not know hereditary rights, and the most humble of faithful men could become pope. In its symbols, sacraments, and sanctuary, the Catholic church offered to the world the most perfect equality.[8]

Hecker grounded his interpretation on two fundamental beliefs. First, the basic principle of American constitutionalism was that "man was capable of governing himself." Puritanism and New England Calvinism, Hecker argued, taught the absolute depravity of the person and the loss of reason and free will in the Fall. It could not then be reconciled with a government based on the exercise of personal freedom. Only Catholicism, with its appreciation of the value of reason and free will and its belief that with the help of grace people could observe the natural law, could support American institutions. Hecker's apologetic, founded on the combination of American natural rights and the Catholic teaching on justification, would not have occurred to John Hughes, Martin Spalding, or John Neumann.[9]

Second, Hecker's interpretation of the Know-Nothing campaign indicated his belief in the providential course of history. Unlike Hughes and Spalding, whose apologetic looked backward to a golden era of American society, Hecker argued that the country had yet to achieve its destiny. "Nations unaided by the powerful influences of Religion cannot realize their destinies. Our own country," he wrote,

> is becoming conscious of this truth. The question now pressing itself upon the American people is, to determine their Religion, as our fathers did the character of their political institutions. These, under the guidance of an over ruling Providence, were based on Catholic principles, and Catholic views of human nature.[10]

Over and over again Hecker returned to this understanding of American history. He believed, from his own experience at Brook Farm and on the missions, that the country offered the greatest possibilities for conversion. He read historical events to discern God's grace operative in social and political life, and he never ceased to look forward to the millennial establishment of the Kingdom of God. He presented the most programmatic statement of this view in his sermon at the Second Plenary Council of Baltimore in 1866. Everything, he preached, was moving to the triumph of the church: the Protestant desire for unity, the development of modern science, and the progress of the physical sciences in developing the steam engine, the telegraph, and the railroad. Could the church capture the hour? Could it read the signs? Here, in the United States, Hecker concluded, "Christianity is promised a reception from an intelligent and free people, that will give forth a development of unprecedented glory. For religion is never so beautiful as when in connection with knowledge and freedom."[11] By "Christianity" Hecker meant "Catholicism."

After 1870, Isaac Hecker's millennial combination of Catholicism, American constitutionalism, and providential interpretation of history received its final modification. Encouraged by Vatican I's definition of papal infallibility to rethink the socioreligious vision of his earlier life, and forced by illness to leave his pastoral duties in New York, he traveled extensively in Europe, Egypt, and the Holy Land from June 1873 to October 1875. During that time, Hecker developed a more theological understanding of the relationship among the person, nature, reason, history, Scripture, and the church. All these dimensions of human life and culture, he believed, were bound together by the creative action of the Holy Spirit. During the past few centuries, the Holy Spirit had providentially guided the church in its struggle against the forces of private judgment and self-interest to concentrate on the definition of its external organization, its institutional structures, and the objective truth of its teachings. The definition of papal infallibility, so Hecker argued, had concluded that era of the church's history.[12]

Always a visionary, what Hecker saw opening up before him during his trip to Europe and Egypt was the broad vista of a universal church, secure in its doctrine and authority, now "led by the Holy Ghost in the peaceful work of the conversion of the world & salvation of souls, and the advancement of Christian civilization." What was needed to accomplish this, he believed, was not the exercise of ecclesiastical authority or the reliance on unity with the civil power, but the active, diligent, and inspired work of individual Christians. The divine agent of the transformation would be the Holy Spirit working through the church for personal conversion. Hecker summarized his reflections in three basic principles:

1. The life of the Church is the indwelling of the Holy Spirit, who is the Guide and Initiator of all her actions.
2. The Holy Spirit as a saving grace acts in and through the Church only, and is the sole immediate and direct divine action in the world.
3. It is only through the divine action of the Holy Spirit in the Church that the soul is regenerated, saved and sanctified; society ameliorated, and progress possible, attainable, and attained.

Seen from the perspective of political developments, the providential human agents of this universal unity, according to Hecker, were the "Greek-Saxon" races. Unlike the Latins and Celts, who guided the church through tradition, authority, obedience, and loyalty, the harbingers of the new civilization represented intelligence, freedom, activity, and individuality. The United States, in Hecker's mind, was the "experimental laboratory or workshop of Divine Providence" for the accomplishment of this great "kingdom of God" on earth. Thus by 1874, Isaac Hecker's belief in the unity of personal, social, religious, and political reform, which he had reached during his conversion of the 1840s, and his millennial mixture of Catholicism and American civilization in the 1850s and 1860s, received its universal application. Providentially guided by the Holy Spirit, the union between Catholicism and the political and social institutions of the United States foreshadowed the progress of the church and the world. This was the "mission of America."[13]

During the last ten years of his life, Hecker struggled to communicate his vision both to a wider audience and to the members of his own religious community. He was, to a large extent, unsuccessful, but the vision itself became influential among the churchmen most deeply associated with the Americanist movement of the 1880s and 1890s: John Joseph Keane; John Ireland, the archbishop of Saint Paul (1838–1918); and Denis O'Connell, rector of the North American College (1849–1927).[14] The differences between these people need not be elaborated here. They seemed to have shared with Hecker two basic convictions that differentiated them from their opponents, the inheritors of the vision of Hughes, Spalding, and Neumann.

First, Keane, Ireland, and O'Connell shared with Hecker an apologetic that discerned the presence and action of God in the contemporary world. On the level of the person, they argued for a convergence of the God-given yearnings of humanity, the natural rights of American constitutionalism, and the doctrines of Catholicism. Taking the historical perspective, they believed that the providential movements of the time revealed a mission to catholicize the United States and to americanize the future church. To accomplish this task, some of them purposely emphasized the points of agreement between Catholics and Protestants.

Second, in a way similar to the approach of Brownson and Hecker in the 1840s, the Americanists continued to stress the unity of social and religious reform. This view clearly emerged in the 1887 *Memorial* defending Catholic participation in the Knights of Labor union organization. The strongest statement of the position came in an 1891 article by John Keane, Hecker's protégé and, at that time, rector of the Catholic University of America. Keane argued that the constant aim of the Christian church had been to bring about a "synthesis and harmony of the religious, the ethical, the economic, and the political elements in the life of mankind." He rested his "social system" on seven major principles. These may be taken as summarizing the general Americanist position, showing its divergence from the corporate and apologetic vision of the immigrant church:

First, the universal Fatherhood of God. This is the source of human dignity and human rights. The rights of man are "inalienable"; that is, beyond the power of man to take away, because they are not bestowed by man, but by the Creator.

Second, the universal brotherhood of men. This follows necessarily from the first. It is placed in clearer light and on a higher level by the mystery of the Incarnation in which Christ makes all men not only his brethren, but his members, and members one of another. This is the source of human duties to one another. . . .

Third, the universal interdependence and mutual obligations of the members of human society. All are agents of the providence of God. Whoever have more than others of power or talents or wealth are bound to be to others "stewards of the manifold bounty of God."

Fourth, the special right of the poor and the working classes not only to justice and charity, but also to respect, because of their special relation to Jesus Christ, who voluntarily chose to be poor and to be the carpenter of Nazareth.

Fifth, the divine authority of enlightened conscience, as arbiter of right and wrong in human dealings. It is the voice of the natural law which flows from the eternal law of divine wisdom and love; and the justice of the eternal Lawgiver is its sanction.

Sixth, the divine authority of civil government and law, for the protection of human rights, the repression of injustice, and the furtherance of human welfare. It was no longer the individual that existed for the State, but the State existed for the individual, the only reason of government being the welfare of the governed. But individuals are bound to co-operate for the common weal, and individual convenience and gain must often yield to the public good.

Seventh, that as all things come from God, so all things must make for God or be referred to God, as the Beginning and the End of all perfection and of all happiness.

Keane called this system the "individualism of Jesus Christ." Building on the insights of Hecker, Keane spent much of his early life trying to elaborate an understanding of piety, asceticism, and prayer that would support this view. It is that area of the Americanist vision that will now be examined.[15]

CHAPTER
9
Piety, Asceticism, and Prayer

*A*ll outward reforms presuppose an inward regeneration of the heart as their cause and foundation," Isaac Hecker wrote to Brownson in March 1844. From the year of their conversion until the 1870s, both men, but especially Hecker, labored extensively to foster this "conversion of the heart" that would support their socioreligious program. In his 1855 apologetic work, *Questions of the Soul*, Hecker presented the outlines of his view. Consciously trying to appeal to Protestants, he reflected on the connection between the desires of the heart, Christ as the model for humanity, the necessity of communion with the Roman Catholic church, and the existence within that church of all the means necessary for human fulfillment in divine life: the sacraments, especially confession, Communion, and extreme unction; the profession of obedience, poverty, and chastity; and practices of mortification. A year later, Brownson's article, "The Mission of America," called for the development of a "robust faith" and "robust piety," one that would encourage a free, self-reliant, and intelligent spiritual life consonant with the American character.[1]

During the 1860s and 1870s Brownson published several critiques of "old world" piety, and Hecker fostered an "American piety" through sermons, the foundation of the *Catholic World*, parochial activities, and the publication of numerous works on mysticism. Both Brownson and Hecker bequeathed their union of social reform and spiritual regeneration to John Joseph Keane. The program of spiritual reform fostered by Brownson, Hecker, and Keane departed from the asceticism of Hughes, Spalding, and Neumann in two significant areas: the relationship between piety and modern society, and the emphasis placed on personal transformation.

In the October 1860 issue of his *Quarterly Review*, Orestes Brownson outlined what he saw as the connections between the history of modern civilization and the piety of Catholics. He noted that Protestants often accused the church of "overlaying faith with a mass of errors, and smothering true piety with a multitude of superstitious practices and observances." While defending pilgrimages to Our Lady and the use of medals, the apologist acknowledged that those Protestant charges were true: Catholics often performed external practices as "substitutes for genuine virtue." He cited as an example the proliferation of devotional guides in which the "indirect and external devotions predominate over the internal and direct." Brownson believed that this type of devotionalism was allied to a system of excessive reliance on external practices that had developed in the church since the sixteenth century. Reacting to heresy and perceiving the strength of non-Catholic tendencies in the world, the church had come to depend on the external support of the civil power to maintain its influence over the people. Like the state, the church had adopted a bureaucratic system of government emphasizing order, routine, and obedience to authority. This left the internal life of faith weak, kept the influence of the faithful laity from becoming strong, and promoted a mechanical rather than an intellectual piety. Under this regime, according to Brownson,

> We become timid, weak, and imbecile; we lack energy and courage, we lack self-reliance and feel that we cannot move without the assistance of a dry-nurse. We have the characteristics of a conquered people, a people who once held and exercised the empire of the world, but are now reduced to slavery, and what is worst of all, are becoming resigned to their condition.

Such a system presupposed an unnecessary dependence of the temporal on the spiritual, a hierarchical political settlement, and the confinement of church government, education, and intelligence to the clerical elite.[2]

The modern world, Brownson argued, had outgrown these conditions. Essentially laic, it proclaimed the autonomy of the temporal, the rights of all as citizens, and popular education. In the religious sphere, the controversy with Protestants no longer took place on the theological level but in the social arena. As a result, "in our own country, if we mean religion shall prosper, the Church take root and flourish in the land, we must leave laymen free to do all that laymen can do, and we must exact of the clergy, few in numbers, too few for

our wants, only those labors which none but clergymen can perform."
To promote this task among the laity, Brownson proposed a revision
of the ecclesiastical relationships between the temporal and the spiritual. He saw no reason why the laity could not own church property,
demand an accounting from the clergy, or control the disposition of
funds. Why, he suggested, should the church control public legislation
on the "just rights of the wife, the *status* of the children, the ownership,
the transmission, inheritance, or the division of estates?" Why were
Catholic colleges governed exclusively by the clergy? In their new
social and ecclesiastical role, the laity could no longer be governed
by a monastic principle of obedience. What they needed was a piety
that would recognize the compatibility between Catholicism and "just
self-respect," "true manly dignity," and freedom.[3]

Brownson's placement of devotionalism within a particular historical epoch and his vision of a piety that would free the laity for
action in the world established the lines along which both Hecker
and Keane would develop their more practical efforts at reform.
Hecker worked extensively as a parish priest at Saint Paul's Church,
New York, and as a mission preacher.[4] Preaching to the Irish immigrants, both the prosperous and the poor, the founder of the Paulists
attempted to shape his listeners to the contours of the new piety. In
1863 he preached on the "Saint of Our Day," in which he noted that
each age produced its own unique form of sanctity. The martyrs of
the primitive church, the desert fathers emphasizing solitude, the
cloistered saints "dwelling in the enclosed gardens of the spiritual
life," and Ignatius of Loyola forsaking the customs and garb of monasticism to establish a new type of Christian perfection—each of
these personal "types" had responded to the wants and promises of
their own age. "None but those of narrow capacities, and a restricted
education," Hecker wrote,

> or under the contracting influences of sectional prejudices, fail to see
> this. It is likewise a monstrous tyranny of opinion to arraign the past,
> judge and condemn it, by the standards of the present; and we resist it
> with no less energy than the spirit that would mould the lips of the present
> into the antiquated forms of bygone ages.

The preacher then went on to describe the chief characteristics of
the present age. It claimed to be a period of enlightened intelligence
and true liberty of will, marked by scientific discoveries and the advancement of civilization. In such an age, Hecker believed, the ideal
of Christian perfection would model the unity between religion, intelligence, and liberty. Saint Joseph exemplified this fullness of
sanctity. Although not a martyr, Joseph exercised the martyr's fidelity
to convictions of conscience and purity of faith; not a solitary, he was

in the world and made the cares and duties of the world subservient to divine purposes. Drawing together the characteristics of the age, the model of sanctity, and the picture of his congregation, Hecker then concluded with one of his most famous statements: "Our age lives in its busy marts, in counting-rooms, in workshops, in homes, and in the varied relations that form human society, and it is into these that sanctity is to be introduced. Saint Joseph stands forth as an excellent and unsurpassed model of this type of perfection."[5]

The Paulist preacher gave a social perspective to his historical understanding of piety when he spoke to the Irish parishioners on Saint Patrick's Day, 1869. He began by appealing to his listeners' nationalism by calling to mind how Ireland, as a nation, had preserved the faith during three centuries of persecution. The Irish had withstood adversity and had died for their religion. The question was: "Will they know as well how to meet prosperity?" Hecker noted that many believed the free institutions and prosperity of the United States would accomplish in two or three generations what persecution had not been able to do. For the Irish immigrant, gone were the monuments, battle fields, cathedrals, worn Irish crosses, and ruined abbeys that had been constant reminders of the faith for their ancestors. Gone also were the social influences of "family, relations, and neighborhood." "It is evident," Hecker argued,

> that the Catholic religion cannot rely on the aids which exist in Ireland for its support in the U.S. Other foundations must be secured, not in contradiction, but in harmony with those already existing. While the religious traditions of the old country and all the old social influences that are possible must be retained, at the same time it is necessary that a stronger intellectual hold must be gained, a better and more complete knowledge of our religion.

In this new context, Hecker concluded, publication societies, the study of religion, reading, a Catholic education, home catechism, and a library for children became significant features of the Christian life; "ordinary piety" simply would not "keep the fervour of faith in your souls under our circumstances."[6]

The Paulist embodied much of his thinking, with its criticism of ecclesiastical externalism and social passivity, in an essay on Saint Catherine of Genoa (1447–1510).[7] The great Italian saint, in Hecker's mind, demonstrated the major characteristics of a piety suited to the contemporary world: reliance on the immediate inspiration of the Holy Spirit; a balance between individual inspiration and obedience to the church; social concern; and the active role of women in society and the church. Upon his return to New York after two years in Europe, Hecker continued to present this plan to his Paulist community.

His fond hope was that these men might be guided by the Spirit and commit themselves to the conversion of America.[8]

Hecker's consistent desire to relate sanctity to the needs of society through mission preaching, sermons, and publications, received a much more practical focus at the hands of his friend, John Joseph Keane. Born in Ireland, Keane had immigrated with his family to Newfoundland, Canada, in 1846, and then to Baltimore, Maryland, in 1848. He was ordained in 1866 and assigned to work at Saint Patrick's Church, Washington, D.C. While there, Keane met Hecker, who had a lasting impact on his personal and intellectual formation. Keane served as bishop of Richmond from 1878 to 1888, when he was commissioned to establish the Catholic University of America as its first rector. He finished his years as archbishop of Dubuque, Iowa, and, having resigned his see in 1911, died in June 1918.[9] An examination of some of his activity as bishop shows the pastoral nature of his Americanist vision in two distinct areas: the promotion of associations to foster social reconstruction through the activity and piety of the laity; and the support of the Confraternity of the Holy Ghost.

John Keane focused much of his pastoral ministry on the promotion of associations to build up society through the action of the laity. He lived in a political environment that emphasized grouping together for a common purpose. In 1866 the National Labor Union was formed, and in 1869, the Noble Order of the Knights of Labor. Throughout the period numerous fraternal organizations emerged in response to social and economic instability. Keane reacted to the proliferation of secret societies and to a view of government that saw relationships between people as a balance of interests or a machinery of counterbalances. He believed that such an economic and political view had contributed to the Civil War. As an antidote to this view, he wanted to promote a social reconstruction that would be organic, enabling people to relate in an ordered, free, and harmonious whole. Catholic unions, Keane argued, could best fulfill those requirements. Modeled on religious orders, they combined the ideal of Catholicity and universality by blending many different communities into one order regulated by a central authority. The Saint Vincent de Paul Society, temperance unions, and various mutual aid associations exemplified these principles.

The most significant example of the unity Keane promoted between religious and social reconstruction occurred in the case of the Knights of Labor, a union composed chiefly of Catholics that was in danger of being condemned in Rome. In 1887 Cardinal Gibbons submitted a *Memorial* on that organization to the Holy See. The document, written by Keane and Ireland, dealt almost exclusively with the church in its relationship to the working class, but it also argued that in aligning itself with the people, the church needed a "new spirit" and "a new law of life," one that would hold the "affections" and "heart" as much as the understanding of the multitudes. Keane probably wrote that section of the *Memorial*, and the language that he used about "heart," "affections," and the "spirit" was telling. For Keane, "heart" carried significant connotations of interiority and spiritual yearning; it was explicitly related to religious sentiments, often as these were expressed in people's devotional associations. If the spirit of truth enlightened the mind, the spirit of love touched the "heart." Just as people joined societies in the church to ensure "time and heart" for God, so they could join together in society to promote a unified social and religious reconstruction. The church could bind individual sentiment, society, and religion together by creating "a new spirit and a new way of life." When the associationist view of society promoted by Brownson and Hecker is recalled, then Keane's support of the Knights of Labor as an instrument of reform can be seen in all its depth.[10]

In addition to the political and social benefits of Catholic societies, Keane also argued for their ecclesiological purpose. In his inaugural sermon as bishop of Richmond, he noted that Protestants often imagined the church to be a "set of contrivances to take the place of Our Lord" or a "mighty power dragging men into its clutches." He believed, instead, that the church existed to dispense the treasures of faith and grace to the world; its best proof was the example of Christian holiness. The formation of societies served this end by encouraging the intellectual improvement of the laity and their growth in charity and morality. Keane took an active role in the Catholic Young Men's National Union, a group whose purpose was to further practical Catholic unity. When the bishop spoke before the group in 1879, its umbrella organization covered sixty-three different literary, social, educational, beneficial, and pious societies. Keane saw it as an example of Catholic associationism, a coming together that expanded the mind and heart in possession of truth and love. "There must be an element of unity," he said, "consisting of truth that all can believe, principles which all can admit, a rule which all can acknowledge their obligation to follow, an authority to which all can acknowledge their accountability in their dealings with their fellowmen."[11]

John Keane fostered Hecker's vision of the unity between spiritual renewal and social reform through the promotion of associations; he also made the primary agent of Hecker's renewal, the Holy Ghost, the focus of his special attention. In October 1879, the bishop issued a pastoral letter requesting that the Confraternity of the Servants of the Holy Ghost be established in every mission of the diocese. He printed enrollment cards and in 1880 wrote a sodality manual for the use of the laity. The bishop asked his priests to note the growth or decline of the confraternity in their annual report. In 1883 he again emphasized its importance in the formation of the laity and in 1886 passed synodal legislation encouraging its development. The pastoral reports indicate that between 1880 and 1885 eighteen missions began the devotion, with the Richmond cathedral boasting 643 participants in 1881.

In his publications Keane argued that devotion to the Holy Ghost was the perfect antidote to the materialistic bias of the age. Emphasizing individual interiority and the development of a free and intelligent piety, it was also not liable to the Protestant charges of a "formal and mechanistic Catholic devotionalism." To enroll in the confraternity one had only to have a "sincere desire and resolution to love and honor the Holy Ghost, to think of Him more frequently and fervently, and to correspond to His grace more faithfully." Although no formal prayers were attached to membership, the bishop advised the people to recite every day some prayers in honor of the Holy Ghost: "Glory Be," prayer for the seven gifts, *Veni Creator*, or some portion of the "Little Office of the Holy Ghost."

The bishop organized the local sodalities of the Holy Ghost in such a way as to reconcile the demands of American republicanism with the hierarchical constitution of the church. A council of one cleric and at least six lay members governed the group. The lay prefect and two assistants, after being elected in private ballots by the members at large, appointed the other lay members of the council. If the sodality was composed of both male and female members, all officials except consultors were male. Outside of the duties of the cleric rector, who presided at the meetings and preached, the lay members were encouraged to take the initiative. The prefect led the members in recitation of the office, and individual consultors promoted regular attendance and reported to the council. Last, the members of the sodality were encouraged to take part in every Catholic work of charity established in the locality. Keane described at length the charitable relations that should exist among members of the sodality, such as visiting the sick, attending funerals, and finding employment for those who needed it. His promotion of the Confraternity of the Servants of the Holy Ghost represented the most far-reaching attempt of any Americanist to shape the people's piety to the needs of the age.[12]

The unity that Hecker and Keane promoted between piety and an active role in social reform was ultimately founded on their notions of personal asceticism and prayer. Again, the roots of this attitude clearly go back to the 1840s. John Hughes had been willing to base his Catholic political economy on self-interest and therefore argued for an external authority capable of assigning duties as well as rights to the individuals. Orestes Brownson, in contrast, recognized the self-ish sentiments but became convinced also of a nonselfish order within the person: benevolence, disinterestedness, and sacrifice. In the context of his anthropology, what was needed was a power that could call forth this disinterestedness by promoting both self-mastery and interior transformation. Christianity existed to accomplish just that end; it was a "system of means divinely devised and instituted for the recovery of man from sin, his restoration to justice and sanctity, and his growth in knowledge and love." Brownson presented the heart of his understanding in an essay of 1847. "All our faculties," he wrote,

> even our sensibilities, taste, fancy, imagination, wit, and humor, were given us for a purpose, and are proper to be exercised, used,—only not to be exercised and used for their own sake, for low, worthless, or sinful ends, but for God, for the great and solemn purpose of life itself. Christianity commands total self-denial; but the self-denial it commands is moral, not physical,—the moral annihilation, not the physical annihilation, of ourselves. We retain as Christians all our faculties, essential qualities and properties as men, none of which are bad in themselves,—for nothing bad ever came from the hand of the Creator; but we retain and exercise them no longer for their own sakes or for the sake of ourselves, or the pleasure which results from their exercise. We retain and exercise them only for God.[13]

This philosophical and theological base, shared by Hecker and Keane, would lead to an asceticism that combined both transformation and discipline. This was the center of the Americanist alternative to the "triumph of the purgative way."

In August 1861, Isaac Hecker preached to his congregation at Saint Paul's on the Transfiguration of Christ. He took the occasion to explain the Christian meaning of *renunciation*. Hecker began with a description of how the Lord had prepared the disciples for his death by granting them a foretaste of heaven. Jesus had taken them to a high mountain separated from the world, a place necessary for high favors and perseverance in the Christian life. The preacher then asked: What is the world the individual is asked to renounce? Surely not the world of nature, which our Lord himself had used to illustrate the gospel; nor the world of art and science that the apostle James commended; nor the ties of families and friends or the common pursuits of life that *wisdom* enjoined on us. "It is a false idea of the Christian religion," Hecker noted, "and one that is most injurious, to imagine that it requires us to stifle all natural affections, and to escape from society, in order to lead a Christian life." No, the world Christians were asked to forsake was not God's creation but the world "fabricated of error, of the abuse of created things, and engendered by inordinate desires." Hecker listed several specific examples of this "world" that people had created: a society built on the sacrifice of self-respect, bribery, seeking of pleasure, and a desire for distinctions and places of honor; a world in which science tried to undermine the religious convictions of the soul. Hecker closed, finally, by returning to what he considered the "real world" in which the Christian lived, the world God had reconciled through Christ: culture, art, science, and beauty.[14]

The transfiguration that Christians were called upon to make present in the world also applied to themselves. In Hecker's sermon on "Self-denial," he argued that the life of Christian perfection introduced people to "spiritual advantages and pleasures as they never conceived of." The point was that anything good in the human condition could be reconciled to God. Self-denial, like the renunciation of the world, meant "renouncing all misdirection of the powers of the soul," regulating the disorderly, repressing the excessive, forsaking what is evil, and holding the animal instincts in subjection to reason. Religion, in Hecker's view, did not exist to supersede nature but to recreate it. "Christianity," he preached,

> finds us men, and leaves us men; gentle, not cowardly; child-like, not childish; amiable, not effeminate; zealous, not fanatical; earnest, not narrow minded; pious, not weak; humble, not subject; full of faith, and yet rational; obedient, not slavish; mortified, not mutilated; for Christ died to save man, and not to transmute man into something else. Christianity demands for its fullest manifestation the most complete nature. The more we are men, the greater our capacity for Christianity.

Penance, Hecker concluded, emancipated the soul, rendered people invisible to their spiritual foes, furthered the practice of prayer, and filled the soul with spiritual consolation.[15]

In these two sermons, Hecker placed the central values of immigrant asceticism—mortification, penance, self-denial, and sacrifice—within the context of his overall project to create a new society. In contrast to the vision of the immigrant church, the Paulist's presentation significantly rooted the values of the spiritual life in the inner life of the person. Whereas the hostile "world" for Hughes and Spalding had focused their attention on corporate sanctity, Hecker's "world," fabricated by people, could be recreated by people who pursued the path of holiness. The leaders of the immigrant church, presupposing a more rebellious streak in human nature, described the corporate church as the primary agent of discipline and restraint. Hecker, in contrast, placed primary responsibility on the individual, his or her self-control, and thirst for virtue. Last, the immigrant church's emphasis on the "purgative way" had been balanced by the eschatological attraction of the communion of saints. In Hecker's vision, the draw of the spiritual life occurred both within a world where people could build culture, art and science, and within the experience of their own transfigured humanity.

It is important to recognize that Hecker did not deny traditional asceticism; he merely restructured it onto an anthropological base. The Paulist always presupposed the doctrinal, ascetical, and devotional structures that the immigrant church had fostered. For example, he converted to Roman Catholicism precisely because it answered the inner dynamic of his mind and heart. People yearned, he argued in *Questions of the Soul,* for an unerring, divine authority; an external guide; confession and sacramental forgiveness; the real presence in the Blessed Sacrament; a place to pursue religious perfection; disciplines to purify them of selfishness; and a life of worship that could offer everything in nature to God.[16] He applied this same joining of the inner movements of the person with the outer structures of the church when he came to discuss the issue of spiritual guidance. "The direct action of God upon the soul, which is interior," he wrote,

> is in harmony with his external providence. Sanctity consists in making them identical as motives for every thought, word, and deed of our lives. The external and the internal (and the same must be said of the natural and the supernatural) are one in God, and the consciousness of them both is to be made one divine whole in man. To do this requires an heroic life—sanctity.[17]

Hecker's system of the spiritual life attempted to reconcile within the person what the immigrant church had joined on the level of the institution. If conflict arose between the inner and the outer, as conflict did arise on occasion between Hecker and his own Paulist confrères, then it had to be resolved on the level of a person whose suffering, in imitation of Christ, reconciled both.

John Keane presented a similar view of "holiness of life" in his 1883 *Pastoral Letter.* The bishop carefully noted that holiness implied the fulfillment of duties, the crucifixion of the flesh, obedience to regulations. But he also argued that holiness was more than morality of life. It implied a spiritual superstructure of a pure conscience, loving heart, and prayerful soul. For Keane, not to realize and reflect on interior change would be "to run the great risk of making our spiritual life a mere motion of forms and externals, without internal meaning and life and soul, such as God reprobated of old." Everything existed, as it had for Hecker, to establish God's kingdom within the person. "This is what God made us for," Keane wrote. "This is what our Divine Saviour redeemed us for; this is what the Holy Ghost lives and works in our souls for. This is what the Church exists for, what her Sacraments are dispensed for."[18]

One final element in the Americanist understanding of piety begs consideration. From the earliest years of his conversion Isaac Hecker yearned above all for union with God. His spiritual life, which developed over many years, was a deeply personal one caught up in the wonder of God's indwelling in the individual. "What blindness," he noted, "and what gross stupidity for many who are always seeking God, always sighing for Him, frequently desiring Him, daily knocking and clamoring at the door for God by prayer, while they themselves are all the time, as the apostle says, temples of the living God, and God truly dwelling within them." Hecker's biographer, Walter Elliott, summarized the heart of the experience in these words:

> His doctrine of Christian perfection might be formulated as a profession of faith. I believe in God the *Father* Almighty; I believe in Jesus Christ the only Begotten *Son* of the Father; I believe in the Holy Ghost the *Life Giver*, the spirit of adoption by whom I am enabled to say to the Father, *My Father*, and to the Son, *My Brother*.[19]

A similar sense of divine communion also became the center of John Keane's understanding of the spiritual life. He stated the teaching most boldly in his *Pastoral Letter* of 1883: "To bring one's whole being and life more and more completely under this control of grace, more and more intimately into this union with God, is the chief object of our vocation as Christians."[20]

Given this goal of divine communion, Hecker naturally turned to the tradition of Catholic mysticism for his understanding of life and prayer. He wrote in his diary for August 23, 1844:

> Where shall we find God? Within.
> How shall we hear the voices of angels?
> Listen with the inner ear.
> When are we with God? When we are no
>   more with ourselves.
> When do we hear the music of heaven?
> When we are entirely silent.
> What is the effect of sin? Confusion.
> Where does God dwell? In silence.
> Who loves God? He who knows nothing and
>   loves nothing of himself.
> What is prayer? The breath of silence.[21]

Writing to Brownson two years later, Hecker noted the existence of different ways in the church by which God led a soul to perfection: the passive and the active, or the "Theology mystic and the Theology scholastic." Hecker did not understand the two ways as mutually exclusive, but simply acknowledged that different individuals found one or the other more dominant in their experience. "In the one grace is acquired by the means of the activity of the faculties of the Soul, in the other it is as it were infused immediately into the Soul. The one is governed by its intelligence and reflection, etc., the other by the simple instinct of grace." The young convert went on to describe the different stages of the "mystic way" by relying on the writings of John of the Cross (1542–1591) and Catherine of Genoa. He later clarified his own beliefs through a study of the seventeenth-century French mystic Louis Lallemant (1587–1635) and the works, among others, of Teresa of Avila, and the English spiritual writer, Augustine Baker (1575–1641).[22]

Hecker assimilated the more profound tradition of contemplative prayer into his personal vision in very simple ways. He above all aimed to acquire the dispositions necessary to discover the presence and guidance of the Holy Spirit in the soul. The methods were simple: interior recollection, purity of heart, meditation, prayer, silence, and fidelity to conscience. The development of this interiority lay at the heart of all activity. While receiving the sacraments, practicing prayer (liturgical, mental and vocal, particular devotions), and reading spiritual books, the person needed to "bear ever in mind, that the steady impelling force by which one does each of these outward things is *the inner and secret prompting of the Holy Ghost, and that perseverance in them is secured by no other aid except the same hidden inspiration.*"[23] John Keane reduced this method of Christian prayer and living to three basic principles:

> The first requirement is, that we should have, and should keep habitually before us, at least an elementary idea of the relation between God and our soul which is produced by the grace of Christ.
>
> The second requirement is, a firm resolution to shape one's life by this knowledge of our relation to God and our duty towards Him.
>
> The third requirement is, to desire and endeavor to draw nearer to God as life goes on.[24]

Both men labored extensively to make people aware of the indwelling Spirit who made them children of God and heirs of the kingdom: Keane through his pastoral letters, his support of the Confraternity of the Servants of the Holy Ghost, and his diocesan visitations; Hecker through his numerous publications of mystical works, mission preaching, and spiritual direction.

The focus on the mystical communion of the soul with God exemplified once again the gulf that divided Hecker and Keane from Hughes, Spalding, and Neumann. The latter had avoided the more contemplative and mystical elements in personal prayer. They chose instead to emphasize the presence of the Spirit in the corporate structures: the Spirit guaranteed the inerrancy of doctrine, the hierarchical constitution of the church, and the efficacy of the sacraments. Holiness belonged to the church. Devotionalism provided the institutional balance to these objective, rational, and ordered elements. In the communion of saints the more personal, relational, and subjective elements came to the fore. In this way, for the leaders of the immigrant church, the masculine and feminine dimensions of religious experience were integrated primarily on the level of the institution.

Hecker and Keane, in contrast, united the objective and subjective, the institutional and personal, the rational and affective, not so much on the level of the institution, but within the person. Thus Hecker talked about the individual, male or female, finding personal fullness in the interior reconciliation of both obedience and freedom, authority and individuality, the external and the internal elements of the church. He spoke about himself in both male and female terms and believed in the equality of men and women. Keane, in a similar fashion, advocated a personal religion that met the demands of both mind and heart. Here was another instance of the anthropological shift occurring in Americanism, a shift in spirituality that implied significant institutional changes.[25]

In conclusion, Hecker and Keane's understanding of piety, asceticism, and prayer formed one single piece with their general vision of conversion and the mission of America. The emphasis on disciplined interiority correlated well with their more optimistic anthropology and their attempt to reconcile the church with republican institutions. The doctrine of the Holy Ghost supported the concentration on individual responsibility and action in the social sphere. The reality of communion with God in the individual soul provided the spark that would ignite the social regeneration for which they hoped and worked. This was the practice of the virtuous life that supported John Keane's "individualism of Jesus Christ." While incorporating the values of the immigrant vision of the Christian life, the Americanist view located them in the person not the institution. Before turning to the "crisis of Americanism" in the 1890s when the two different views most sharply focused their disagreements, a central symbol of the Americanist vision needs to be examined, its image of Jesus Christ.

CHAPTER
10
The Mystery of the Incarnation

*J*esus Christ is the same yesterday, today, and forever." Commenting on these words from the Epistle to the Hebrews (13:8), John Keane described the presence of Jesus Christ in history. The Lord, he noted, when asked if the powers of the earth should be pressed into his service, entered Jerusalem riding on an ass. He appeared in the Passion as the "most abject of men." It was in this humble and human way that he was "the same forever."[1] With this short description, Keane captured the heart of the image of Christ that pervaded the writings of many of the Americanists. For them, Christ's unchanging identity was focused on his presence at historical events and among people, and, operating from within history, his desire to reconcile all things in himself. This image summarized much of their understanding of the relationship between the church, the person, and the mission of America. Its progressive and reconciling tone contrasted sharply with the image that Hughes, Spalding, and Neumann used to exemplify the steadfast nature of an embattled Catholicism.

It would be impossible to synthesize all of the Americanists' writings on Christ. Perhaps the most popular image was drawn by Walter Elliott, who published a *Life of Jesus Christ* in 1901. Born in Detroit, Elliott had entered the Paulists after a stint in the Union army and a career as a lawyer. He was ordained in 1872 and spent the greater part of his life at Saint Paul's Church in New York, from which he developed a distinguished reputation as a preacher of missions. He lived on close terms with Isaac Hecker, became his most ardent disciple, and published Hecker's biography in 1891. Elliot's *Life of Jesus Christ* sold over fifty thousand copies between 1901 and 1925. At the end of the *Life* he printed a short epilogue entitled "Jesus Christ is God." This short piece together with the *Life* may be taken as an accurate guide to the image of Christ also present in the writings of Hecker and Keane.[2]

Elliott began his reflections on Jesus Christ by referring to the act of creation. He acknowledged the existence in the person and in the human race of a "reaching after the possession of the divine," a "yearning," a "desire for elevation," and "eagerness of desire," an "overflowing heart." This was implanted by God as a "gift superadded to the high endowments of innate nobility." Elliott wrote: "Man's capacity of knowing craves a divine knowledge; of loving, to enjoy the ecstacy of union with the Deity; of action, to increase the honor and glory of the infinite God; of life, to live as long as God." Elliott saw this yearning witnessed to in the traditions of the East, the Greeks and Romans, and the Hebrew prophets. He noted: "Christianity is historical. It deals with the life which the human race has lived. It is not a theory to be considered in the abstract. It is a fact. It has been a fact. It belongs to that narrative of man's lives and deeds which we call history."[3] Throughout his writing Elliott presented Christ as the culmination of the providential workings of history. Christ's activity was centered not above and beyond time, "sitting at the right hand of the Father," but in and through it. "The dignity of man suggests the possibility of the Incarnation; the aspirations of man suggest its probability; the degradation of man cries out for it, and implores its immediate gift."[4]

In meditating on the Lord as the fulfillment of human longings, Elliott pictured Jesus first of all as a good man, a truthful man, an enlightened man, one who testified to his own divinity. Christ was the human race's "only perfect hero." Jesus was the fullness of love, knowledge, joy, freedom, and purity. He found the world in a state of lust, violence, tyranny, and idolatry, but conquered it, thereby infusing a new spiritual reality: the completion of the yearnings. "All who try *this* object of burning human love," the Paulist wrote, "exclaim together, in an ecstacy, that they have received a fullness of satisfaction beyond the scope of created power to bestow. The object is divine—it is the only end of man." In Elliott's perspective, if humanity was to find out who it truly was, it must look to Christ. His work, in turn, as fulfilling and redemptive, *personal* and *invisible*, regenerated the inner person.[5]

The link that Elliott made between the creation and the incarnation and his stress on the "mystery of Christ's humanity" was common among the Americanists. Hecker, building on his Transcendentalist inheritance, pioneered the use of the method in his *Questions of a Soul.* In an 1864 sermon, he spoke of an "obscure idea of God," embedded in the human breast, and becoming clear in the life and work of Jesus Christ. Jesus, he noted, "has lived a human life, submitted to our wants, toils, humiliations, taken part in our griefs, carried our sorrows, and sympathized in our joys." In *Emmanuel,* a book that he considered the culmination of his spiritual life, John Keane challenged his readers to "study well the mystery of the Lord's humanity." "All is consummated in the Mystery of Love, by which I am truly Man, while ever truly God. For this is the will of My Father, that thus all our work of Creation, summed up in Man, should be lifted into the Bosom of the Godhead, and there abide." In the view of Elliott, Hecker, and Keane, Christ exemplified obedience in his willingness to take up the condition of being human, to embrace the historical condition of poverty, hiddenness, seeming nothingness, and, by uplifting it, to transform the natural goodness of the person into eternal beatitude. The image did not concentrate on the two natures of Christ, as had Spalding, but on the unity of the two natures in one divine person.[6]

By emphasizing the longing hidden in the hearts of different peoples, and presenting Christ as the fulfillment of human aspirations, Hecker, Keane, and Elliott argued for a theological image corresponding to their political views. Their political Americanism accepted values centered in the person: equality, inalienable rights, the necessity of consent, the sovereignty of the people. Republican institutions, recognizing rights and working to complete human aspirations in the social sphere, were designed in turn to serve the person. In such a view there could be no split between the secular and sacred spheres of existence. Everything emanating from the person found its completion in the one person, Christ. Keane graphically pictured this understanding when he asked his readers to behold this vision from Calvary:

> . . . the Mystery of the Incarnation.
> And we saw how, as Man doth unite the
>   whole Creation in his twofold being,
> So the Eternal Wisdom, taking Humanity to
>   Himself in personal union, and being thus
>   the God Man,
> Would bring all things into unity, and
>   would lift the whole Creation into the
>   Creator's Bosom.[7]

How different from the vision of Calvary that Martin Spalding had imagined! But where was this God-Man, who reconciled all things in himself, to be found? Where could people discover this mystery of the Incarnation?

Elliott, Hecker, and Keane argued that the church was "the extension of the Son of God into the open life of men so as the better to honor the Heavenly Father publicly, and to save men privately and one by one." As a continuation of the Incarnation, the church existed to "create and maintain" the inner power of Christ in the person and community. The church, Hecker wrote in his "Notes on the Holy Spirit,"

> is that body authorized by Christ to convey to souls the grace, the divine actions, which He came down from heaven to convey to men. The Church is that institution which exists from the time of Christ, established by His authority, to continue the work for which He came down upon earth and became man in the womb of the Virgin Mary.

Like Christ, the church's actions needed to be *personal* and *invisible*, infusing, not superimposing or imputing new life. "Apart from the graces attached to office," Elliott wrote, "the real power of religious organizations to convince is not in the spectacle of disciplined masses, but in the influence of regenerate persons; let *them* move forward in unity, and everything bows before their banners." Finally, like Christ, the church gathered up all the yearnings of humanity and completed them: "She alone is the complete body of truth, possessing what the sects hold in scattered fragments, and she alone has the vital organic force which is to render her life and her evolution commensurate with the ages that will need the Redemption."[8]

The emphasis on personality and communion, which flowed from the understanding of the church as the extension of the Incarnation, also shaped the view of asceticism, authority, and sacraments in the vision of the Americanists. "Since the only unitive virtue is love," Elliott wrote,

> therefore the original, the perpetual, the all powerful, the exclusive means of bringing men into friendship with God and keeping them there must be love: how then can one who does not love hope to save souls? If we yield a place to fear, it must be an introductory one, the minor orders of that divine priesthood and hierarchy of persuasion and conversion and perseverance which is conferred upon sanctified souls. The official hierarchy of the Church's ministry was founded by Christ to arm this unofficial hierarchy of personal virtue with a divine authority in the external order. By sacraments and dogmas, indeed, the Church is constituted; but sacrament and dogmas generate prayer and patience and zeal and every other form of holy love, which in turn reacts upon them and makes them more fruitful. Happy is the family, and the parish, and the religious community, and the diocese in which this rule of Christ prevails, and obedience and love are so blended as to be indistinguishably one.

Hecker and Keane concurred, since in their view the real end of all asceticism and authority was "to teach the soul how it can remove all obstacles and prepare itself to become a perfect instrument of the Holy Ghost."[9]

A practical application of their general view of the church presented itself in the Americanist understanding of religious life. As early as 1855 Hecker had rooted the pursuit of the religious state in the personal yearnings of the individual, thus placing the vows of poverty, chastity, and obedience in the broader context of the community's longing for perfection. Keane adopted the same treatment in his discussion of societies in the church. Elliott's *Life of Christ* made the point explicit. In commenting on the call of the rich young man, the mission preacher noted that the "test of perfection is not in what one does, much or little, but in the mighty purpose to do everything, as soon as God's spirit points the way." The Paulist did not mention the call to religious life in his exegesis of this passage but immediately followed it with two chapters, one on the sacrament of matrimony and one on Christian virginity. Elliott stressed the fact that Christ "restored the marital relation to its original condition, which is the equality of husband and wife," and ranked marriage with the other sacraments. He noted that the state of Christian virginity was "a state of holiness higher than even Christian matrimony" but modified the difference by arguing that both existed for the purpose of sanctification, the one of society, the other of the individual. In his treatment Elliott emphasized the dignity of sexual longings. What was significant about all of these interpretations was that they rooted the importance of one's vocation in the quality of the person's response to the interior movements of the Spirit, not in the place each occupied in the hierarchical society. This was a republican vision of the vocation of the Christian.[10]

The Americanist understanding of the image of Christ and the nature of the church carried significant consequences for the inner life of the Christian. By imaging Christ as the exemplar of what it meant to be human, to be wise, loving, joyful, free, pure, and at the same time, holy, Hecker, Keane, and Elliott presented a spirituality that moved from the inner dynamics of the person to outward expression in the institution. Elliott typified the approach when he argued that "Christ's kingdom is not exclusively external," and that "belief and hope and love and repentance, if worth anything for eternal life, must be preceded in the soul by the inspiration of the Spirit of God, which is the Spirit of Christ."[11] This was opposite to the focus of the leaders of the immigrant church who stressed the subordination of the inner person to the outer rule of faith.

In summary, reconciliation, or "the things that make for unity," was the key to the system. Christ had reconciled the world to himself; the church carried this mission to the ends of the world; and the person, the agent of reconciliation, embodied the whole: Spirit and matter; church and world; the internal and the external. Elliott summarized the approach in these words:

> So with the men and women of Christ's flock. Their life is the knowledge and the love of Jesus Christ more and more abundantly enjoyed. The Church of Christ is the fold, the shelter of the people from error and vice, the ministry of the Church is Christ's company of shepherds to guard them. And apart from all figures of speech, the Divine Spirit within the Christian's soul continually demands the same Divine Spirit in an external brotherhood as a safeguard of its own inner life—a criterion and test of the validity of its inward guidance; just as the soul of man craves a voice to speak to his brethren and an ear to hear their voices in reply. Both orders of life must be divine, a divine interior life united to its divine expression in the Christian Church.[12]

In the context of the later nineteenth century, this stress on the interior, the participative, the unitive, and its basis in the image of Christ, the church, and the person went to the heart of Americanism as a crisis in spirituality.

CHAPTER
11
The Crisis of Americanism and the Structures of Catholic Spiritual Life

$\mathcal{F}$or almost twenty years the Americanist vision of the Christian life and the immigrant church's view developed side by side in the post–Civil War Catholic community. At the Second Plenary Council in 1866, the prelates who received a "Pentecostal fire within their bosom" when Isaac Hecker announced the "Future Triumph of the Church," also passed legislation making Martin John Spalding's understanding of the Christian life normative for Catholic institutional development. Hecker preached "transfiguration" to an emerging middle class of lawyers and businessmen, and civic responsibility to Irish laborers in the parish of Saint Paul's. At the same time, a fellow New York convert and priest, Thomas Scott Preston reminded his equally mixed group of parishioners that the spiritual life required obedience to ecclesiastical authority, and that the "triumph of the Church" meant the ascendancy of a corporate body whose purity, truth, and ordered life contrasted sharply with the society around them. Using Hecker's missionary techniques, Walter Elliott traveled far and wide in an effort to convert his Protestant neighbors; but groups of Jesuit and Redemptorist mission preachers, speaking mostly to Catholic congregations, spread the message of John Hughes's church. In 1884 the Third Plenary Council repeated the legislation of 1866 enjoining the priests to wear the clerical collar and forbidding them to attend horse races and the theater. The same council, at the

119

behest of John Keane, asked that "devotion to the Holy Ghost be cultivated continually and fervently in the seminaries, so that the Spirit of Christ the High Priest may enter into the clerics, abide in them, and operate in them." Last, in 1889, one year after Keane finished promoting his "intelligent Christian piety" in the diocese of Richmond and moved to the Catholic University of America, an Italian immigrant woman, Frances Xavier Cabrini (1850–1917), arrived in New York City. She would be for her generation what John Neumann had been for his.[1]

By way of summary, the vision of the immigrant church and the Americanist view—both of which shared a common doctrine, discipline, ritual, and commitment to Catholicism—might be schematically juxtaposed in this way:

	Vision of the Immigrant Church	Americanist Vision
Social Experience	religious persecution free-market capitalism americanization	religious unity associationism mission to America
Person	passions industry rebellion from God	spiritual yearning natural virtues image of God
History	ideal of Middle Ages early republic	providential development
Christ	Redeemer Crucifixion	Reconciler Incarnation
Church	divine constitution corporate institution moral teacher	extension of Incarnation organic communion agent of personal sanctification
Asceticism	sacrifice obedience to authority mortification self-interest	free and intelligent piety self-reliance transfiguration self-denial
Prayer	methodical meditation resolutions of will	contemplation discernment
Devotions	Eucharist Immaculate Conception communion of saints	Holy Spirit social/religious confraternities interior communion
Social Reform	institutions for the poor parochial schools protection of the immigrant	Knights of Labor common education reconstruction of society

The common conditions of social reconstruction, industrial expansion, and a weakening of Protestantism as a public force, conditions that allowed these two views to coexist, began to change rapidly in the late 1880s. The "plague of the city" with its tenements and poverty, economic depressions, and industrial conflicts between the

"Gilded Age" managers and their employees rocked the society at large. The Protestant churches, recovering slowly after the Civil War, demonstrated new life in urban evangelical missions and institutional growth. The American Protective Association, formed in 1887, revived the institutionalized nativism that had lain dormant since the 1850s. By 1896 it boasted over 1 million adherents. Josiah Strong, a Congregationalist minister, published *Our Country* in 1891. It was a full-scale attack on Catholicism and argued that the church "opposed the basis of national life: it was critical of popular sovereignty, free speech, free press, free conscience, free schools, separation of Church and State." Within Catholicism, increased Irish and German immigration heightened Protestant fears and occasioned ethnic conflicts of sharp intensity. Catholic participation in secular (Protestant) schools became once again an issue of divisive significance. This school debate symbolized the relationship between the church and the culture. Liberals and conservatives jockeyed for position and influence in the Roman congregations that were themselves embarking on a policy of centralization in the wake of Vatican I's definition of infallibility.[2]

Within this changing context, the two different approaches to Americanism and Americanization came into sharper focus. Thomas Scott Preston, the vicar general of the archdiocese of New York, presaged the heart of the conflict when he wrote in January 1870 to Archbishop Domenico Jacobini:

> Here in New York we are loyal Catholics. We are devoted to the Holy See, we do not believe in the great folly and absurdity of Americanizing the Catholic Church. We propose to Catholicize America. We are entirely Roman in all our actions and affections. We believe in the temporal power of the Pope and we advocate it, and we feel certain that in God's good time it will be restored.[3]

It would soon appear that the vision of the immigrant church and its inheritors and the vision of Hecker, Keane, and others could no longer peacefully coexist; in the heat of battle, they became diametrically opposed.

During the course of the 1890s, the conflicts over education, ethnicity, and the relationship between church and state dominated the public discussions in the United States. Issues of the spiritual life dropped into the background. Walter Elliott published the *Life of Father Hecker* in 1891 and attempted to synthesize the Paulist founder's spiritual doctrine, but the work received scant notice. This concentration on political and social issues changed only in 1897 when the book was translated into French with an introduction by Archbishop John Ireland. French commentators recognized Elliott's *Life* as a work of some significance in the history of Catholic piety. They began to draw some connections between the Americanists' view of history and politics and their understanding of the spiritual life.[4]

Abbé Felix Klein, a professor of literature at the Catholic Institute of Paris and ardent defender of Hecker, published an article in October 1897, in which he synthesized the major characteristics of this "new American asceticism." He repeated the general contention that in the modern world, the sanctity suited for the cloister could no longer prevail. The regime of passive obedience dominated by rules and a predetermined program of life was finished. The times demanded something new: a recourse to self, a dependence on personal responsibility, a searching of the will of God in the depth of people's hearts. Individuals, Klein argued, needed to listen to the inspirations of the Spirit and be guided by the habitual presence of God in the soul. This French republican believed that the Americanist position opened up a new chapter in the history of the spiritual life.[5]

The French monarchist Abbé Charles Maignen responded to Klein in a series of articles published in book form as *Le Père Hecker: Est-il un saint?* (1898). He addressed at length the issue of sanctity and its social dimensions. Noting the current interest in mysticism, Maignen quickly affirmed that the mystics themselves had always followed the doctrine of Jesus Christ and his church. In one of his most telling comments, he referred to the close connection between republican political convictions and this mystical emphasis on individual experience and guidance. Reacting to the "new asceticism," Maignen spent a large portion of his work defending the discipline needed for a spiritual life: monasticism, the evangelical counsels of poverty, chastity, and obedience, and devotionalism. He presupposed throughout that the Americanist perspective carried important implications for the daily life of the Christian. Maignen was joined in his critique by the Jesuit Père A.-J. Delattre, who argued that the Christian life was characterized primarily by docility and obedience to authority. Delattre rejected Hecker's intimation that the age of martyrs, monks, and hermits was over. He believed that the "American model of devotion"—independent, republican, democratic—contradicted papal statements calling for support of the present structures of church and state.[6]

These battles that began in the United States and raged in France between republicans and monarchists also found fertile ground in Italy. Both sides struggled for approval in Rome. A decision was rendered with the publication of Leo XIII's encyclical letter sent to Cardinal Gibbons, *Testem Benevolentiae*, in January 1899. The letter was designed to condemn Americanism as a body of opinions affecting Catholic spiritual life and was essentially framed within the context of the French debate. Written with the help of Camillo Mazzella, a

Jesuit who had spent some time in the United States, the encyclical devoted only two short references to American customs and the condition of the commonwealth. The rest concentrated on opinions "concerning the manner of leading a Christian life." Throughout the text, the discipline and rule of life that should govern the daily conduct of the Catholic received the most attention. The importance of *Testem Benevolentiae* for the future development of Catholic spiritual life in the United States can be discovered by examining its understanding of the church and the state, the spiritual life, and Christ.[7]

In its presentation of the spiritual life, *Testem Benevolentiae* presupposed Leo XIII's analysis of the relationship between the church and society. Leo had developed his view in his major encyclical letters "On Civil Government" (1881), "On the Christian Constitution of States" (1885), and "On Human Liberty" (1888). He evolved his position in the context of the struggles of the church in Italy, France, and Germany, against the laicist state and the more revolutionary, socialist ideas of "liberty." In Europe, the growth of the modern state and the adoption of "democratic liberties" was accompanied by outbursts of anticlericalism, suppression of religious orders, forced secularization of church property, and the closure of religious schools. The sovereignty of the people in the laicist state had no reference to God or revelation, and public law tended to confine religion strictly to the realm of the individual conscience. In order to combat these opinions Leo took a very definite position on the nature of the state and the church.[8]

Leo first emphasized the origin of political authority in God and the duty of citizens to obey their lawfully constituted rulers. To protect society from the ravages of revolution, he concentrated on the authority of the ruler as the "tutor and guardian of virtue in the body politic." "God has always willed," he wrote, "that there should be a ruling authority, and that they who are invested with it should reflect the divine power and providence in some measure over the human race." He described the rulers as "fathers" and the citizens as "subjects" or "children," who show obedience, reverence, and fealty. In its own sphere of concern, when it acted in conformity to right reason and natural law, the state, according to Leo, was divinely constituted and supreme in authority. This view of a divinely constituted order in civil society emerged very clearly in *Testem Benevolentiae* when it noted: "From the word of God we have it that it is the office of all to labor for the salvation of the neighbor in the order and degree in which each one is."[9]

The same context that led Leo to emphasize the subordination of the citizens to the rulers and subordination of the latter to the law of God also encouraged him to define the church in similar terms.

Testem Benevolentiae referred explicitly to Leo's "Christian Constitution of States," in which he argued that the church

> is made up of men, just as civil society is, and yet is supernatural and spiritual, on account of the end for which it was founded, and of the means by which it aims at attaining that end. Hence it is distinguished and differs from civil society, and, what is of the highest moment, it is a society chartered as of right divine, perfect in its nature and in its title, to possess in itself and by itself, through the will and loving kindness of its Founder, all needful provision for its maintenance and action. And just as the end at which the Church aims is by far the noblest of ends, so is its authority the most exalted of all authority, nor can it be looked upon as inferior to the civil power, or in any manner dependent upon it.[10]

The pope had reaffirmed this understanding of the church in his 1898 encyclical *Satis Cognitum*. It concentrated on the immutability of the corporate and hierarchical society. Given this view, it was not surprising that *Testem Benevolentiae* criticized those who wished to imitate civil society and to introduce into the church a certain liberty "so that, limiting the exercise and vigilance of its powers, each one of the faithful may act more freely in pursuance of his own natural bent and capacity." Ecclesiologically, Leo's vertical relationship between the rulers and the subjects had been translated into the relationship between the hierarchy and the laity.[11]

Testem Benevolentiae's presuppositions about the state and the church shaped its approach to the spiritual life in five major ways. First, the encyclical acknowledged that the "Holy Ghost, by His secret incoming into the souls of the just, influences and arouses them by admonition and impulse." Still, these impulses could not be discerned without external guidance. According to the common law God had decreed that people for the most part should be saved by people. Given the encyclical's presuppositions about church and state in conflict, an emphasis on the external, organizational elements in the church was naturally forthcoming. Leo had already elaborated this understanding of the importance of external guidance in an earlier encyclical on the Holy Spirit, *Divinum Illud* (1897). There he had noted that the Spirit constituted the bishops "and by their ministry are multiplied not only the children, but also the fathers—that is to say, the priests—to rule and feed the church by that blood wherewith Christ has redeemed her." The Spirit was mediated to people through the sacraments since "our whole nature had fallen into such guilt and dishonor that we had become enemies of God. We were by nature the children of wrath. There was no power which could raise us and deliver us from ruin and eternal destruction." Building on this earlier view, *Testem Benevolentiae* emphasized the role of the spiritual director as "teacher and leader."[12]

Second, Leo had defined the state and the church as separate entities, each with its origin in God, but with a different purpose: the state to insure peace and civil harmony; the church to labor for the glory of God and the salvation of souls. This understanding informed the presentation in *Testem Benevolentiae* on the relationship between the natural and supernatural virtues. On the one hand, the individual possesses natural virtues, and the encyclical merely castigated those who extolled these virtues as being more suited to the modern age because "they make a man more ready and more strenuous in action." This nuanced presentation preserved a natural order of things corresponding to the natural ends of the state, giving the latter some autonomy. On the other hand, as *Testem Benevolentiae* argued, the person was also disturbed by passions "sometimes of a violent nature, for the persevering conquest of which, just as for the observance of the whole natural law, man must needs have some divine help." In the practical order, the natural virtues "have more the appearance than the reality of virtue." Also, of what use were the natural virtues, *Testem* asked, unless "the gift and strength of divine grace be added." Virtues exercised with the help of divine grace, in contrast, became "productive of a supernatural beatitude; and become solid and enduring."

By emphasizing the weakness of the natural virtues and the need for grace to make them "productive of blessedness," the encyclical significantly founded the church's function on the anthropological base of human concupiscence and sinfulness. It made no mention of the natural yearnings for blessedness, and how these desires found their completion in the gospel. In the natural order, the person needed the authority of the ruler to insure virtue; the ruler, in turn, needed the law of God as interpreted by reason and natural law and, if there was confusion, the authority of the church to interpret the law. In the supernatural order, the person needed the church to teach truth and provide the way to salvation. In both orders, obedience became the key virtue of the Christian life. The church was the mediator of grace to sinful humanity, the protector of a public order that could not preserve virtue without supernatural aid, and the agent of the final, supernatural end of the person.[13]

Testem Benevolentiae's treatment of the religious life flowed from this understanding of natural and supernatural virtues and the importance of the church as a divine authority. For *Testem*, it was the religious, those who had vowed the perfect pursuit of Christ, those who were humble, obedient and docile, who truly enjoyed the freedom "whereby Christ has set us free." From the religious, *Testem* noted, the people received preachers of the Word of God, directors of conscience, teachers of youth, and most importantly, examples of holiness. The encyclical rejected those who argued that the spirituality of former times was not suited to the present age or that it emphasized the "wrongly called *passive*" virtues. In fact, all virtues were active, and those who professed the evangelical counsels presented themselves to "Christ as his prompt and valiant soldiers." The underlying point was simple: religious, as exemplars of perfection, witnessed to the principle of hierarchical mediation and to the active virtue of obedience.[14]

Last, given the encyclical's presupposition about the integrity of the church, its perfection in doctrine and constitution, it naturally disparaged any new methods of public preaching that attempted to appeal to Protestants by passing "over certain heads of doctrines, as if of lesser moment, or to so soften them that they may not have the same meaning which the Church has invariably held."[15]

The heart of *Testem Benevolentiae*'s vision of the Christian life was presented in its image of Christ. Christ was, first of all, "the Author and Master of all the truths that Christian teaching composes." In this capacity, he was the one who addressed the apostles to "go, teach all nations, teaching them to observe all things whatsoever I have commanded." Second, Christ was the one who bestowed on the church "a kind and merciful disposition," by which she made modifications in discipline according to diverse times and places. Third, Christ was the "Master and exemplar of all sanctity." To his rule all who wished to attain to the throne of the blessed must adapt. The encyclical used five scriptural passages to describe Christ and the action of those who lived in him: Christ was the "only begotten who is in the bosom of the Father" (Jn. 1:18). He was the same "yesterday, today and forever" (Heb. 13:8). He showed himself "obedient unto death" (Phil. 2:8) He taught the people for all ages: "Learn of me, for I am meek and humble of heart" (Matt. 11:29). Last, the ones who lived in him have "crucified their flesh with its vices and concupiscence" (Gal. 5:24). According to *Testem Benevolentiae*, therefore, Christ, in the bosom of the Father, was always the same. The abstract truths of discipline, of which he was the author and the apostles the custodians, never changed in themselves but were relaxed because of his mercy. In turn, the true Christian, modeled on the exemplar, was one whose life was marked by humility of spirit, obedience, and mortification. Christ, in short, recapitulated *Testem Benevolentiae*'s understanding of the church, the person, and the asceticism necessary for the spiritual life.

THE STRUCTURES OF CATHOLIC SPIRITUAL LIFE

Taken by itself, *Testem Benevolentiae* did not make that great an impact on the Catholic community in the United States. The Americanist bishops and Paulist community soon submitted letters of loyalty and denied the condemned opinions had ever been accepted in this country. Their opponents lauded the encyclical as "admirable" and expressed gratitude that the errors that they believed existed among the clergy and laity had been identified and repudiated. In general, public discussion of the encyclical seems to have rapidly abated. Nevertheless, *Testem Benevolentiae* was communicated directly to the acknowledged leader of the American church, Cardinal James Gibbons, and when John Keane received the letter appointing him to the see of Dubuque in August 1900, Pope Leo XIII explicitly asked him to reflect on the condemned errors. The pope felt that the piety of the faithful had been endangered. "Nor do we doubt," he wrote, "that you will work hard to suppress the errors spreading there and to foster the union of souls with this seat of infallible truth."[16] Also, inasmuch as *Testem Benevolentiae* presupposed Leo XIII's general approach to the relationships between church and society, it combined with his other encyclicals to encourage the growth of a uniform style of spiritual life more compatible with the European social and religious scene. The way had already been prepared in the United States for the reception of the papal understanding by increased emphasis on papal authority in such theological and devotional writers as Thomas Scott Preston and Otto Zardetti. These developments would be further encouraged by the institutional reaction to modernism under the pontificate of Pius X (1903–1914).[17]

Even more important than these three factors for the future development of Catholic spiritual life in the United States was the convergence of *Testem Benevolentiae* with the already well developed immigrant vision of the Christian life. In the encyclical the American and European traditions joined for the first time on the level of official church teaching. Both positions had developed within a context of religious persecution: nativism in the United States; the laic state in Europe. They agreed on a definition of the church that emphasized its corporate and hierarchical nature, its unchanging doctrine and practice. They tended to view the relationships between church and state as the interaction of two corporate wholes that were juridically separate. Within the person, both sides divided nature from grace and concentrated on the weakness and sinfulness of human nature. As a consequence, they argued on the one hand for human action in obedience, loyalty, sacrifice, and mortification, and on the other for the importance of institutional authority to guide and direct aberrant humanity. In the spiritual life, this view emphasized the teaching and sacramental functions of the church, the mediating role of the priest, the exemplification in religious life of the "way of perfection," and the importance of devotions as "symbolic dogma." Historically, *Testem Benevolentiae* and the immigrant vision looked backward to a time when church and society had been integrally connected. Clearly, in many ways Leo's encyclical strengthened the position that Spalding, Hughes, and Neumann had elaborated in the 1840s and 1850s.

This convergence of the immigrant and papal traditions was extremely significant. Still, it would be historically naive to presume that they were the same. Between the time of Hughes, Spalding, and Neumann and that of Leo XIII, papal infallibility had been declared a doctrine of the faith, and neo-scholastic theology had undergone a revival. Thus, while affirming many of the developments that had marked the synthesis of the immigrant church, *Testem Benevolentiae* and the general view of Leo XIII also modified the American immigrant tradition in a significant way. The encyclical, following Leo's earlier statements, made a very clear distinction between the state (society) and the church. It explicitly rejected those who attempted to introduce into the church, "which is of divine right," that liberty "which is now the law and the foundation of every civil community." When translated into the American scene this distinction heightened the differences between American political traditions and the structures of the Catholic church. In contrast, the builders of the immigrant community, while accepting the divine constitution of the hierarchy, also noted parallels between American constitutionalism and the elective and conciliar processes in the church.

Second, within the context of Leo's argument, the right to religious freedom was inconceivable; one of the chief duties of the ruler was "to favor religion, to protect it, to shield it under the credit and sanction of the laws, and neither to organize nor enact any measure that may compromise its safety."[18] Yet Hughes and Spalding had insisted that one of the strongest links between Catholicism and American identity was the latter's constant support of religious liberty from colonial times to the nineteenth century. On both the institutional and personal levels the leaders of the immigrant church pushed for some integration of church and culture; this integration corresponded to their policy of Americanization. It was one area in which they and the Americanists agreed. By completely divorcing the political and ecclesiological dimensions of life, *Testem* denied one of the underlying dynamics of the immigrant tradition. This necessitated a new version of what it meant to be Catholic and American; the spiritual life, accordingly, underwent some significant changes.

Three responses to the encyclical may be cited to indicate how it influenced and modified the understanding and practice of Catholic spiritual life. In May 1900, John Ireland wrote an article under the pseudonym of J. St. Clair Etheridge for the *North American Review*. He distinguished between "political Americanism" and "religious Americanism" and argued that only the latter had been condemned in *Testem Benevolentiae.* The archbishop of Saint Paul listed five distinct elements in this "crude body of heretical opinions": 1. the minimization of Catholic doctrine in order to gain adherents to the church; 2. the exaltation of the natural qualities of character at the expense of supernatural virtues; 3. giving to the individual a liberty of thought and action incompatible with the scope of ecclesiastical authority; 4. support of the absolute separation of church and state in all countries and circumstances; 5. false principles of piety that depreciated the moral value of the vows and argued that the spirituality of religious orders was no longer suited to the age. Ireland denied that these opinions had ever existed in the United States.

Ireland also put forth what he called "political Americanism," a body of opinions left untouched by *Testem Benevolentiae.* This view encouraged every Catholic to be a good citizen; worked to uplift the masses "politically and socially"; desired to leaven all of private and public life with the principles of Christianity; strove to cooperate with non-Catholics for the general welfare of the people without losing one jot of Catholic doctrine; and adapted the external methods of the church to the needs of the times without sacrificing an essential element of Catholic organization.[19]

By making such a sharp distinction between political and religious Americanism and denying that the latter had ever existed in the United States, Ireland was indicating one significant avenue along which Catholic spiritual life in the United States could develop. The archbishop pointedly indicated that "the things that make for unity" in the social sphere (political cooperation and economic reform) could not influence Catholic doctrine, organization, or piety. The spiritual life in this view could only be strictly ecclesiastical, developing along the lines indicated by the institutional church. As a phenomenon within the church, spirituality was unconcerned with social reform. This emphasis on the institutional church would strengthen the Catholic tendency to confine the spiritual life to the "purgative way," to define "perfection" in moralistic categories. Ireland had departed from John Keane's "individualism of Jesus Christ" and the integrated understanding of "No Church, No Reform," but given the perspective of *Testem Benevolentiae,* his view was a post-Leonine version of Americanism. While isolating the spiritual life, it allowed socially for cooperation between Catholics and Protestants, separation of church and state, greater lay initiative, and keeping the church as the "Church of the people."

Joseph McSorley, a young Paulist who as a novice had listened to Walter Elliott read the chapters of his *Life of Father Hecker,* presented another approach to *Testem Benevolentiae.* In 1900, McSorley wrote an article on "Devotion to the Holy Spirit" in which he reaffirmed

Hecker's emphasis on the indwelling Spirit, obedience to individual inspirations, and the voice of conscience. McSorley argued that the pursuit of perfection could often conflict, as it had for Ignatius of Loyola, with prevalent notions and cherished traditions. Since Leo XIII had described liberty as one of the greatest natural gifts, the Paulist reasoned, the devotion to the Holy Spirit admirably suited the earnest, intelligent, active, and liberty-loving present age. In a passage reminiscent of John Keane's address before the Third Plenary Council of Baltimore in 1884, McSorley paralleled devotion to the Holy Spirit and devotion to the Sacred Heart as the two foundations of a vital spirituality. He even repeated Brownson's and Hecker's contention that post–Reformation Catholicism had emphasized external authority in reaction to Protestantism. "The frequent advice of others," he wrote,

> may be perfectly indispensable to our success, and consequently is to be sought; but we should not neglect opportunities of useful work, merely because no one has suggested our embracing them. Nor can we always have a director within call, unless indeed it be the indwelling Spirit. And therefore the best direction is that which trains men in prompt and spontaneous fidelity to the guidance of God's Holy Spirit, as the normal spiritual life is that where the soul, instead of merely shaping itself on the minute details of a model provided by an adviser, uses its own intelligence to recognize, and its own will to execute God's particular design in its regard.

To support his position in all of these areas, McSorley used theologians whose orthodoxy could not be questioned. He also referred extensively to the encyclical letters of Leo XIII. The Paulist was clearly trying to show that the condemnation of Americanism had not included Hecker's teachings on the spiritual life and the primacy of the Holy Spirit.[20]

What was missing from McSorley's article was any reference to Hecker's program of social regeneration, any attempt to relate devotion to the Holy Spirit to economic and industrial reform. The Paulist mentioned the close connection between the natural yearnings of the individual and their completion in grace, but when he discussed the perfection of the social order he explicitly acknowledged Leo's philosophy and presupposed the pope's emphasis on reason and natural law as the basis of a just society. In other words, McSorley labored to preserve Hecker's notion of individual experience and mysticism on the personal level, but he could not adopt the social unity between Catholicism and Americanism that had marked the vision of Brownson, Hecker, and Keane.

In a later essay, McSorley related his understanding of personal religious experience with the need for social reform through the "sacrament of duty." "Duty," he argued, meant "all that conscience demands," and "sacrament," everything that symbolized and imputed God's blessing to the soul of the person. Thus, by performing the ordinary duties of life, by acting according to conscience, a person could be encountering the grace of God and living a life of perfection. The "sacrament of duty," in a world that confined secular activity to the sphere of natural virtue, enabled the ordinary person to pursue holiness. "The mind which meditates on the rewards of duty," he wrote,

> will see beauty, holiness and eternal worth in lives of patient suffering and honest toil, to rank vocations noble in proportion to the selflessness for which they call, to discern the possibilities of divine perfection in the monotonous round of man's daily duties, and to regard the soul's everlasting struggle with temptation as the true building up of the kingdom of God.

The "sacrament of duty" also left room for the operation of individual conscience in an ecclesiastical world that emphasized obedience to authority. It was a post-Leonine adaptation of Hecker's sermon on "The Saint of Our Day."[21] If Ireland had taken Americanism in its social direction, McSorley elaborated on its anthropological basis. The two, however, met only in the slender area of "duty."

The pastoral letter of Benjamin J. Keiley (1847–1925), bishop of Savannah, on "Devotion to the Sacred Heart" in May 1901, furnished a third example of the assimilation of *Testem Benevolentiae* into Catholic life. The bishop argued that Sacred Heart devotions were properly founded in three dogmatic truths: the dual nature and unity of person in Christ; the divine maternity of the Immaculate Mother; and the real death of the Lord and his love that directed the sacrifice of Calvary. Would not such a devotion, he asked, draw back the hearts of people by making an appeal to their gratitude? Keiley also noted that Sacred Heart devotion had sometimes met with "secret and open opposition." Its final triumph meant the victory of "faith over error; of the Church over recreant children; of principle over expediency; of authority over insubordination." The devotion above all should inspire people to a "loving submission to the Vicar of Christ on earth," who represented the authority and the tenderness of the Lord.

In the middle of his pastoral, Keiley repeated the strictures of *Testem Benevolentiae* and reiterated the Catholic acceptance of the divine constitution of the church and its authority in faith and morals. He concluded by establishing a link between the rejection of Americanism and the practice of Sacred Heart devotions. "Our submission to the Holy Father," he wrote,

> must not be merely a lip service, but sincere and from the heart, and it should be our prayer that God may increase in us this simple loyal faith. The basis of our submission to the Holy See is the fact that He is the

Vicar and Representative of Christ Jesus on earth. Let us strive then, Rev. and dear Fathers to encourage a devotion which speaks so eloquently and tenderly of our blessed Lord, and by fostering among the faithful a greater love for the Sacred Heart, let us remind them that the voice of Peter has blessed and sanctioned this devotion; and that the love which he taught by the Sacred Heart, and found therein, has prompted him, to care for the sheep of His fold by placing them under the guidance and direction of an earthly Vicar.

The bishop directed that Sacred Heart devotions be held every day in June, and that the Litany of the Sacred Heart and act of consecration be said in the presence of the Blessed Sacrament during the novena in preparation for the feast.

In his pastoral letter Bishop Keiley clearly focused on the institutional and juridical definition of the church as a perfect society. Devotion to the Sacred Heart, often linked in the thought of the time with eucharistic devotion, symbolically portrayed this truth. As if sensing the implications of this support of *Testem Benevolentiae*, the bishop affirmed his "loyalty to our constitution and obedience to the laws enacted in pursuance thereof." On the one hand, he noted that the republic "has brought no new principles of Government for the Church; has developed no theory of revelation which we accept; has not changed the old landmarks." On the other hand, Keiley argued that Catholics were good Americans precisely because they were Catholics first.[22] He could do this because he strictly limited the things that belonged to Caesar and extended the things that belonged to God. His tendency was to emphasize Catholic identity so as almost to ignore the secular world. This view always subordinated the development of personal spiritual life and involvement in social reform to the directives of ecclesiastical authority.

The interpretations that Ireland, McSorley, and Keiley offered for *Testem Benevolentiae* obviously indicated that a pluralism of approaches would continue to characterize Catholic spiritual life in the United States. *Testem* had clearly not forestalled future variations. But the three churchmen, despite their different convictions, also presupposed an overarching unity to Catholic life. In this respect, it is important to note that they responded to *Testem Benevolentiae* as a papal document. The encyclical had marked for the first time the entrance of the Roman magisterium into the self-definition of American Catholic spiritual life. Future developments would continue to be guided by papal statements. All three respondents also presupposed that the church was a divinely constituted, immutable, hierarchical "Body of Christ." This common framework indicated that the next generation of Catholics would develop their spiritual life in such a way as to include a strong concept of priesthood, an emphasis on discipline and the ascetical life, devotional practices, and an image of Christ as Teacher and Lawgiver. Variations would occur only within this context; the Catholicity of ethnic groups not emphasizing these elements would be questioned.[23]

Finally, living within the American context, all three churchmen stressed the mutual independence of the state from the church. Leo XIII clearly preferred a situation in which the church "enjoyed the favor of the laws and the patronage of the public authority," as he had stated in *Longinqua Oceani*, his encyclical letter to the American hierarchy in 1895.[24] But *Testem Benevolentiae* had steadfastly avoided commenting on these secular matters. "We cannot approve the opinions which some comprise under the head of Americanism," the encyclical concluded, but

> if, indeed, by that name be designated the characteristic qualities which reflect honor on the people of America just as other nations have what is special to them; or if it implies the condition of your commonwealths, or the laws and customs which prevail in them, there is surely no reason why We should deem that it ought to be discarded.

The generation after *Testem Benevolentiae* would interpret this phrase and some of Leo XIII's other statements tolerating separation of church and state to show the compatibility of Catholicism and American institutions. But the price was great: the affairs of the church and the affairs of the state, the sacred and the secular, existed side by side, contiguous but not commingled, two separate compartments of a fractured Catholic spirit.

Testem Benevolentiae, as a summary of Leo XIII's understanding of the Christian life, definitely transformed the two traditions that had developed in nineteenth-century American Catholicism. The immigrant vision, although providing the institutional, ascetical, and devotional structures that would undergird the twentieth-century church, lost its bite of Americanization and unity of approach. The Americanist vision, forced to adjust to the accusation of heresy, continued by splitting its social and personal dimensions into two distinct approaches. What disappeared in both instances was a vision of the Christian life that could in some way integrate personal experience, Catholic identity, and American culture. In the twentieth century, the shapers of Catholic spiritual life would put forward a variety of approaches, but all of them in some way would be dealing with a fractured inheritance bound together by the structures of the institutional church. The ways in which they tried to unify the person, the church, and the world within those structures will be the subject of the next section.

PART FOUR

A Fractured Inheritance, 1900–1930

The three currents of the nineteenth-century church that had come together in the crisis of Americanism continued to provide the foundation on which twentieth-century Catholicism would construct its vision of the Christian life. The skeletal structures of schools, parishes, and dioceses that in the immigrant church had embodied Americanization programs now became solidified under the managerial revolutions associated with big business and centralized government. A new generation of prelates led by Cardinal William O'Connell of Boston (1859–1944) and Cardinal George Mundelein of Chicago (1872–1939) were known for their administrative talents and their tendency to view the church as an efficient corporation capable of operating in an increasingly professional world. The thrust of Brownson, Hecker, and Keane to create a more militant and active laity as a sign of the church's mission to America, now directed by an overarching commitment to hierarchical authority, still contributed a significant element to the apostolic programs of parishes, dioceses, and national federations. William O'Connell summarized the mood of an era in 1901:

> We have passed the day and passed forever, when we quietly stole unnoticed to our humble little chapel and were grateful for being ignored. The Church has grown to immense proportions—its cathedral spires tower above our great cities—our men are a power in the nation . . . the voice of our best, most influential laymen, must be heard and felt in

135

public life, indicating and proclaiming to all the highest Catholic public sentiment.[1]

Last, the vision of a Christian life fully reflective of papal teaching permeated the programs and the mentality of the church in the United States. An era that began with Leo XIII's *Longinqua Oceani* (1895) and *Testem Benevolentiae* (1899) continued to be shaped by Pius X's *E Supremi* (1903) and Pius XI's *Ubi Arcano* (1922) and *Quas Primas* (1925). This papal vision of a unified social and spiritual renewal functioned as an illusive but attractive ideal for the church in the United States.

Yet the three streams did not combine easily, and the most vital Catholic movements of the era reflected the fractured inheritance of the Americanist crisis. Willing to accept papal direction and joining it with the institutional structures of the immigrant church, Catholics nevertheless struggled to fashion a spiritual life of faith within the context of American society. The following pages will describe this struggle that dominated Catholic spiritual life from 1900 to 1930 by examining the thought of one representative figure, John A. Ryan, and the development of two major movements of spiritual revitalization, the eucharistic and retreat movements.

CHAPTER
12
Spirituality and Social Reform

*J*ohn Augustine Ryan was born on the Minnesota frontier in 1869. Having grown up near Saint Paul, he studied both as a collegian and as a candidate for the priesthood at Saint Thomas Seminary. During his educational years, he became familiar with political populism and John Ireland's call for a resurgent Catholicism led by an active laity. In 1894 he read, for the first time, Leo XIII's social encyclical, *Rerum Novarum*. Ordained in 1898, he received a licentiate in theology from the Catholic University of America and returned to teach at the Saint Paul seminary. His doctoral dissertation was published as *A Living Wage* in 1905, and from that time until his death in 1945 he was perhaps the most influential Catholic social reformer of his era. In 1915 he joined the faculty at the Catholic University of America. In the following years he took an active part in shaping the social policies of the American hierarchy and training future generations of teachers. He became a foremost proponent of the New Deal. His biographer summarized Ryan's spiritual life in these words:

> Though he wrote a great deal during his career, he rarely touched on mystical or even purely religious topics. . . . His journal spoke only of a practical view of perfection, directed outward rather than inward. If we cannot attain the perfection of loving our neighbors as ourselves, he wrote, "let us see that our love and appreciation for self does not become openly injurious and offensive to others. In this way we shall avoid sin against others if not against ourselves." Christianity embraces both a call to individual perfection and a social ethic.[1]

Although a social progressive and often at odds with more conservative churchmen, John Ryan in his combination of a private spiritual life and a social ethic witnessed to the religious self-understanding of a generation of Catholics. The son of Irish immigrant parents,
an inheritor of Keane and Ireland's Americanist vision, and an ad-
herent of Leo XIII's view of the relationship between the church and
the social order, Ryan received all three traditions but bore them in
an uneasy synthesis. His representative position and its departure
from the nineteenth century can be understood through an examination of four key elements that shaped his understanding: the intellectual context of rationalism, the social problem, the battle with liberal Protestantism, and difficulties in the Catholic community itself.

Unlike his nineteenth-century forebears, Ryan fashioned his
Christian life not in the context of nativism or in the transcendental
quest to unite freedom and authority but in response to much broader
contemporary intellectual and social issues shared by both Protestants
and Catholics. The enemy in the intellectual order was rationalistic
skepticism, a philosophical position that had grown in popularity
since the time of Isaac Hecker. "The ages of simple faith are gone by
forever," Ryan wrote in the journal he kept during his theology years
at Saint Thomas Seminary, Saint Paul.

> In their stead we have the age of criticism, of scepticism, if you will.
> Which is to be preferred? Is our time more fortunate in its questionings
> and its doubts than the good old days of yore? On the whole, yes; simple
> faith was alright when the horizon of men's knowledge was as limited
> as that of his aspirations, but it would never do now, when both have
> become incomparably widened. Scepticism and distrust are perhaps less
> ideal than simple faith, but they are also less liable to be imposed upon
> by superstition; and they are certainly better adapted to the spirit of our
> times. By their aid we shall accomplish the greatest amount of good,
> even though it be at the expense of the poetic in life.[2]

In his theology lecture notes at the Catholic University in Washington,
Ryan would link the inheritance of rationalism with political liberalism, "modern liberties," the secularization of government in the
schools and family life, and the social ills of the age.[3] While Hughes
and Spalding and Hecker and Keane had battled with rationalism
only in its religious dress, Ryan felt that it permeated the atmosphere.
His response was all that much more vehement.

In the same way as Vatican Council I, which had affirmed both
that God could be known by reason and that faith was a supernatural
gift, Ryan reacted to the intellectual climate by emphasizing reason
as a legitimate avenue of truth; but he also argued that Christ was
needed to teach what even the "Greeks and Romans" had failed to
grasp. A knowledge of truth that was at once natural and superna-

tural—within reason and above reason—became a central structure of his thinking. In response to contemporary currents, he wrote, "the immutable principles of the divine and natural law had to be established by reason and authority. The principles of morals have to be applied to the new economic, physiological, and political questions. The separation between morals and politics has to be combatted." Ryan experienced a secularization that Hughes, in the public school debate of the 1840s, had only sensed.[4]

In this context, the structure of Ryan's religious thinking tended to divorce reason and faith, while trying to protect both. His apologetics, for example, became one of facts and proof texts; the resurrection proved "faith to be reasonable." "Our faith is based upon knowledge. We have faith in Christ because we have the knowledge of the Resurrection." Reason and knowledge dwelt together at the center of experience, at the expense, as he had noted, "of the poetic in life." "The Christian," he wrote, "knows with infallible certainty what he is, where he comes from, whither he is moving, and how he ought to live."[5] Faith, on the other hand, came as a gift from a God who could only be "reasoned about at a distance." It was "bestowed only upon those who have the proper dispositions of heart and will. Men must have the will to accept and embrace the truth at any sacrifice of prejudice, comfort, or affection." Significantly, Ryan associated faith with the heart and affections, and knowledge with the intellect. Faith and reason were not so much interrelated, as they had been for Hecker, as juxtaposed. The conflict with secularism was making a more profound impact than Ryan supposed.[6]

The plight of the worker and the growth of socialism were other major forces shaping Ryan's religious experience. In some respects, he inherited the identification with the worker characteristic of the immigrant church and articulated by Hughes and Brownson in 1844. But a world of experience and change separated the generations. Ryan's identification, stripped of the personal romanticism that had led Hughes to equate Christ with the poor and Brownson to emphasize the sentiments of associationism, was articulated in terms of the virtue of justice. His lifelong struggle to right the social order took on the tone of workmanlike analysis. "What a world is this of ours!" he wrote in his journal. "We struggle and strive, and plod and plot day by day, often for years without adequate recompense." He repeated similar sentiments in a sermon on self-denial, the spirit of which would have been unknown to Hughes or Hecker:

> Suffering is also the law of life for society. We are assured that throughout the world of living things there is carried on a constant struggle for existence, in which only the fittest survive. Now the very words "struggle"

and "survival" suggest that social life is maintained only at the cost of pain. No discontent and no suffering in society mean stagnation and retrogression. Consider the matter from another point of view. The law of progress for the human race is the moral law. The better the moral law is observed the greater will be the meaning of human advancement. And every violation of the moral law, every sin that is committed, is a check to humanity's onward march. Think of any sin that you will, trace out its consequences as far as you can, and you will conclude that human society would occupy a higher place today if that sin were unknown. But to avoid sin, to obey the moral law, costs us inconvenience, pain, suffering, therefore, social life and social progress are impossible.[7]

Ryan, while inheriting the mantle of social criticism, also inherited the fruits of policies of Americanization; the competitive industrialism that he rejected had entered into his very self-perception.

Early twentieth-century socialism also contributed to Ryan's religious understanding. Following Leo XIII, Ryan argued that socialism throws aside "religious discipline, scorns duties and clamours only for rights." Yet he did not reject it completely; he tried rather to draw a fine line between materialistic socialism, the evils of individualism, and Leo's teaching on the right to private property. The significant issue for the spiritual life, he believed, was the need in the face of so many conflicting opinions and so much social unrest to establish an authoritative teacher of moral conduct. How, in fact, could a person *know* what to *do?* Fortunately, Ryan preached, Christ made the truths of individual, family, and social life absolutely clear. Following Christ, the Christian would not become a cog in a machine but could "decide for himself the kind of life that he shall live in the hereafter." In this way, the law of Christ mediated the true values of socialism but preserved the dignity of the individual. Given the industrial problem and the need to combat radical socialism, *action* became for Ryan, as it had been earlier for Hecker, Brownson, and Keane, a criterion of faith; but he differed from them in the deeply moralistic tone of his position. "To know the truth and to live the right life," he wrote, "are the deepest and noblest and most enduring of man's aspirations. Truth and righteousness are the only ends worth seeking in this earthly life."[8]

In addition to combating the intellectual issues of rationalism and the social forces spawned by industrialism, Ryan also fought religious liberalism. In his journal he compared the Protestant and Catholic faiths, arguing that the former was "a splendid effort of the human mind to appreciate religious truth." Ryan believed that the most vital Protestantism of his day equated religion with humanitarianism. In a sermon on Jesus curing the leper (Matt. 8:2), he noted the Lord's compassion but argued that God became man not to look after bodily comforts but to save souls. A philanthropic view of Christianity was wrong. Jesus suffered because "he wished to reopen heaven for men, to show mankind how to suffer, and to make full reparation for Adam's disobedience, and thus give to the world an idea of the awful enormity of sin."

At this point, Ryan's battle with philanthropy joined his polemic against rationalism to provide a certain structure to his religious experience, a structure emphasizing the distance between reason and faith, body and soul. This represented a spiritualization that Hughes and Spalding would have found strange, and Hecker and Keane unacceptable. They had not battled with liberal Protestantism but with evangelicalism and Transcendentalism. For them, Christ had come not to "save souls or teach men how to suffer" but either to provide some consolation or to build the kingdom.[9]

Fourth, two major difficulties within the Catholic body itself divided Ryan's experience from that of his predecessors. Reared on the doctrine of *Rerum Novarum*, Leo XIII's encyclical addressing the problems of capital and labor, Ryan always argued the necessity of individual Catholics actively engaging in social affairs. He severely criticized the tendency to practice the spiritual life without the "practical duties of justice and charity." The Lord, he preached, insisted on the keeping of the commandments: "He wishes men to *work* out their salvation." Belief, profession, and the observing of pious forms without good deeds were only the shell of religion.[10] As a second major issue, Ryan identified what he called "moral autonomism" prevalent in the community. Influenced by political and industrial freedom and the principle of private judgment, Catholics, he complained,

> are *to some degree practical* autonomists. That is to say, they acknowledge the teaching and governing authority of the Church as a general proposition, and accept on her authority many doctrines and precepts which they do not fully understand, and yet refuse to be in compliance with, certain other beliefs and commandments which do not seem to them reasonable.[11]

Hughes and Spalding and Hecker and Keane had criticized Protestantism for dividing faith from works and had lauded the Catholic principle of authority in opposition to private judgment. The argument had enabled them, in different ways, to pursue Americanization. Ryan, fifty years later, needed to turn the same polemic against his fellow believers. The difference in the community—its individualism and lack of social concern—was a crucial element in the formation of early twentieth-century Catholic spiritual life. Ryan's enemies, to some extent, lived within his own house.

John A. Ryan clearly shared many of the characteristics of the faith with his immigrant and Americanist predecessors: with the immigrant tradition, an emphasis on the structures of the institutional church and a concentration on the moral law as a guide to life; with the Americanist tradition, a passion for social reform and the desire to create an active lay apostolate; with both, a desire to unite faith and works, a critique of capitalism, an identification with the worker, and an argument for the compatibility of Catholicism and American society. Yet contemporary trends in philosophical rationalism, the social question, liberal Protestantism, and the Catholic community itself differentiated Ryan's Catholic experience from that of his predecessors. He battled not so much with Protestantism as with a secular society. He presupposed in the Catholic community an individualism and division of faith from works that would have surprised his predecessors.

Influenced by rationalism and the very industrialism he criticized, Ryan's view of life took on a reasonable, moralistic, and dutiful tone not present to the same degree in his romantic predecessors. Last, he divided reason from faith, nature from grace, and body from soul with a new sharpness. These elements gave his spiritual life a shape that allowed for some continuity while enabling it to be responsive to a changing environment. The theological framework that he used to integrate all of these characteristics, and which in turn shaped his understanding and practice of the Christian life, must now be briefly examined.

Scholastic moral theology provided the basic structure for John Ryan's understanding of the spiritual life. Thomas Bouquillon (1840–1902), a leading proponent of the revival initiated by Leo XIII, was his major professor at the Catholic University of America. When Ryan returned to the seminary at Saint Paul, he relied on Bouquillon and presented an approach to religion that essentially followed Thomas Aquinas as mediated through Francisco Suárez, Aquinas's sixteenth-century commentator. Ryan took the same approach after he became professor at Washington in 1915. He defined religion as a potential part of the virtue of justice. "A person is said to have religion or to be religious," he wrote, "if he fulfills all the duties which religion imposes." On God's part, religion signified absolute dominion; on man's part, total dependency. The habit of religion encompassed all of the acts of worship: devotion, adoration, prayer, sacrifice, use of the sacraments, and so on. Following Aquinas and Suárez, Ryan argued that the individual possessed one final end, supernatural beatitude, but that there also existed intermediate ends, demanding only the use of reason and natural law, on which people could cooperate.

The final, supernatural end could only be obtained through grace that lifted the person to a new plane of being.[12]

An important component of Ryan's acceptance of an intermediate (natural) and final (supernatural) end to human acts was his understanding of the church and society. Following Leo XIII's encyclicals, Ryan defined the church as "an organized group of persons connected with one another, and with the head of the society"; "a perfect society, having within itself all the authority and means necessary for legislation." Divinely constituted by God, the church was supernatural in its ends and instruments, universal and necessary, perfect and independent. Civil society was also instituted by God but only as a necessary part of a reasonable and well-ordered life. Its ends were temporal, concerned with intermediate, natural goals.[13]

Several significant consequences for the understanding and practice of the spiritual life flowed from Ryan's adoption of the framework of moral theology. First, this concept placed all relationships in a juridical context: Creator to creature, church to society, person to person. Thus acts of religion were acts of justice expressing a person's duty. "Again, we cannot live upright lives without God's grace," Ryan preached, "and grace is given principally through the sacraments. If we do not approach the sacraments frequently, we are neglecting one of our principal duties." When discussing hope and charity as theological virtues, the moralist argued that the precept of charity obligated a person as soon as the obligation to love God above all things was understood.[14]

Second, given the definition of church as a supernatural society, Ryan emphasized the sanctity of ecclesiastical laws. The law was intrinsically perfect from the moment of its promulgation; it proceeded from Christ and its power did not depend on reception by the faithful or by civil society. It produced an obligation in conscience; any law directed to a divine end was gravely obligatory. Ryan offered the following commentary on the practice of the Christian life:

> When the end is very useful or morally necessary and the law is very conducive, we have grave matter. E.g. public service of God, penance, sanctification; to these ends the observation of festivals, abstinence and fasting are very conducive. Similarly, in regard to celibacy, the recitation of the breviary, the celebration of the Mass for faithful.

Finally, "since the end of the Church is internal sanctification, it can quite properly command internal acts."[15] Underlying much of Ryan's emphasis on law, obligation, and internal assent was a presupposition that the church, composed of individuals, could only be unified through the power of law. Given Ryan's emphasis on human action and obedience to moral law, this juridical conception of the church led to what has been described as "muscular Christianity." Ryan's view shared a common root with the immigrant church's "purgative way" but could more properly be termed an "ecclesiastical athleticism."

As might be expected, given the inheritance of the "purgative way," the moralist balanced his emphasis on juridical relationships and legal obligations with a strong devotional life, especially devotion to the Eucharist. The Sacrament, Ryan preached, realized fully the aim of union and love: "His heart becomes knit to our heart, His soul to our soul, so that He *lives* in us and we, in Him." In the Eucharist Jesus experienced the pleasure of doing us good, showering favors upon us, and feeding us. The Eucharist also "preserves us from mortal sins by curbing our passions, and by strengthening us against the assaults of temptation. Thus we are enabled to overcome our besetting sin, to restrain our violent desires, and to keep our souls pure, and tranquil, and strong."[16] A stronger combination of ecclesiasticism and personal communion could not be imagined. Devotionalism thus remained a significant element in Ryan's spiritual life, even while his synthesis lacked the organic quality associated with the immigrant church's "communion of saints."

A final consequence of Ryan's perspective should be noted. He clearly accepted Leo XIII's definition of the relationship between the church and society and indicated this acceptance when he talked about intermediate and final ends to human actions. This classic position ultimately implied the union of church and state since the supernatural end to which the church directed people subsumed the natural ends of the state. Leo had mentioned union as the most desirable state of affairs in his encyclical to the American hierarchy, *Longinqua Oceani*. Ryan, following the logic of his own position, took the same stance in his 1922 book, *The State and the Church*.[17]

However, in the context of the United States, where separation of church and state, religious liberty, and constitutionalism were the law of the land, Catholics could hardly follow the implications of Leo XIII's teaching. It would have confirmed the worst fears of the nativists, something Leo had recognized in *Testem Benevolentiae* when he noted that he was not condemning "the condition of your commonwealths, or the laws and customs which prevail in them." In the practical situation, Ryan was thus led to take his reasoning in another direction. Instead of emphasizing the dynamic between intermediate and final ends, he followed another statement in Leo XIII's "Christian Constitution of States." The church and the state, he argued, existed in two different spheres. They were, if not separate, at least independent. This interpretation paralleled on a social and institutional level the separation in his thought between faith and reason, grace and nature, soul and body. Existing within this structure, the American Catholic, acknowledging two allegiances, was a citizen of two worlds, an ecclesiastical and a civil one. In areas where the two spheres might overlap, the laws of the supernatural society took precedence. In either case, the primary virtue to be cultivated in the life of the individual was obedience to the divinely constituted authorities.

This dualistic structure of his thinking indicated that John A. Ryan participated in the fundamental fracturing of the American and Catholic identity that had occurred in the crisis of Americanism. Using the intellectual categories offered by moral theology, Ryan fashioned a religious system that allowed for the coexistence of two distinct realms of experience. At the heart of his experience lay the fundamental question: How could the spiritual life, an ecclesiastical affair directed by the church, be related to the concerns of social charity and justice? He labored his whole life to bridge this gap, which he perceived as growing larger in the Catholic consciousness. At times he related the two poles through a concentration on reason and natural law, thus establishing a social ethic common to Catholics and Protestants; at other times, through the agency of the church itself and the growth of her organizations of charity. In both cases the intrinsic relationship between the spiritual life and justice was established through the mediation of law and authority.

The solution that John Ryan proposed to the question of how to be both Catholic and American was not unique. Many of his contemporaries turned to authority and the framework of moral theology to provide a structure for the Christian life. They shared with Ryan an emphasis on duty and a belief in the divine authority of the institutional church as remedies to socialism and individualism. At the same time they had also grown up in the wake of *Testem Benevolentiae* and the confluence of the immigrant, papal, and Americanist traditions. The dilemma confronting Ryan also confronted them, and the fracturing of the spiritual life from justice in society, faith from works, the church from the world, shaped their understanding and experience. Paradoxically, this position, which separated the Catholic and American identities and was designed to protect the structures and truth of Catholicism, promoted at the same time the secularization of thought and the accommodation of the church to the practical, worldly values of society. Given this background, the Catholics of the 1960s and the 1970s would need to struggle for an integration that could somehow discover the sacred within the secular. But before the forerunners of those changes can be examined, two of the more vital spiritual movements, indicative of the position of Ryan and his contemporaries, need to be examined.

CHAPTER
13
The Eucharist, Symbol of the Church

᷍᷍᷍

$\mathcal{E}$merging from the devotional revival in the second half of the nineteenth century, the eucharistic movement was the most vital spiritual movement of the first fifty years of twentieth-century American Catholicism. The growth of tabernacle societies between 1865 and 1888 has already been noted, and the late nineteenth century also witnessed the flourishing of devotions and associations to promote the centrality of the Eucharist in Catholic life. Nocturnal adoration groups, begun in Boston (1882), Baltimore (1884), and New York (1891), were officially organized by 1903. In 1893 Propaganda Fide issued a rescript for the Confraternity of Perpetual Adoration. These groups, whose primary purpose was "to adore the divine Lord in the Sacrament of His love and to make reparation for the many indignities offered this Holy Sacrament by ungrateful mankind," promoted frequent communion, attendance at benediction, visits to the Blessed Sacrament, and eucharistic processions.[1] The practice of forty hours became a major social event in New York in the last quarter of the nineteenth century. At the appointed time, "the priests gathered at the place of celebration, to preach, to hear the innumerable confessions, to carry out the ceremonies; the people attended in such large crowds as made hard labor necessary; and in the intervals of labor the assembled clergy discussed the passing history of the Church, the points of pastoral theology, and the local conditions."[2] Eventually, the People's Eucharistic League grew out of smaller associations in New York parishes. Its monthly organ, *The Sentinel of the Blessed Sacrament*, first appeared in January 1898. Ten thousand people had joined by the following year. By 1904 the league included one hundred parishes and twelve thousand members. Father Francis Xavier Lasance, spiritual director of the Tabernacle Society in Cincinnati, compiled one of its most popular prayer books, *Visits to Jesus in the Tabernacle: Hour and Half-hours of Adoration Before the Blessed Sacrament* (1898).[3]

During the same period, the priestly identity of the clergy also came to be more and more focused on the Eucharist. In 1887 Father Bede Maler, O.S.B., of Saint Meinrad's Abbey, Indiana, came across the Statutes of the Priests' Eucharistic League, a movement begun by the French cleric Pierre Julian Eymard (1811–1868) to promote the interests of the Blessed Sacrament. Under Maler's direction, the league grew in the midwestern United States. The first convention, attended by 6 bishops and 150 priests, was held at Notre Dame in 1894. There were five more general conventions between 1897 and 1920, and four regional ones in the next decade. The purposes of the Priests' Eucharistic League with its periodical *Emmanuel* (January 1895) were twofold: to sanctify "the priesthood by an increase of practical faith in and efficient love for Eucharistic God in our own hearts"; and to benefit the flock by interchange on the best way to reach the hearts of people. Within four years almost 2,000 people belonged to the league; by 1929, 50 percent of the priests in the United States belonged, and *Emmanuel* boasted of 100,000 affiliates.[4]

The league's most enduring legacy, supported by the reforms of Leo XIII and Pius X, was the sponsorship of five National Eucharistic Congresses between 1895 and 1911. These gatherings foreshadowed the much larger and more impressive International Eucharistic Congress at Chicago in 1926, and four more national convocations between 1930 and 1941. A good portion of the league's practical thrust can be gathered from the resolutions passed at the Third National Eucharistic Congress in 1904. The assembly challenged pastors to encourage the people to attend mass, not just on Sundays and holy days but also on weekdays; to keep churches open for daily visits; to recommend frequent communion; to correct the apparent irreverence shown the sacrament; to preach regularly on eucharistic subjects; to support devotion to the Blessed Sacrament in seminaries; and to establish the People's Eucharistic League in their parishes.[5]

A study of the church in Boston indicates that this eucharistic revival had far-reaching effects. Signs of the revival included an increase in the frequency of daily mass during Lent, the reception of holy communion several times a week, visits to the Blessed Sacrament, the establishment of confraternities in each parish, and increased membership in nocturnal adoration societies. In 1922 Boston counted 2 million daily communions; 4 million on first Fridays and feast days.[6]

Looking back at fifty years of work, the editor of *Emmanuel* attributed much of this increased devotion all over the United States to the Priests' Eucharistic League.[7]

What did all this interest in eucharistic devotion mean? How did it reflect and contribute to the culture of the Catholic community? Given the enormous success of the movement and the tremendous numbers of organizations and literary activities that supported it, its understanding of the Eucharist may be taken as indicative of the structures that dominated Catholic spiritual life in the twentieth century. The whole phenomenon was a symbol of the church, its self-perception and struggle for identity in American society. The overall significance can be seen by examining the movement's understanding of the priesthood and the relationship between the spiritual life and social reform.

The understanding of the priesthood in the Eucharistic League reflected the prevailing concentration in the United States on the structures of the institutional church. After the Civil War, a movement for priests' rights, the adoption of the Roman collar, the founding of periodicals specifically directed to the clergy, the celebration of ordination anniversaries, and the call for the dedication of Pentecost as a special feast honoring the clergy reflected a growing awareness of role differentiation within the Body of Christ. There also appears to have been a concern about the clergy's financial state and need for financial acumen. "The American priest," William Stang wrote in his *Pastoral Theology*, "does not comply with the requirements of his position by preaching and administering the sacraments: he must be a successful manager of church revenues, the sacred offerings of the faithful." The clergy were both spiritual and temporal lords.[8] Their ministry was established to communicate to people the sanctity of God: "To these ministers He gave all His doctrine, the whole Gospel, and secured to them its possession. He gave them a Sacrifice and Sacraments for the sake of His people, He made them priests, dispensers of the mysteries of God, and rulers of His church." The eucharistic revival symbolized, in this context, the triumph of the "reign of Christ on earth, the Church which he founded on the primacy of Peter."[9] The alliance established during the period between Sacred Heart devotion and the Eucharist reinforced this institutional view.[10]

The Priests' Eucharistic League embodied the spiritual heart of this ecclesiological vision. When joining the movement, the clergy were encouraged to "visit and adore the Blessed Sacrament, in order to hasten by their supplications the triumph of the church, to expiate the sacrileges of unfortunate priests, and to promote among the faithful a tender devotion to our Lord in the adorable Eucharist."[11] Numerous authors described the priest in glowing terms of spiritual identity. He was a "shepherd of souls," a "sign of contradiction," an *"alter Christus,"* a mediator standing between the people and the altar. Like Mary, he was overshadowed by the Holy Spirit; like Joseph, he was the guardian of the Lord. The priest and the Blessed Sacrament were correlative terms. During his weekly hour of meditation, the priest could offer himself as a victim, expiate for the sins of others, and avert the anger of the infinite. His vocation was the most exalted one on earth. "Holy Mass," one author wrote, "is the celebration of that mystery wherein the priest by the word of consecration changes the substance of bread into the Body of our Lord and the substance of wine in the Blood of our Lord, with all the rites and ceremonies that accompany the sacred act."[12] Through proper thanksgivings before and after mass, visits to the Blessed Sacrament, and consistent adoration, the priest could go to his "Faithful Friend, the Prisoner of the Tabernacle, and commune with Him, heart to heart, mind to mind, and thus find solace in this vale of tears."[13]

The priest's closeness to the "Divine Captive" and the "Tenant of the Tabernacle" demanded a certain style of sanctity. His words were to be ever grave and instructive, "dignified and discreet," both in and outside of the pulpit. In his dealings with people the priest could never abstract from his sacred calling. A model of holiness, his life contrasted sharply with the feuds, fraud, oppression, and turbulence of the world of the laity. In all actions, the "ambassador of Christ" was bound by the rules of ritual cleanliness. "In building a beautiful Church," H. J. Heuser wrote, the Catholic priest "makes his measure of utility the greater glory of God; but the measure of God's greater glory is to him the liturgical law of the Church." The dignity of the priestly office required the "purity of an angel." As one who took and consumed *"hostiam puram, hostiam sanctam, hostiam immaculatam,"* the priest should lead a mortified and watchful life. His holiness consisted, above all, in two things: "purity, which separates from everything that may stain; firmness in virtue, which cannot be obtained but by unison with the sovereign good, which is God."[14]

The presence of our Lord in the white host of the Blessed Sacrament reinforced the exalted and separate nature of the priest's calling. But Jesus was also present in another way. He was there as incarnate food, father, and guide, "who loved the poor preferentially," gave mercy to the erring and repentant, and was kindly to those who suffered. Our Lord loved a hidden life of good works. As *the* priest, he was an obedient and humble servant, zealous for people's smallest needs, taking on their greatest burdens, identifying out of love with their weakness and confusion. Kneeling before the Blessed Sacrament, the priest also proclaimed this Lord as his model. He strove to know "Christ's mind, heart, conduct towards men, methods, and virtues."[15]

Several significant elements in this vision should be noted. First, the eucharistic revival's focus on the purity, obedience, humility, and charity of the "tabernacled Lord"—someone separate from the world but available to it—functioned in the United States during the twentieth century to balance the increasing institutional focus on the priest as both spiritual and temporal "keeper of the keys." While reinforcing their hierarchical role in the community, praying before *Jesus hostia* called the clergy back to the spiritual origin of their authority and power. As long as the Eucharist was there at the center of his life, the priest could be both manager of the school and liturgical leader, voice of revelation and humble servant, paragon of purity and counter of collections. Lived well, his identity was truly a eucharistic one for the creation of the church. Lived poorly, his eucharistic identity became a justification for spiritual and temporal divinity.

Second, the image of the priest as *alter Christus* implied a great deal about the laity within the church. There can be no doubt that they were often pictured as passive recipients of the *ecclesia docens*, consumers, not producers, in the economy of the Eucharist. Their lives, too often marked by poverty, ignorance, and disarray, needed the model life of the priest to promote unity and doctrinal integrity. Exposed as they were to the prevailing Protestant culture and necessarily preoccupied with business interests, the laity's commitment to monthly holy hour, to periodic visits to the Blessed Sacrament, and to nocturnal adoration represented their allegiance to a parochial community and their obedience to its leaders. "The observance of Sunday," one commentator wrote, "the attendance at Mass on the Lord's day is the connecting link between the toilers of the workaday world and the Church which represents Christ on earth."[16]

On the other hand, frequent reception of the Eucharist, the reality of the priest as a model of holiness accessible to them, and their participation in parish confraternities, sowed the seeds among the laity for a more active ecclesiological role. Recognizing this, some of the speakers at the early national congresses, which the laity did not attend in any numbers until 1920, called for a more active participation in the Mass. Walter Elliott discoursed on how the real presence made true missionaries of the laity.[17]

This double function of the eucharistic movement in the life of the church could be clearly seen with respect to the role of women. *Emmanuel* presented the following guidelines for priestly purity:

Holy priests are inflexible on the point of avoiding unnecessary intercourse with persons of the opposite sex. They are dreaded, accused of coldness, blamed for excessive severity: but they are in veneration and a protection to the holiness of the sanctuary. Those who wish to be praised for their nice and pleasing manners, and willingly mingle in conversations with women, should they be pious women, assiduous at church, charitable and devoted to good works, will be the instruments of their own ruin, but not without bringing disgrace upon religion whose ministers they are.[18]

Another author conjured up the image of Delilah and the wife of Uriah to illustrate the dangers of the world.[19] "Woman," Leo XIII wrote, "is by divine counsel and decree of Holy Church, formally excluded from what directly regards the Adorable Body of Christ, in the offering of Holy Mass, the custody of the Blessed Sacrament, the celebration of the Holy Mysteries." She could not serve, touch the vessels, "pass the limits of the Holy of Holies," extend her hand over the eucharistic bread. In short, she had "no part in the act, by which, enveloped in a mysterious cloud of faith and love, the Man-God daily renews upon the altar the divine Holocaust of Calvary."[20] In such a world, the ideal image of female sanctity was the nun, who dispensed "the good things of Christ to a hungering and impatient world." She became "the bursar of heaven," "the half closed tabernacle, where God's presence dwells."[21] She, like the Eucharist and the priest, was the symbol of purity.

Still, as has been noted, the Arch-Confraternity of Perpetual Adoration was controlled by women, gave them a sense of mission beyond the confines of home and parish boundaries, and contributed to the financial and material support of poor churches. Leo XIII commented on this function also:

> Her industrious, her happy piety has, in a certain way, broken down the barriers which separate her from the altar; it is her generous offerings, her apostolic zeal, the labor of her hands, which have prepared the sacred vestment and linens and provided all that pertains to the divine sacrifice, to the august Prisoner of the Tabernacle. . . .
>
> Here is a new horizon opening out before you, pious ladies, a new dignity which elevates you, withdraws you from the crowd; consecrates you more intimately to our Lord; associates you with the grandeur of the Catholic priesthood.[22]

In calling women to frequent reception of the Eucharist and giving them a sense of "God's specialized love," the eucharistic movement also formed the backdrop for a vision of women in church and society that would begin to emerge in the 1930s. For example, what happened when a woman, kneeling before the Blessed Sacrament, prayed:

> My cherished Rabboni, it is sweet to kneel here in Thy presence. It is a joy to know that Thy dear eyes are resting upon me.—that no part of my soul is hidden from Thee.—that every aspiration, every longing, every desire is known to Thee. . . .

I long to be a storehouse from which others may draw the strength and encouragement to reach Thee.

I yearn to be filled with peace so full, that it may overflow into the hearts of others.

I pray that every one who comes near me may be attracted to Thee, my cherished Rabboni. . . .[23]

Could it be that in some way this act of unitive prayer signified that every "Christian is preeminently a living temple of the Godhead in such an intimate way that he [or she] is caught up and associated with the actual life of God himself." For example, Katharine Mary Drexel (1858–1955), founder of the Sisters of the Blessed Sacrament and a great missionary to the native Americans, combined a strong commitment to the institutional church, a pioneering and independent spirit, and contemplative devotion to the Blessed Sacrament.[24]

In summary, the Blessed Sacrament, from this perspective, served as the sign not only of Christ's presence but also of the identity of the priest, the role of the laity, and the place of women. Frequent communion, nocturnal adoration, benediction, and visits to the Blessed Sacrament represented between 1895 and 1930 an ecclesiological vision. Clement Thuente, O.P., stated the issue very clearly at the 1904 National Congress:

> Without the Light of the Tabernacle, the whole Church remains dark and mysterious. The many questions asked; why convent life? why cloistered nuns? why so many devotions? why the celibacy of the priesthood? why the Latin language in the liturgical services? find their final and full explanation in the Real Presence. The tabernacle in the sanctuary of the church is substantially the answer to the "Question Box" in the vestibule of the church.[25]

Simply put, the Prisoner of the Tabernacle was the one who made the church one, holy, catholic, and apostolic.

A second important issue in the eucharistic movement was the relationship between the spiritual life and social reform. From the time of the First Eucharistic Congress in Lille, France, 1881, through the 28th International Congress in Chicago, 1926, the movement carried social and political overtones. As might be expected, the significance varied from country to country. In France, the movement capitalized on the popular interest in pilgrimages, with their political connotations, and widespread discontent with the secularist policies of the government. At Lille, Father Joseph Leman, a converted Jew, argued for the extension of Christ's reign over society and a restoration of the penalties against blasphemy. In 1893 at the Congress of Jerusalem, the delegates heard a stirring call for an act of reparation for blasphemies to be recited throughout the world after benediction. This eventually became universal church law in 1893.[26] Although Leo XIII rejected the excessively monarchist tones of many of the eucharistic adherents, he also linked devotion to the Eucharist to a restoration of the "Christian constitution of states." "Everyone is aware," he wrote in his 1902 encyclical on the Eucharist,

> that no sooner had *the goodness and kindness of God our Saviour appeared* than there at once burst forth a certain creative force which issued in a new order of things and pulsed through all the veins of society, civil and domestic. Hence arose new relations between man and man; new rights and new duties, public and private; henceforth a new direction was given to government, to education, to the arts; and most important of all, man's thoughts and energies were turned towards religious truth and the pursuit of holiness. Thus was life communicated to man, a life truly heavenly and divine.[27]

This life, present in the Eucharist, came through the church. Adoring Christ in the host proclaimed publicly one's belief in the ascendancy of the church over the state.

In the United States it was impossible for the eucharistic movement to take a church-state position similar to its European counterpart. Social issues were noticeably absent from the proceedings of the early congresses. More evident was Leo's charge to pray that "all who differ from us may be brought back to the unity of faith and charity."[28] At the 1895 congress Walter Elliott linked devotion to the Eucharist, conversion to the church, and a missionary laity. "Persuade a Protestant," he charged his listeners, "that his Catholic neighbors have Christ the Lord personally present in the Church building, and what obstacle remains for faith to overcome? By such a soul a Roman dogma of authority, every way easier to believe than the Real presence, will soon be understood and accepted." One of the resolutions of the congress explicitly referred to the return to Christian unity as a purpose of the league's prayers. William Stang at the 1904 congress insisted that it was the "will of Christ that all should belong to His Church, that all should listen to the great White Shepherd in Rome, the visible head of His Church." In this context of the "unsettled mind of [the] modern Protestant world," eucharistic devotion symbolized an active faith in Christ and his doctrine, as that was mediated through the hierarchical church.[29] The primary social activity was proselytism.

The inability of American commentators to express the political and social meaning of eucharistic devotion along the lines used by Leo XIII structured the movement, even more than in Europe, toward the personal sanctification of the priest and the encouragement of individual piety among the people. Thus the movement in the United

States concentrated almost exclusively on the relationship between Jesus and the believer. The Tenant of the Tabernacle was food for a soul, a guest in the heart, a personal friend, a consoling presence. Some groups might recite a liturgical office during nocturnal adoration, but more representative was the popular *Visits to Jesus in the Blessed Sacrament* of Father Fràncis Xavier Lasance (1860–1946). Lasance's work included numerous private meditations and encouraged an allegorical interpretation of the Mass. Although the individual was instructed to identify mystically with the sacrifice of Christ, he or she prayed alone in the body of the church.[30] Similarly, a typical theme of the Priests' Eucharistic League was the Eucharist and the personal life of the clergyman. This individualistic emphasis characterized *Emmanuel* and *The Sentinel of the Blessed Sacrament*.

After 1920 the individualism of the eucharistic movement was significantly modified to include some dimensions of social reform. As one of the influential interpreters of the congresses has noted, eucharistic devotion now became linked to Pius XI's proclamation of Christ as king over individuals and nations. This highlighted the heritage of politics and devotion that had marked the early days of the movement in France.[31] The encyclical *Quas Primas*, December 11, 1925, preceded by six months the 28th International Eucharistic Congress at Chicago. This latter event dramatically shifted the national movement into a more socially self-conscious direction. The Chicago congress, according to one writer, "bids fair to help America to realize its ambition of becoming a Eucharistic people." It accented the supranationalism of the church, created general enthusiasm for "faith in Jesus hostia," demonstrated how effectively the church could use modern means of organization and press coverage to further its message, and interpreted "the genius of American Catholicism to those brought up in the conservatism of older countries."[32] Subsequent national gatherings became mass celebrations of the unity of the Eucharist, Catholicism, and Americanism. For example, at Omaha in 1930, "American flags floated from housetops and buildings;" 60,000 people received communion at Sunday masses; 11,000 watched the governor of Nebraska and the mayor of Omaha receive the apostolic delegate in the local coliseum; Herbert Hoover sent a telegram lauding "the value of spiritual ideals and of religious observance in the life of our nation."[33] Five years later the congress in Cleveland took as its theme "the Eucharist and Catholic Action." Trying to "shake off the memories of individualism," the congress aimed first to quicken Christian life through the Eucharist and then to organize it into action. New Orleans in 1938 and Minneapolis-Saint Paul in 1941 followed a similar pattern. The Eucharist became associated with Catholicism on the march, a phenomenon well-documented by recent historians.[34]

In this context, there were two ways of associating the Eucharist and social reform. First, people concentrated on the practical effects that frequent Communion should have in the life of the individual. The church raised up saints by feeding the soul spiritually, and once fed, the "Catholic instinct" led to the transformation of the world. By bringing the family within the circle of Christ's arms, early and frequent Communion could make the ideal of Christian marriage possible, thus addressing the evils of divorce, birth control, denial of authority, and companionate marriage. A religion "in which matter is taken up and irradiated by the indwelling Presence of the Son of God" was considered the answer to modern materialism.[35] In 1928 *Emmanuel* carried an article on the social value of frequent communion. Through the individual reception of the Eucharist, it was argued, mankind or society is brought nearer to God, finds a remedy for its needs, gathers together on more equal terms, and is assured of its future prosperity, happiness, and ultimate salvation. While attempting to address "society or mankind," the article referred only to Christ's presence in the individual soul. Reform of the person leads to reform of the world.[36]

Emphasizing the Eucharist as sign of the triumphant church became a second way of showing its social function. In Catholic Action, *Jesus hostia* was directly related to the "marvelous organization of Catholic societies." The national congresses in the 1930s took on aspects of a "military movement" fueled by "vigil of battle amid the night-silence of the sanctuary before the Altar of the Eucharistic King."[37] Samuel Stritch, archbishop of Milwaukee, summarized this relationship between eucharistic devotion and social reconstruction in a remarkable speech he gave at New Orleans in 1938. "It would be to miss the full meaning of this Eucharistic congress," he sermonized,

> to rest with the thought that we have come here merely to give eloquent expression to our individual piety and to draw from it profit merely for ourselves. It is the Church of Christ which prays and worships here. . . .
>
> Christ willed that His Church should be coterminous with human society. The Church is His plan of social unity: He asks all men's cooperation in this plan of all men. In it, nations and groups and families and individuals can find true social unity. In this society of Christ we are asked to live and co-operate as men and sons of God. Ours must be the service of man, a reasonable service, and our lives must be commingled organically and supernaturally with His life. In a new sense we are asked to live and have our being in Christ and through Christ.
>
> The Holy Eucharist among the Christian Sacraments is *par excellence* a great social Sacrament, the symbol of true social unity in the Mystical Body of Christ and the pledge of that unity to men of good will.[38]

A vision of a Catholic America, this statement presupposed the social conditions of the 1930s and the struggle against totalitarianism. It was the logical outcome of the principles enunciated at Lille over fifty years before, presumed to be ideal in Leo XIII's encyclicals, and furthered by Pius XI's program of Catholic Action. The Prisoner of the Tabernacle could take on his full significance when church and society were one.

Although the force behind the eucharistic movement dissipated by the end of World War II, its general understanding of the church and the structures that supported a vital spiritual life would continue into the 1950s. For the first half of the century, its Lord of the Tabernacle occupied center place in Catholic spiritual life and embodied the church's dominant self-perception. Symbol of a cultural worldview and presupposing the fractured inheritance endemic to its generation, the eucharistic movement would naturally undergo a sharp decline if not collapse in the tumultuous decade of the 1960s. The same would be true of the other movement so much a part of the spiritual life of the period, Catholic Action.

CHAPTER
14
The Cenacle, Soul of Catholic Action

$\mathcal{R}$ooted in the nineteenth century and designed, as was the eucharistic movement, to reform the mind and heart of the common person, the retreat movement was the second major initiative of organized religious revival to span the first half of twentieth-century American Catholicism. The movement joined spontaneous developments among the laity with organized commitments on the part of dioceses and religious orders to create new mediating institutions in the community. On the part of the laity, the retreat movement built on the foundations established by the voluntary associations of the immigrant church, the parish mission system, the program of the Americanists to involve an active and responsible laity in the mission to America, and the various lay-initiated groupings of the late nineteenth century, such as congresses, fraternal societies, and federations of Catholic societies. The idea for a national retreat movement, as will be seen, originated in New York with the laity themselves (1911). At the same time, Boston Catholics, encouraged by the Passionists, formed an organization constituting a guild of officers and an advisory board for retreats. This later developed into one of the largest and most influential of the lay organizations, the Saint Paul of the Cross Laymen's Retreat League (1926). In Philadelphia, another group, led by John Ferrick, John J. Sullivan, and Richard T. McSorley, sponsored a similar movement. They founded the Laymen's Weekend Retreat League (1921) and purchased an estate in Malvern, Pennsylvania, becoming one of the few lay groups actually to own the retreat house property. Other organizations flourished in Louisville (1921), Los Angeles (1924), Atlantic City (1926), and Wichita (1929). Among the women, guild members became actively associated with the cenacle retreat houses and followed a similar path as the men, with the laity establishing their own system of contacts and groupings.[1]

At the 1910 Eucharistic Congress in Montreal, when he first proposed the retreat movement as a general program of spiritual and social renewal, Terence Shealy, S. J. (1863–1922) described the twentieth century as the "layman's century." The retreat, he argued, was directed to the formation of "a vast army of the true sons of the Church, a strong body of loyal Catholic lay-captains and soldiers." From the very beginning of the movement, its adherents self-consciously heralded the hour of the Catholic laity. If the twentieth century was, as Joseph McSorley described it, the time of the "common person," then the retreat movement was to be the focal point for the development of the laity's American Catholic spiritual identity.[2]

The spontaneous demands came from the laity; the organized response came from the religious orders and dioceses. After the modest beginnings of retreat houses at the initiative of the Religious of the Sacred Heart (Philadelphia, 1847) and the Redemptorists (Baltimore, 1852), the half-century from 1860 to 1910 witnessed the foundation and spread of religious orders dedicated to revitalizing the spiritual life of the laity through the practice of periodic recollection days and retirement from the world to a "place apart." Women's retreats had their beginnings with the Dominican Congregation of Saint Catherine de Ricci, founded in 1880 by Lucy Eaton Smith; in 1893 the Religious of the Cenacle began work in New York; and in 1908 a convent was founded in that city by the Society of Mary Reparatrix. By 1936, 22 permanent houses hosted 267 enclosed retreats and served over 11,000 women; by 1954, 46 houses reached over 65,000 people; and within the next decade 24 additional houses had been established. For the men, the Passionists began retreats for high-school students in 1860; by the 1890s the Jesuits and the Society of the Divine Word had pioneered foundations in Louisiana, Ohio, and Illinois. In the early twentieth century, San Francisco (1903), New York (1911), and Boston (1911) boasted similar establishments. By 1929 the number of men's retreat houses had grown to 55. A survey taken in 1939 indicated that 59 of the 110 houses polled reported a total of 2,340 retreats in the previous decade with an attendance of 131,004. The twenty years after World War II saw the establishment of thirty more diocesan centers, and in 1965 a total of 176 houses served 189,000 men and 70,000 youth.[3]

In the retreat movement, clergy, religious, and laity cooperated to shape twentieth-century spirituality not only on the local level but nationally as well. The First National Congress of the Laymen's Retreat League was held in Philadelphia in 1928; 51 delegates representing 15 centers attended. The following year 27 centers were represented. By 1962 the national leaders, laymen and priests, had gathered nineteen times. The First National Conference of the Women's Retreat Movement, attended by over 800 women and representing 14 states and 11 permanent houses, met for the first time in 1936. This national organization met 11 times between 1937 and 1955. Both men's and women's organizations hosted regional conferences as well. After Vatican Council II, Retreats International was formed (1972) and the men's and women's divisions were combined in 1977.[4]

The whole retreat movement, in its numerical and financial growth, its propertied base, organization, and close cooperation between laity, religious orders, and priests reflected the growth of the American Catholic community and its development, in the first half of the twentieth century, of relative stability and economic security. The significance of this movement for the underlying structures of Catholic spiritual life, then, cannot be ignored. Although its complete history remains to be written, the structures of the spiritual reform can be discovered by examining the origins of the national organization in New York in 1911 and then discussing how the movement coalesced with the papal program of Catholic Action. Examined under these two aspects, it is clear that the movement as a whole reflected the fractured spiritual inheritance that lay at the heart of the community's twentieth-century religious experience.

A FRACTURED SPIRITUALITY: AMERICAN AND CATHOLIC

When the first Congress of the Laymen's Retreat League met in 1928, the speakers traced the origins of the national movement to the work of Father Terence Shealy, S.J., and some prominent Catholic laity of New York. Shealy, who had received a bachelor's degree from the Royal University in Ireland, immigrated to the United States and entered the Jesuit novitiate at Frederick, Maryland, in 1886. He studied philosophy at Woodstock College and, after teaching at Fordham University and Holy Cross College, returned to Woodstock for theology and ordination. The Jesuit spent a good part of his life (1902–1922) at Saint Francis Xavier College, Fordham, where he taught jurisprudence and medical ethics. Like John A. Ryan, he set himself resolutely against the laissez-faire individualism of nineteenth-century liberalism and argued for the importance of government and law in controlling human greed. Sharing, as did Ryan, many of the socialists' criticisms of industrial capitalism, Shealy also rejected their solutions. Instead, he supported a return to the natural law tradition of Thomas Aquinas and his Counter Reformation Jesuit commentators, Robert Bellarmine and Francisco Suárez. Like many of his generation, the Jesuit combined his ethical convictions with a "reasoned appreciation of everything American."[5]

In 1912 Shealy summarized the social context for his thinking in an address to the New York Catholic Club on "Socialism and Its Dangers to American Institutions." In graphic terms, the Jesuit referred to the pauperization of labor, the concentration of wealth in the hands of a few, unregulated competition, the "cut-throat economy of supply and demand," and the oligarchy of capital that dominated the social scene. He believed that such a situation spawned a climate in which socialism could flourish. To counteract this possibility, Shealy argued that if the tenets of socialism were adopted, they would destroy the "right to private property—a right enshrined in the common sense of the Fathers," erect a work-state for the "superman of the future," and destroy the "natural law of right and wrong." In tones every bit as critical as Hughes, Brownson, and Ryan before him, Shealy rejected every attempt, whether capitalist or socialist, to reduce the person to the level of the machine. "In the light of the materialistic conception of history, or economic determinism," he wrote,

> according to which the whole soul-life of man in all its social, political, moral and religious concepts is nothing but the response of material stimuli and necessarily changing with changing economic conditions, the charter of our liberty, our rights, natural, inherent and inalienable, are not worth the paper they are written on. And the common sense of the Fathers, so far from being clear intuitions of original justice, and the strong consciousness of natural law, is but the necessary resultant of industrial development in the British colonial system.

In concluding his address, Shealy pointed to one last evil of socialism: its externalism, the looking for the causes of things "in external conditions and environment." In contrast, he noted, "the law of the heart is life's supreme determinant and unless the heart be vitalized, unless men are educated to the discipline of self-control from within, State control from without cannot save us."[6] As the spiritual source for this social reconstruction, Shealy turned to the retreat.

Coming from the nineteenth-century tradition of Jesuit mission preachers and within the context of the emergence of the retreat movement in Belgium, France, Germany, Ireland, and England, Shealy had always been interested in strengthening the spiritual life of the laity through the adaptation of the *Spiritual Exercises* of Ignatius of Loyola to a weekend experience. He believed that by spending this short time in "instruction, meditation and prayer, away from the 'grind' and perplexities of business, worldly cares and the distractions of everyday life" people could develop true Christian character.[7] These personal interests coincided with the demands of the laity themselves when, in 1909, Sidney Finlay, the secretary of Fordham's Xavier Alumni Society, requested that the Jesuit superior appoint a retreat master to work with lay people. Shealy was chosen. He conducted the first retreat at Fordham, July 9, 1909, and from then until late December, 175 men participated in the weekend events. In 1910, nineteen retreats were given to 300 men, and Shealy responded by calling for the general "revitalization of the Catholic heart" through the retreat movement.[8]

United through Shealy's leadership, the laity began to organize. In 1911, a "committee on organization," consisting of prominent Catholic laymen formed the Laymen's League for Retreats and Social Studies. Its purpose, reflecting Shealy's interests, was twofold: to establish the yearly retreat based on the spiritual exercises as a "feature of Catholic life in this country" and to study the social question. The league obtained an estate on Staten Island, renamed it Mount Manresa, and began the first retreat on September 8, 1911. Two months later the league opened the school of social studies at Fordham University Law School. This school, designed explicitly to train lay leaders to apply Christian social principles to current economic problems, inaugurated a series of lectures given by Shealy, John A. Ryan, and influential laymen. The leaders were then expected to go out to spread the message in secular organizations of both men and women, as well as to parochial societies and clubs. In conjunction with the school, the league established the Social Reform Press, published *The Common Cause* (1912–1913), and a weekly paper, "The Live Issue." Although the publications were short-lived, the school itself was affiliated in 1915 to the Fordham University school of sociology and social sciences, of which Shealy became the dean. Throughout this period he continued to give retreats in the eastern United States. It was from the two centers in which he labored most extensively, New York and Philadelphia, that the leadership emerged for the organization of the First National Convention of the Laymen's Weekend Retreat League. By 1928 what had begun as a small spark had thus become a roaring fire.[9]

In forming the laymen's league, both Terence Shealy and the lay people under his influence adopted a certain approach to the spiritual life, one that reflected the fractured inheritance of twentieth-century American Catholicism. While accepting the ecclesiastical framework and intellectual categories offered by Leo XIII's Thomistic revival and the social philosophy implied in *Rerum Novarum*, they also adopted wholeheartedly the constitutional separation of church and state and the principles embodied in the Declaration of Independence. This combination of traditions forced them to affirm the separate integrity of both Catholicism and Americanism and then to struggle to unite their religious life with their social responsibility. The underlying dynamic was the same as that which had shaped the life of John A. Ryan and the course of the eucharistic movement, and it formed the basis of Shealy's and the laity's understanding of spirituality.

On the one hand, within the context of the separation of church and state, Shealy and the Catholic writers of *The Common Cause* affirmed the independence of the natural order. The context of socialist unrest contributed to this almost secularized emphasis on nature and nature's God by impressing on Shealy and others the necessity of cooperation among all people if the right of private property and the sanctity of the family were to be protected. In his conference Shealy extolled the ideals of citizenship and individual rights. " 'I am an American citizen,' is a proud boast," he preached, "and in this certainty we may have a justifiable pride—that we are citizens of a land whose mercy and justice have ever made her a haven for the oppressed. . . ."[10] In a similar fashion, *The Common Cause* eschewed sectarianism and emphasized the natural virtues. "Its mission," the editors acknowledged,

> is not to parties or systems as such, either to advocate, defend or uphold, but rather to declare Right, Truth, Honesty, Justice, Righteousness, Purity, Brotherhood, Freedom, Kindness, Charity, believing that the real success of nations as well as of individuals is built upon these foundations and principles, and that all social reforms to be enduring and successful, must not ignore them nor violate them.[11]

The result of such a position, as it had been with Ryan, was a structure of thought that tended to separate reason and faith, the natural and the supernatural, the secular and the sacred. Thus, in his conference on "citizenship," Shealy paralleled but did not unite the duties, privileges, and rewards of being an American with those under the "Constitutions of Christianity."

On the other hand, building on the ecclesiological inheritance of the immigrant church and Leo XIII, Shealy and the laity combined this emphasis on the integrity of the natural order with an equally strong focus on a separate Catholic identity. The same people who could write for *The Common Cause* could also live in a religious world that extolled the supremacy of Catholicism. In his 1910 address Shealy summarized the basic principles of the retreat movement in four major points:

1. The Retreat Movement for laymen has the warmest blessing and

God-speed of our Holy Father, and of all the bishops and pastors under whose jurisdiction and favor it has been instituted.

2. It is a wondrous instrument of Divine Providence for the saving of the Catholic layman, amid the grave and peculiar dangers which beset our modern life.

3. It is a great social force directly leading to Catholic union and organization, in an age of serious and threatening social problems.

4. It is a great spiritual power-house from which the parish and its various societies and clubs draw new strength and vitality, and the Altar is made the Mountain of life by the frequentation of the Sacraments.

Shealy's description was clear: the retreat, like the nineteenth-century mission, was designed to create a stronger and more organized institutional church. The Jesuit referred to the pope, bishops, and pastors who possessed jurisdiction; the social force of Catholic unions and organizations; the renewal of the parish and other societies. He presented examples from France and Belgium where the retreat had fostered the practice of frequent communion, thus joining the movement with the eucharistic revival. He explicitly named the Knights of Columbus, the Central Verein, the Saint Vincent de Paul Society, and the Holy Name Society as having grasped the idea of retreat most readily.[12]

Shealy showed a similar emphasis on the hegemony of the church when he lectured at the opening of the school of social studies. "There is no power on earth to compare with" the church of God, he said. "She has the widest experience, meeting with men in every age and directing them in all their understandings. Kneeling down at her clinic, knowing all the diseases, and applying the medicine to all the Social Ills. That is the Teacher we are going to have." Among the laity, the same people who could praise the Declaration of Independence also relied on papal statements as the authoritative answer to the social and religious questions of humanity.[13]

It was not surprising, given this dual affirmation of Catholicism and Americanism, that the laymen's league with Shealy's leadership founded Mount Manresa, the school for social studies, and the Social Reform Press. The retreat house was a place where Catholics, separated from the world, could gather together to pray, celebrate the sacraments, and listen to the voice of the institutional church. *The Common Cause* was a publication, basically secular in tone and spirit, that tried to unite people under the banner of Americanism. In between lay the school for social studies, "designed to train a body of lecturers in a thorough knowledge of Socialism and send them out among the Catholic societies to tell Catholic men and women the truth about Socialism."[14] The three institutions portrayed in a symbolic way the fracturing of spirituality from social reform in the civic forum and in the life of the person. Spirituality and society could only be united through the agency of a Catholic organization: a parish, a pious society, a union, an educational institution. To be integral, a person needed to belong to all three institutions.

Within this basic structure, Shealy and the laymen's league struggled to establish a spiritual identity that could unite the separate spheres of existence. They did this by placing at the center of their lives, as had John A. Ryan, those values that could promote both the ecclesiological integrity of the perfect society and the demands of American society. Thus "duty," "character," "law," and "work" were exalted as the most ennobling traits of the Christian. This perspective surfaced in Shealy's conferences to both women and men.

In one of his reflections to the women at Marymount College, Tarrytown-on-Hudson, Shealy commented on the Pauline phrase, "whatever a man shall sow, that also shall he reap." The preacher began by noting that the harvest time of the world was at hand. It was clear that the seeds of sin, sown long ago, had borne a "horrible fruition": the diversity of sects, impurity, the greed for gold and power, the world war. "There is a law," Shealy preached,

> God's law stamped in Nature, that governs life itself. It is the law of sowing and reaping. Men sow the seeds in the bosom of the earth, and when the smiling days are done, when chill and dark are about to come again upon the fields, men reap the harvest, and garner it into their granaries. Year after year they sow and reap,—and God's law never changes. And as the moving centuries creep on, and the kindly earth moves on, then in happiness and thanksgiving man reaps the fruits of the field.

The Jesuit then asked the audience to look at their hearts, to "examine your character. Who had made you cranky, mean or sour, and the plaything of passion? God has not made you thus. You have made yourself into this harvest. You have reaped what you had sown." Instead, Shealy challenged his listener, if the law of God guided life, then "when winter comes and strips you of earth's best gifts, you shall reap in gladness what you sowed."[15] This emphasis on initiative and strength of character typified Shealy's preaching to the young women. Catholic women possessed "character," and "character" meant good citizenship.

Given this approach, which so linked Catholic and American values while at the same time separating them, it was inevitable that the primary feminine virtues advocated by Shealy both accepted the present status of women in society and also stressed the "ideal" nature of the Catholic woman. Shealy described the young women who had enrolled themselves under the banner of Mary in the following terms:

> Now, you must all one day take your places among the women of the world, many of whom have a far different ideal of life from that which you, and Children of Mary, possess. It is then that the real strength of your character will be tried as gold in the fire; then it is we shall see whether your promise to Christ was sincere or not. To retain the modesty of Mary in the midst of a society which has lost the blush of shame; to persevere in the simple truths of the Church, when new ideas and religions are being taken up on all sides; to keep your place in the home when other women are entering the lists of politics and civic affairs to the detriment of their first obligation to their home and family—all these are tests by which you may know if you are still living up to the ideals which were instilled into your hearts as Children of Mary.[16]

The link that Shealy made between personal modesty, the truth of the church, and confinement to the home was highly significant. From a social point of view, such an ideal was in conflict with the campaign of the radical socialists and suffragettes. But taken ecclesiastically, if Mary is understood as a symbol of the church, then the ideal is seen as reinforcing strong external boundaries (mixing in society, relationships to Protestants) for Catholic self-identity. Combined with Shealy's emphasis on the "manly" virtues, such an ideal corresponded to the definition of the church as a perfect society and implied a spiritual life structured by two separate but compatible Catholic and American identities.

Shealy's presentation of virtues compatible with American society to his men retreatants was also indicative of his compartmentalization of identities. Thomas F. Woodlock, a prominent member of the laymen's league, noted that instead of following the schema typical of the Ignatian *Exercises* (the foundation, the Kingdom, two standards, three classes of men, the three degrees of humility), "topics such as Efficiency, Business, Preparedness of Manhood, were made to carry full freight of the Exercises. . . ." Shealy was, in Woodlock's opinion, an organizational genius. "For the business of the week-end," he wrote,

> Father Shealy had some sixty-two hours at his disposal—namely, from 6 P.M. on Friday to 8 A.M. on Monday. Of these sixty-two hours there were needed for sleep, three nights, twenty-four hours; meals required four hours; for recreation eight hours had to be allowed; this made thirty-six hours, leaving twenty-six for business. Into these twenty-six hours had to be packed as much of the Spiritual Exercises as was possible with time left for Holy Mass, for Rosary, for Way of the Cross, for night prayer and for Benediction.[17]

The Jesuit, a true son of the institutional church, apparently exemplified to the men "those qualities that we commonly note as the special endowment of the modern American man of affairs." This approach to the retreat reinforced Shealy's emphasis on individualism, self-control, *"the power of realization,"* success, discipline, order, and "manly character." His retreat conferences and meditations indicated the extent to which he presented Catholic spiritual life to be the model of good Americanism. In his last meditation for the laymen, he summarized his ideal under the Ignatian image of the Captain and the soldier: "You must have obedience and discipline. The presumption is always in favor of authority. There is another class. They do a full day's work, a full day's fight, are obedient, loyal. These are our support. Such we want in the army of Christ."[18] It was only in practicing these virtues that the individual could combine his American and Catholic identities, doing justice to two separate spheres of existence.

The spiritual vision associated with Terence Shealy and the laymen's league indicated how the fractured inheritance of American and Catholic identities could shape one of the overarching movements of twentieth-century Catholic life. This very unique attempt to join Mount Manresa and *The Common Cause* demonstrated in a graphic way the heart of the twentieth-century problem: Given the inheritance of the papal, immigrant, and Americanist traditions, how could the Catholic create a unified spiritual life? With the death of Shealy in 1922, the social thrust of the retreat movement died, and as one historian tellingly remarked, only the spiritual vision continued.[19] From that time on the vision that would shape the retreat movement would be the papal program of Catholic Action. This was an approach with which most of the retreat houses would find themselves already compatible.

THE CENACLE: SOUL OF CATHOLIC ACTION

Pius XI was elected pope February 6, 1922. His vision of society and the church, built on foundations elaborated by Leo XIII and Pius X, reinforced the split between the spiritual life and social reform that had troubled the retreat movement in the United States. In an apostolic constitution of July 25, 1922, *Summorum Pontificem*, Pius named Ignatius of Loyola as patron of all spiritual exercises or retreats. The motto for the pope's pontificate, articulated in *Ubi Arcano* (December 1922), became the "Peace of Christ in the Reign of Christ," a theme elaborated in *Quas Primas* (December 1925). Pius emphasized the importance of the retreat movement for his vision in the encyclical *Mens Nostra* (December 20, 1929). The retreat movement was defined as the "soul of Catholic Action." To understand the course that the retreat movement took in the United States, it is necessary to review some of the major elements of Pius XI's program of spiritual and social renewal.[20]

In *Mens Nostra* Pius argued that the retreat movement was meant to touch the different classes of people: the pontifical curia, bishops, priests, and religious, the Catholic Action laity. He wrote:

> There is a need for elect groups of men, both of the secular and regular clergy, who shall act as faithful dispensers of the mysteries of God. *In addition to these we must have compact companies of pious laymen, who united to the Apostolic Hierarchy by close bonds of charity, will actively aid this by devoting themselves to the manifold works and labors of Catholic Action.*[21]

The perspective indicated here reveals the place of the laity in the church of Pius XI. He had written earlier in *Ubi Arcano* that the laity were to promote under episcopal direction and that of the clergy the knowledge and love of Christ. In other words, if the retreat movement was the "soul of Catholic Action," the determinants of the content of "soul" *came from the Spirit as mediated through the hierarchical church.*

In contrast to the early days of the retreat movement and the attempt of the layman's league to establish a close connection between spiritual renewal and social reconstruction, Pius XI defined the relationship between the retreat and action in the world in almost exclusive terms. *Mens Nostra* presented the model for the retreat-society relationship in terms of the upper chamber where the apostles hid themselves before the day of Pentecost. Pius took the words of Jesus as the key: "Come apart into a desert place and rest awhile" (Mark 6:31). He described those making retreats as people in search of "placid solitude." Tossed by the tempests of the time, . . . moved by the solicitudes of life, . . . beset by the frauds and fallacies of the world, . . . fighting against the deadly plague of rationalism, . . . allured by the fascination of the senses, these were people drawn by "the beauty of a more holy, perfect life." They entered from this world of anxiety into the retreat, where "meditating on heavenly things, they have ordered their lives in accordance with supernatural lessons." Having thus rejuvenated themselves in the midst of a hostile environment, the laity then reentered society and attempted to reconstruct it by participating in such instruments of Catholic Action as Catholic Evidence guilds, the Legion of Decency, classes in sociology, study clubs, and adoration societies. In other words, the retreat concerned itself with personal sanctification and the discussion of the inner life. Catholic Action, which took place outside of the retreat, concerned itself with social issues, such as the labor market, redistribution of goods, union organization, legislation, and the reconciliation of capital and labor. The retreats provided spiritual resources but did not enter into the discussion of and action toward social change.

Pius XI's vision of church and society came together in his presentation of Christ the King. Pius saw the unrest of the day as primarily the result of the lessened respect for justice and authority. The remedy was a return to the counsels and precepts of Christ's teaching on the dignity of man, purity of morals, the duty of obedience, the divine origin of society, the sacrament of marriage, the sanctity of the Christian family, "as well as all such other truths as He brought from heaven to earth" and "confided to His Church." Such a view of Christ was perfectly comprehensible in the context of the 1920s and 1930s. Pius saw a return to Christ the King as the remedy for the social ills of misery in the Near East, economic dislocations, class warfare, breakup of the family, widespread restlessness, the irritability of peoples, spiritual maladies, immoderate desire for temporal goods, excessive nationalism, and general lapse into barbarism. He presented Christ in his threefold office as Lawgiver; Judge, all judgment having been given by the Father to Christ; and Executive, i.e., the one whom all people must obey. Although Christ's power and kingdom was spiritual, still he had absolute power over all creatures. For Pius it was the church, hierarchically structured with the clergy directing and guiding the laity, who was the agent and witness to this threefold dimension of the ruling Christ.[22]

Pius XI's program of Catholic Action with the definite place that it gave to the retreat movement was summarized by its interpreters in four major elements:

> 1. there must be created in the faithful fidelity in striving after personal perfection; 2. they must be led to a more frequent participation in public worship; 3. the zeal thereby aroused must apply itself to Christian reform; and 4. the organized outlet must be planned by the Ordinaries for their respective districts under the guidance of the Holy See.[23]

Underlying this conception was the assumption of a strong distinction between the spiritual and temporal. Both church and state were considered as "perfect societies," with the realm of the spiritual influencing the temporal order only through the action of the laity. The lay person was, at the same time, both Christian and citizen, responsible to both societies. The social concerns of Catholic Action were channeled through parochial structures, and the retreat, as the "soul of Catholic Action," existed to prepare people for work, its primary aim being personal sanctification and the creation in the people of a spirit that would align them with parochial and diocesan works.

There can be very little doubt that Pius XI's program of Catholic Action provided the structures for the spiritual vision of the retreat movement. In 1928 Father Nilus McAllister, O.P., one of the leaders in the movement, graphically described how Pius XI's ideas could apply in the United States:

The most characteristic likeness, however, the one which gives the most complete idea of the effects of a retreat; the one idea that tells us at once that the work of a closed retreat ends not merely at the portals of a retreat house, is that wherein we style it the *Training Camp of the Lay Apostolate.*

When our great nation entered the World War, almost over night training camps for our soldiers sprang up all over the country. We realized the need of equipping our men with the science and disciplines of warfare, if we were to come through victorious. In these training schools our boys were filled with an enthusiasm for our *nation's cause.* Even as those students of military tactics passed from those training schools out onto the field of battle to fight for the honor of their homes and country; so likewise today, a vast army of well-trained, retreat-trained men, filled with the zeal of the early Apostles, animated with a personal enthusiasm for their leader, Christ, are going forth from the sacred precincts of our retreat houses, to join the glorious army of the Lay Apostolate which is engaged in battling against the spirit of unbelief, injustice, and immorality so rampant in the world today.[24]

McAllister went on to describe a host of parochial and extraparochial societies that would accomplish this social reconstruction: the Holy Name societies, the Saint Vincent de Paul Society, the Confraternity of Christian Doctrine, the Knights of Columbus, Catholic societies for men, boy movements, Catholic lecture bureaus, and home and foreign mission work. The retreat gave the impetus, zeal, and enthusiasm for such endeavors.

As the decade of the 1930s wore on, speaker after speaker at the national congresses proclaimed the connection between the retreat and Catholic Action. The approach was very similar to that taken by the eucharistic congresses of the period, and the problem was the same: In the United States, where Catholics had allied themselves so strongly with the separation of church and state, they could not accept Catholic Action as a program that attempted to restore Christendom through the union of spirituality and social reform under the direction of the church. While speakers could talk about the fourfold purpose of the retreat as personal perfection, the perfection of the family, the perfection of the church (i.e., loyalty to pastors), and the reconciliation of capital and labor, the retreat itself became a place for predominantly spiritual concerns focused on individual conversion, prayer, and participation in the sacraments. Referred to as "the plain man's postgraduate course in religion," the "time away" lost its connection with the problems of society; social concerns were the domain of parish organizations.[25] Sensing the problem, numerous speakers at the congresses urged the retreat to include some discussion of practical labor problems, to move away from stressing simply the salvation of the individual soul. But by 1946 one of the lay participants could summarize the situation in these terms:

It appears to us of the Diocese of Buffalo that the viewpoint of the average Catholic layman who has not participated in closed retreats, is simply this: It is one of many pious practices, efficacious in nature, desireable in its effects, refreshing in substance, but nevertheless a practice subject to the vicarious factors of present day living. It is thought to be well worth while, but an activity to be fitted into the complexities of modern living. . . .

If one were to psychoanalyze the layman in this frame of mind it might be found that a factor is the widespread belief that retreats are held for the sole purpose of attaining personal reform and sanctification. This basic view of the retreat is, of course, true because it is fundamental. This conception, considered by itself without the many implications involved, appears to us to be the immature viewpoint of, shall we say, the high school retreatant.[26]

Participants at the 1948 conference voiced even stronger criticisms.[27] With the advent of the secularism of the postwar world, it was becoming clearer that the structures that had shaped American Catholic spiritual life since the early twentieth century were no longer viable.

This structure of thinking and action that separated the retreat from social reform had four dominant effects on the spiritual life of the individual person. First, since the retreat itself was preached by priests and the houses operated by religious, it symbolically reinforced the notion of the church as a "perfect society." While the laity could be apostles in the world, within the church they remained passive recipients of salvation. Logan Bullitt, a prominent member of the movement in Philadelphia, summarized the general belief in this way: "Because a man is asked to bring men to Malvern, he is not an embryo St. John the Baptist, but rather like a cowboy going out on the plains to round up 'beef on the hoof.' When delivered to the market place [the retreat house], the responsibility ends; if these 'beeves' have immortal souls, that is the responsibility of the Retreat Master."[28] Second, the particular brand of spirituality promoted by the retreats reinforced the individualistic devotional practices associated with the eucharistic movement and parish societies. Indulgences, papal blessings, stations of the cross, benediction, prayers to the saints, and rosaries tended to dominate the horarium of the weekend.

Third, this approach, which encouraged the practice of private devotions and the teaching role of the priest, implied a certain practice of prayer. The weekend schedule left little time for personal assimilation, reflection, or meditation. While some speakers encouraged the retreat masters not to preach but to guide the laity to exercise their own spiritual faculties through meditation and silent reflection, this was not the dominant style.[29] The context reinforced the disparagement of contemplation in the American church. Last, the structures

of the retreat, which split the spiritual life from social reform, institutionalized the separation between action and prayer. At the 1948
conference, James Fitzgerald, a layman from Detroit, identified the
issue in these terms:

> What does a man do on retreat? He devotes himself exclusively to a try
> at living the active and contemplative spiritual life; he alternates between
> trying to be Martha and trying to be Mary. The trouble is just there, in
> the alternation. The two lives are separated and lived in separate com-
> partments. Why does he do that? Because that is the way he does his
> daily life. The only difference in his dual life in retreat and his double
> life every day is a difference in emphasis. In his daily spiritual life ACTIVE
> is written in very large capitals and contemplative in very small letters.
> In retreat it is just the other way around—CONTEMPLATIVE is written in
> big letters and active in small ones. What he needs to do is merge these
> two, and blend them into an evener proportion.[30]

While the retreat movement in so many ways presupposed and
promoted the fractured spiritual inheritance of American Catholicism,
it should be remembered that it began as a movement to reform and
revitalize the spiritual life of the laity. As a reform movement, it also
undercut in many ways the world that it reflected. When the retreatants left the busy marketplace and went to the "place apart" for a
revitalization of their spiritual lives, they did so on their own initiative. For a time, they abandoned their parochial boundaries, the
ministrations of the local pastor, and the confines of their home, to
discover themselves in a voluntary community united only by the
action of God's grace. If they wanted, they could seek advice from a
priest other than their pastor, one whose advice they could choose to
follow or not. Vitalized by the retreat, they became active members
of the lay apostolate, Christ-bearers and missionaries in their own
right. As one interpreter put it, Catholic Action presupposed the life
of grace in the individual soul and divine adoptive filiation: It "par-
ticipates in the priesthood of the Church through sacramental incorporation into the life of grace; it is entitled to share in the magistracy
of the Church by virtue of the truth of divine adoptive sonship; it
merits collaboration in the sovereignty or primacy of the Church
through the charity of the Mystical Body."[31]

Confined within the boundaries of the fractured spiritual inheritance, the retreat movement as the "soul of Catholic Action" would
reinforce American and Catholic identities. But what would happen
to the seeds of this reform—so far-reaching in some of its principles—
were the lay person to leave the boundaries of Catholic Action, re-
imagine the church as the mystical body of Christ, and discover the
reality of "Christ in us, our hope of glory"? The retreat movement,
as the eucharistic movement before it, carried the seeds of a different
church and the hopes for a new world.

PART FIVE

Seedbed of Reform, 1930–1965

While the late nineteenth-century struggles associated with *Testem Benevolentiae* fractured the unified vision associated with the immigrant church and the Americanists, the same period also produced the seeds of other types of renewal that would more directly anticipate the restructuring of Catholic spiritual life at the time of the Second Vatican Council. In 1884 the Third Plenary Council published legislation calling for the reform of prayer books and for the revival of Gregorian chant, both changes being designed to encourage the faithful's more active participation in the liturgy. At the Parliament of Religions in Chicago, Thomas O'Gorman (1843–1921), the first rector of Saint Thomas Seminary, Saint Paul, called for a close connection between dogma, experience, and worship. He held out as an ideal the union between God and the person to be achieved in heaven: "There the intellectual basis of the union shall be, not objective dogma and subjective faith, but a knowledge of God quite different from what we now have, called in our imperfect human language, the intuitive vision." During the same period, the Paulist Alfred Young (1831–1900) pioneered congregational singing, and Archbishop John Ireland published the *Saint Paul Hymnal*. Before the first decade of the twentieth century was closed, the understanding of the church as "communion," so evident in Orestes Brownson, would come to be translated into the notion of the "mystical body of Christ" through the writings of Joseph McSorley and the English convert Robert Hugh Benson (1871–

173

1914). Pius X would inaugurate the liturgical movement and call for the frequent reception of communion, reform of the breviary, and restoration of Gregorian chant. Much of this early activity would be drawn together in the work of the Collegeville Benedictine, Dom Virgil Michel (1890–1938), by any account one of the most important forerunners of Vatican Council II.[1]

At the turn of the century, it was the combination of the great conflict between capital and labor and the fear of socialism that helped shape the interpretation of Leo XIII's *Rerum Novarum* and the social-spiritual vision of John A. Ryan and Terence Shealy. These same forces, experienced in a completely different way, contained the germs of another synthesis between spirituality and social reform. Two years before *Testem Benevolentiae*, Dorothy Day (1897–1980) was born in Bath Beach, Brooklyn, New York. As a young journalist, she wrote for the radical periodicals *The Call* and *The Masses*. After her conversion in 1927, Day would bring to the American Catholic community a radical commitment to justice, identification with the poor, and an implied critique of a fractured inheritance that allowed Catholics to claim citizenship in the heavenly kingdom while strongly identifying with the efficiency, productivity, and material success of the American economic dream. Day would turn to the oasis of a retreat movement of the 1930s to nourish her pursuit of a heroic sanctity lived in the world. She would also promote the "little way" of Saint Thérèse de Lisieux as especially suited to the century of the anonymous person and call for an elaboration of the social implications of the saint's teachings.[2]

A modern American missionary movement, inspired by the work of Walter Elliott, also found its roots in the late nineteenth century. Elliott preached a crusade at South Beach, Michigan, in 1893 and challenged his listeners to take a systematic approach to working for the conversion of Protestants. He founded the Catholic Missionary Union to develop a missionary technique that would be expository, not controversial, and that would encourage a missionary spirit among all people, especially the religious and secular clergy. Elliott's methods and approach influenced Father Thomas F. Price (1860–1919), who with James Anthony Walsh (1867–1936) founded the first American missionary society, today known as Maryknoll (1911). Coming out of this tradition, James Keller (1900–1977) would establish the Christophers, a movement that would shape a whole generation of lay apostles after World War II.[3]

Last, the same period that caused the fracturing of the American and Catholic identities engendered a renewal of the interior life. Joseph McSorley, the twentieth-century bearer of Isaac Hecker's spirituality, wrote extensively on prayer. Along with his Paulist companion and friend, Thomas Verner Moore, McSorley through his numerous books attempted to address the problems of lay Catholics as they confronted the materialism and preoccupations of daily life. In an article on Thérèse de Lisieux in 1902, McSorley wondered about the narrow spread and mean results of the spiritual teaching of the church. Why was prayer so poorly understood? Why was spiritual ambition so uncommon? Why were the possibilities of God so little tried? "We must often and loudly reaffirm, in the hearing of the present generation," McSorley wrote in another article,

> that the Church is established for the eternal salvation and the spiritual perfection of humanity; that for the obtaining of this end alone does she profess to be equipped; and that she will never throw the aegis of her divine authority over anything which is not of concern to the health of the soul.

While McSorley was writing these words, the reigning pontiff, Pius X, was busy promoting a reform of the spiritual life influenced by the vision of the French Cistercian, Dom Jean-Baptiste Chautard (1858–1935). Chautard's *The Soul of the Apostolate* called for an interior life nourished by the sacraments, liturgy, and meditative prayer. In fewer than fifty years, Thomas Merton (1915–1968) would introduce Chautard's book to American readers. Throughout the next twenty years, Merton would witness in a special way to contemplation as an integrating force in Catholic life.[4]

The seeds of these approaches to spiritual renewal began to come to fruition after World War I and continued unabated into the post–World War II era. The major proponents shared with the eucharistic movement an emphasis on personal communion with God; with the retreat movement, a commitment to the development of an interior life and the search for a community shaped by a common experience of faith. Catholic Action, with its focus on baptism and the universal call to holiness, also prepared the way for their development. However, Virgil Michel, Dorothy Day, James Keller, and Thomas Merton, each in his or her own way, broke from the dominant spiritual structures of twentieth-century American Catholic life. They struggled against a fractured inheritance that split spirituality and social reform, and argued with the ecclesiastical and juridical categories that supported Catholic Action. Instead they promoted a more mystical-sacramental notion of the church, the priesthood of all believers, the laity's call to heroic sanctity, the community between Protestants and Catholics in mission to the world, and the universal possibility of contemplative experience. No study of twentieth-century American

Catholicism would be complete without these people. Although it is impossible to present a complete analysis of their vision of the Christian life here, it is important to indicate how they anticipated the search for a new synthesis of American and Catholic spiritual life that would be inaugurated in the 1960s.

CHAPTER
15
Virgil Michel: The Priesthood of the Faithful

$\mathcal{R}$eared in the same midwestern populist atmosphere that influenced John Ireland and John A. Ryan, Virgil George Michel pioneered a movement that would carry the vision of an integrated American and Catholic identity into the second half of the twentieth century. Michel, who was born in 1890 in Saint Paul, Minnesota, entered the preparatory school at Saint John's Abbey, Collegeville, in 1903, the same year Pius X published his *motu proprio* calling for the restoration of the Roman liturgy and the promotion of the active participation of the faithful in the life of the church. After entrance into the Benedictine novitiate in 1909, Michel continued studies for the priesthood and was ordained in 1916. He then specialized in philosophy and education at the Catholic University of America and wrote his dissertation on "The Critical Principles of Orestes Brownson." The young monk gravitated especially toward those writings of the American philosopher that joined Christianity, culture, and social reconstruction in a common synthesis. They were the same essays that in a much earlier generation had attracted Isaac Hecker and formed the foundation for his understanding of "renunciation." When Michel returned to teach literature and philosophy at Collegeville, he shared with his students an avid interest in contemporary intellectual movements. He caught the spirit of the times after World War I in a letter to his abbot, August 12, 1918:

> There is certainly going to be a reconstruction of ideas and ideals after

this war in every line of thought and activity. And unless we Catholics are prepared to advertise (in the good sense) our views, we shall be missing a glorious opportunity. Nor will any Catholic's views count for much, unless he shows that he is acquainted with the best prevalent views and theories on any subject. That is only natural.[1]

In early 1924, Abbot Alcuin Deutsch, who had himself begun to work for a revival of the liturgical spirit among the monks, asked Michel to go to Europe, and from spring of that year until August 1925, the philosophy professor studied at Louvain and Rome, and traveled extensively in Italy, Spain, and Germany. The time was a decisive one. Michel was especially inspired by Dom Lambert Beauduin (1873–1960) and the liturgical revival being promoted by the Benedictines at Maria Laach in Germany, Solesmes in France, and Maredsous in Belgium. During this period he began to integrate Leo XIII's social vision and Pius X's call for a spiritual reform with contemporary ecclesiological theories on the church as the mystical body of Christ.

In April 1925 Michel wrote to Abbot Alcuin describing the results of some sleepless nights:

> Another result of those nights was a system of propaganda that was an inspiration (think of the Eucharistic congress in Chicago!). Again, amid attempts (made from a sense of duty) to fall asleep, I went through a meditation on the magnificat, on the mission of women in the modern world, on the close contact between the natural and the supernatural, and on the voice of reason in modern thought.[2]

The letter included the first real outlines of that "system of propaganda" that was to integrate and revitalize all of these dimensions of Catholic life. The "system" was to be focused through the liturgical movement, a popular liturgical library, and a periodical called *Orate Fratres.*

Michel returned to the United States, started *Orate Fratres* during Advent 1926, and, from then until his death in 1938, labored to make Saint John's Abbey, Collegeville, the center of the revival of Catholicism. His contribution through the liturgical movement to the development of Catholic spiritual life can be seen in his interpretation of the Mass and in the conflict between the liturgical movement and its eucharistic predecessor.

When Virgil Michel inaugurated the liturgical movement, he focused his attention on the meaning and function of the Mass in the Catholic community. Father William Busch, professor of church history at the seminary in Saint Paul and one of the liturgical movement's strongest supporters, had published an English version of Joseph Kramp's *Eucharistia* in 1925, and the following year Michel translated

Beauduin's *La Piété de l'église*. True to his original inspiration, Michel next made the insights of these European scholars available to a wider audience in a series of pamphlets, *My Sacrifice and Yours* and *Why Do Catholics Attend Mass* (1926). At the same time he gave a series of public lectures and retreats on such subjects as "Mass: Sacrifice in Christ," "The Life in Christ," and "Liturgical Prayer." Articles and retreat notes from the 1930s indicate that this emphasis on the mass as a ritual act that embodied the community's self-identity continued throughout his life.[3]

In his writings and lectures Michel was above all concerned to reestablish the bonds of community. He asked: Can the mass be attended in mental separation, even isolation, from the priest? Clearly not. The liturgical text itself indicated that the priest acted primarily as the leader of the community (e.g., "Let us pray," the server's answer of "Amen" to several of the prayers, the mention of "those here present" in the canon). Furthermore, everything necessary for the sacrifice of the new law came from the people: the church building, the vessels, the altar, the bread and wine, the priest himself. Liturgical prayer was basically corporate, the "expression of combined spiritual experiences of religious minds." The action of the whole person, it united both the "simple play of the soul" in aspirations of the heart with deliberate, cautious, and reasoned ritual expression. Through standing, sitting, kneeling, and the sign of the cross, the whole community involved itself in this drama of redemption.[4]

Michel's articulation of a common Christian action at the center of the community's self-expression found a ready echo in many of his contemporaries. H. F. Flock, pastor at Saint Patrick's Church, Sparta, Wisconsin, told the Benedictine of the problems he had encountered when he had many years previously tried to inaugurate a parish renewal program based on the same principles. "What started me," he wrote,

> was the total ignoring of the principal parts of the Mass except the elevation, when the children recited the Rosary or sang hymns at the Mass. I began by teaching the children to say the Confiteor with the server; the two Offertory prayers; and a spiritual Communion at the proper times. The idea was to teach them to discern at least the principal parts and to unite in the sacrifice with the priest.
>
> About fifteen years ago I began with the children to say the whole Ordinary of the Mass in English. I bought a supply of cheap prayer books and marked as many of the prayers as could conveniently be said aloud while keeping with the priest at the altar, omitting the words of Consecration from the "Hanc Igitur" etc. A few boys with a good voice were trained to watch the priest at the altar and announce the various parts

and prayers and start them. These boys also would read the epistle and
gospel proper of the day from the English Missal.

A few years ago, when the children were quite well practiced, I had
them say the Mass in this manner for the congregation at early Mass on
a Sunday. The people were very attentive and by this visual and practical
illustration learned more about the Mass and how to "pray the Mass"
than by many theoretical instructions.

We had these congregational Mass prayers with the children at least
once a week until about three years ago, when I found an item in the
American Ecclesiastical Review stating that Rome, in answer to some-
body's inquiry, had forbidden to pray aloud with the congregation any
of the Mass prayers that the priest said "secreto." We then gave up the
practice and have not taken it up since.[5]

Many other Americans and one of Michel's most ardent English supporters, the layman Donald Attwater, agreed that the Mass needed
to become the property of the whole community. Bishop Joseph
Schrembs of Cleveland (1886–1945) summarized the dominant feelings of those involved in the movement: "The faithful must be brought
into a living participation with the liturgy of the Church, to which
today, as a matter of fact, they are practically strangers." Schrembs
went on to note that the laity's public participation was limited to
the recitation of the Rosary and singing of a few hymns like "Mother
Dear Oh Pray for Me" or "On This Day . . ." All of these people, in
conjunction with Michel, attempted to bridge the gap between clergy
and laity, between institutional expression and personal piety—a gap
indicative of the community's fractured self-identity—through support of the *missa recitata*, the publication of missals, liturgical retreats
and missions, and numerous popular publications.[6]

Michel believed that the theological center for this active participation of the faithful in the liturgy was a correct understanding of
the mass as a "sacrifice." In an article on the "true Christian spirit"
in 1930, he argued that the long polemic battle with Protestantism
had led Catholics to emphasize the juridical nature of the church.
Undue prominence had been given "to her external social constitution,
as if she were mainly a corporate person with power to exact certain
dues from her members and to punish non-payment of them." Within
this understanding, religion was considered simply a part of the virtue
of justice with the sacrifice of the mass demonstrating God's right
and dominion through the destruction of the victim offered in payment
for sin. In the Benedictine's mind, the true Christian spirit implied
something different. Instead of being a perfect society, the church
was also the embodiment of the Spirit of Christ himself. The actions
of the church related more to the virtue of charity than to justice. For

Thomas Aquinas, Michel argued, the purpose of sacrifice was not simply the destruction of the victim but also the remission of sin, the conservation of grace, and the perfect union between God and people. From this perspective, the sacrifice of the mass embodied not the "minimum discharging of a debt" but the active participation of all in the priestly action of Christ. As Michel noted on one of his retreats, the object of the offering, the bread and wine, stood for the giver, for the people themselves, and expressed their self-offering in mind and body. At the consecration, this offering became Christ himself: "What stood for our poor selves thus becomes God." In this way, through collective offering of themselves, people were drawn into Christ's work of redemption. This was true sacrifice.[7]

Given this understanding of the mass as a sacrifice, an understanding shared by many of Michel's contemporaries, it was inevitable that the liturgical movement directly conflicted with the aims and presuppositions of its eucharistic counterpart. In 1927 Alcuin Deutsch compared and contrasted the two different approaches in the pages of *Emmanuel.* The eucharistic movement, he wrote, aimed, "to bring priests closer to the Blessed Sacrament" and to make them "apostles of the Blessed Eucharist, who will do their utmost to increase in the hearts of the Christian people faith in and love for the Holy Eucharist." While the liturgical movement also aimed to sanctify souls, it achieved this sanctification through the active participation of the faithful. Deutsch then distinguished between the early church's understanding of the sacrificial nature of the Eucharist and the emphasis in the Middle Ages on the real presence in the host. Pointing to the earlier period as the model, he argued that the liturgical movement sought "to make the Mass the center around which our daily life revolves, and Christ's spirit of self-immolation for the glory of his Father and the salvation of His brethren the model which shapes its course." Christ, he concluded, had instituted the sacrifice; reservation, the work of the church, existed to make Christ's immolated body available for those unable to assist at mass. "For centuries there was no attempt to surround the consecrated species outside of the Mass with the splendor and trappings of glory with which we love to surround them in modern times. . . ." Michel's translation of Beauduin's *La Piété de l'église* indicated that he shared his abbot's criticisms.[8]

The differences between the eucharistic and liturgical movements came into even sharper focus in 1929. In January of that year, William Busch published an English translation of Dom Gommaire Laporta's "Eucharistic Piety." The Benedictine from Mont César, Louvain, contrasted the liturgy as the action of the believing community with popular devotions centered on Jesus hidden in the tabernacle: benediction, visits to the Blessed Sacrament, holy hours, and perpetual adoration. Too often, he noted, the people advocating these devotions "think of communion as a simple visit to the Blessed Sacrament, and of the Mass as that exercise of miraculous priestly power which brings about the Real Presence for the sake of Communion and exposition." In fact, the altar of sacrifice, not the tabernacle, should be the distinguishing feature of Catholicism. The Benedictine then carefully broadened the current understanding of eucharistic presence. "How many know," he asked,

> that the special grace of the Eucharist, that sacramental grace which it both symbolizes and produces, is supernatural charity, that love which unites us with Christ and unites us with each other, and so produces that union and intercommunication of vital forces which constitute the mystical body of Christ, the end and purpose of the Eucharist?[9]

Two months later the *American Ecclesiastical Review* carried a pseudonymous article in response to Laporta. "Senex" believed that the liturgical movement would "seriously disturb the fervor and most holy practices of many devout people." Christ, he argued, had not spoken any "word of collective sacrificial action." Laporta's views conflicted with the tradition of the church, the Council of Trent, and the statements of Leo XIII and Pius X. "To put out the light in the Tabernacle would be to put out the light which marks a Catholic Church to the eyes of men and makes it shine out to all in the world as the Home of God on earth. To minimize its import is to darken the Catholic Faith."[10]

The controversy between the two sides, so clearly articulated by Laporta and "Senex," would continue for the next thirty years. William Busch, John LaFarge, S. J. (1880–1963), Virgil Michel, and, as late as 1952, Clifford Howell, S.J., would struggle with the proponents of the eucharistic movement over the meaning and function of the "real presence." Michel himself best summarized the opposing notions during a retreat to lay people at Saint John's Abbey, Collegeville. In parallel fashion, he presented the "wrong" and "true" notions of the thanksgiving prayer that the Catholic performed after communion.

> *Wrong notions.*
> a) Now Christ is in us. 15 precious minutes. To think in terms of physical presence of Species. We are now tabernacles. As if greatest honor to be for 15 min. what wood or stone of tabernacle is all time.
>
> b) 15 precious minutes. Now have Xt. cornered. Get all out of Him we can while chance lasts. Supreme sponger-attitude. Our prayer-books overflow in sweet sentiments which we do not feel. No tingling in our senses, etc.
>
> c) Fifteen minutes—show due reverence to Xt. in us. But merely gimme

prayer. Nor is physical, spacial presence supreme thing. Something much higher and more lasting occurs.

True Thanksgiving.

a) True thanksgiving take cue from whole sacrificial action. *Res sacramenti* received *ex opere operato:* is more than physical presence. Is supernatural abiding presence increased. We in Christ and Christ in us, special sharers in God—permanent, as long as not chased out by us.

b) Have seen: Communion is God's return gift. Gift for a purpose, i.e., to live Christ. Thank God first of all for that. Renew promises of sacrificial offering, etc. Ask for strength, etc., after mind of Christ, not contrary.

c) Received gift to live out Christ. Not for 15 minutes, but for whole day, week. Hence real thanks more than a prayer. Christ's strength for living out continually. Unless that, our thanksgiving a lip service.[11]

Although this controversy would appear as somewhat trivial to a generation raised after the Second Vatican Council, its focus on the central ecclesiological symbol of the era, the Eucharist, indicated that what people perceived to be at issue was not an attitude toward the Blessed Sacrament but something of much greater significance. The pioneers of the liturgical movement seemed to be restructuring the contours of Catholic spiritual life in at least four different ways. First, by emphasizing the "priesthood of the faithful," Virgil Michel and others challenged the current understanding of the relationship between clergy and laity and thus, it was thought, the very constitution of the church itself. "The Liturgical Movement," one author wrote in the *Sentinel of the Blessed Sacrament,* "aims to take the very heart of the priesthood away from us clergy and give it to the lay ones."[12] Although Michel did not really have this in mind, he certainly was pushing for some different alignment. In February 1929, he wrote to George Shuster, the editor of *Commonweal,* who had complained about the barriers erected between the clergy and laity:

A layman (alas!) must still be very cautious in writing such an editorial, and this editorial could hardly have put things more diplomatically and yet tellingly.—My hearty congratulations. Some day an "official teacher" will have to [restate] the age-old Catholic doctrine that the lay folk are not merely trained dogs but true living members of the Church & in their own way true Apostles of Christ.[13]

Michel elaborated on these comments in a long article in which he argued that "the Church is not made up of those who do only the giving on the one hand, and those who do only the receiving on the other. The Church is the mystic body of Christ in which all members live the life of Christ." In the mid-1930s, true to his original dream of the magnificat, he extended these insights to promote the dignity of women in church and society.[14]

Second, Michel and others dramatically moved the focus for Christ's presence out of the tabernacle and into the minds and hearts of the individual believer and the community. The sacramental correlative of this was an emphasis on baptism and confirmation, those rites whereby an individual was permanently reborn in Christ and grafted onto the mystic body. This shift departed from both individualism and its accompanying moralism that had so shaped the spiritual vision of John A. Ryan, Terence Shealy, and the eucharistic movement. Over and over again in his retreats, the Benedictine called for a new appreciation of the role of grace in the Christian economy. He summarized his general approach in a letter to a colleague in 1938:

> The collect of last Sunday speaks of vitare diabolica contagia and of Deum sectari. Moral theology has told us how to do the former [banish the wiles of the devil], the negative side of Christianity, but it has not bothered about the latter [pursuing God]. And ascetic theology, on which moral theology tries to shift the burden, has been concerned greatly with putting off the old man while often forgetting that this is merely the first step towards the more important putting on of Christ.[15]

Such a view allowed Michel to dissolve the categories of "duty," "character," and "obedience" that had shaped an earlier generation. He defined holiness as the "disposition fertile for fructification of grace," and identified its major characteristics as a spirit of joyfulness, faithfulness in little things, ardor of heart, and the "total giving of self, in imitation of God Himself."[16]

Third, this recognition of the person's life in Christ that he or she could then carry into the world led Michel to argue that Catholic Action need not be confined to working within church organizations under the direction of the hierarchy. The bishop, he noted, "ordains official priesthood and consecrates official apostles (lay). Both high official commission." The lay apostles had the duty of "sanctifying, teaching, governing by example and word of mouth and action." Even in a secular organization, the Christian could practice a wide field of spiritual and corporal works of mercy. Michel's approach was tentative, but it represented a definite break from the structures of Catholic Action that had begun powerfully to shape the spiritual life of the community.[17]

Last, although Michel's early writings concentrated on theological topics, in the course of the 1930s he began to focus his attention on the liturgy as the center of all life. In a lecture on the background of the liturgical movement, he severely criticized the laissez-faire individualism that had grown in society and the church since the sixteenth century. The Benedictine argued that Catholics had been affected in their everyday life in such a way that they separated religion and business and isolated their spiritual obligations from their ordinary affairs. Society itself had lost its mooring in the moral law; people had fallen into atheism. In such a context, the liturgical movement implied social changes of far-reaching consequences.

Michel believed that through active participation in the liturgy a person became immersed in Christ's "sacrificial spirit," a spirit that freed people to be active in the world. On a sociological level, the liturgy portrayed a truly supernatural model of human fellowship, one witnessing to relationships between responsible persons who voluntarily chose to cooperate in a common life of fellowship. Moving between the excesses of individualism and totalitarian collectivism, the liturgy thus became the model for family, community, and social life. Through the action of sanctifying ordinary objects of life (bread and wine), the liturgy also showed that material goods could be put at the service of others for the glorification of God. Reflecting very much the thinking of his time, Michel concluded that all of this could take place only within the context of the Catholic church. "It is the aim of the liturgical movement," he wrote,

> to restore the liturgy so that religion and spiritual culture may again inspire the whole life of the individuals of society. As a movement it seems to bring about the intensification of the spirit of Christ in Christians. How is this to be accomplished? By giving each and every Christian an opportunity to participate in the liturgical movement or in its worship.[18]

When viewed from Michel's perspective, the Mass as the central religious and cultural symbol of the community thus stood for an integration of the different dimensions of life that had eluded American Catholics since the turn of the century.

In conclusion, the structural importance of the liturgical movement for the development of Catholic spiritual life lay in two distinct areas. Reacting very strongly to the fractured state of Catholic life, Michel and others supported a stronger integration between the spiritual life and social reform, between the individual and the community, between the objective piety of the liturgy and the more subjective dimensions of personal participation.[19] Their foundational emphasis on baptism and the ecclesiology of the Body of Christ pushed toward the democratization of the priesthood of Christ and the creation of an active and free lay Catholic community. In these areas the movement tried to fashion a new American Catholic identity and anticipated the changes that would affect almost every dimension of Catholic life in the 1960s. The liturgy, as it had since the days of John Carroll, still served as the central symbol reinforcing or changing the community's identity.

CHAPTER
16
Dorothy Day
The Heroic Ideal

*O*n December 8, 1932, the thirty-five-year-old socialist Dorothy Day prayed at the National Shrine of the Immaculate Conception. She had spent the previous five years since her conversion to Catholicism learning the practices of her faith (frequent confession, daily mass, the rosary) and searching for a vocation within the church. "I was on the brink of losing my faith," she would later tell an interviewer.

> I was very upset by what I saw—the church's apparent indifference to so much suffering. In [the early years of the Depression] people walked the streets, hundreds and hundreds of them, looking dazed and bewildered. They had no work. They had no place to go. Some groups tried to help them, but neither the state nor the church seemed as alarmed as my "radical friends."[1]

Day had come to Washington to cover the story of the Hunger March of unemployed workers and tenant farmers who gathered in the capitol to present stark evidence of the plight of the poor. Watching the protesters, she realized once again the gap that separated her as a Catholic from the practical concerns of those suffering hunger, cold, and poverty. She prayed at the shrine "that some way would open up for me to use what talents I possessed for my fellow workers, for the poor."[2]

When Day returned to New York, she found a French peasant worker, Peter Maurin, waiting for her. Inspired by his Catholic critique of capitalism, his commitment to a personalist and communitarian

186

revolution, and his deep knowledge of the French intellectual and spiritual tradition, Day set out to give flesh to Maurin's vision. The first issue of *Catholic Worker* appeared May 1, 1933, and within a few years houses of hospitality with their distinct blend of food offered and opportunity for the "clarification of thought" sprang up in urban centers across the country. From that time until her death in 1980, Day would labor unceasingly, practicing a "harsh and dreadful love" through her combination of uncompromising Catholicism and equally strong advocacy of social reform. For many, she became an exemplar of holiness. Although her spiritual legacy is too vast and profound to be examined here, her impact on the structures of Catholic spiritual life in the twentieth century can be seen in her attitude toward Catholic Action and her modeling of a heroic ideal lived in the world. Like Virgil Michel, she pointed to an integration and democratization that would anticipate the renewal occasioned by the Second Vatican Council.

Day always considered her activity to be outside the scope of a church apostolate as it was usually defined. She stated the basic principle very clearly in her 1963 history of the Catholic Worker movement, *Loaves and Fishes:*

> We never felt it was necessary to ask permission to perform the works of mercy. Our houses and farms were always started on our own responsibility, as a lay activity and not what is generally termed "Catholic Action." We could not ask diocesan authorities to be responsible for opinions expressed in *The Catholic Worker*, and they would have been held responsible, had we come under their formal auspices.[3]

The origin of the approach seems to have been with Peter Maurin, who had been influenced by the French reformist movement, *Le Sillon*, and by the French personalist tradition from Jacques Maritain (1882–1973) to Emmanuel Mounier (1905–1950).[4]

Peter Maurin recognized that Catholic Action was "action by Catholic laymen in cooperation with the clergy." He also noted the existence of a deep historical separation between the spiritual and temporal orders, between clergy and laity. He believed that the usual approach of Catholic Action left this separation intact, confining religion to the sanctuary and leaving the world of education, politics, and business empty of spiritual significance. "So Catholic clergymen," Maurin began an "easy essay,"

> have ceased to mind the lay-
> man's business
> and the laymen have made a
>   mess
> of their own business.

> And Catholic clergymen have
> tried to mind their business
> with business-like techniques
> borrowed from business-minded people.[5]

This type of situation, Maurin argued, required both the recovery of
a different idea of the church, one not associated with the juridical
categories of the perfect society, and an emancipation of the laity so
that they could act independently with a "freedom illumined by
grace." He synthesized his key ideas in "Catholic Activity—Catholic
Action."

> Love and liberty
>
> which are the foundations
> of the Christian community
>
> often had to give place
>
> to authoritarian ecclesiasticism.
>
> Modern times
> have seen a practical eclipse
> of the idea
> of the Mystical Body.
>
> The Christian Community
> has had to give way
> to a collectivized society
> where the element of hierarchical authority
> is exercised
> in a manner detrimental
> to the liberty of the laity.
>
> The task of the laity
> is the social explanation
> of the words of Saint Peter
> addressed to all Christians—
> "You are a royal priesthood."[6]

Dorothy Day built her apostolic activity on Maurin's insights: "We
are trying to build up the lay apostolate throughout the country,"
she wrote, "but not as an organization but on a personalist basis so
that man whether he is in a lodging house or in a factory or in a shop
can feel that he has a definite job to do to live his faith and influence
others."[7]

    The significance of this approach for the structures of Catholic
spiritual life can be seen when it is compared with that of John A.

Ryan, whose thinking was so compatible with Catholic Action. Ryan's understanding had been shaped by what he saw as the external threats of socialism and secularism. Working within this apologetic context, he tended sharply to separate the natural and supernatural orders, the world and the church. Dividing Catholicism and Americanism, he united them not on the level of the person but through the abstract principles of natural law or under the aegis of a Catholic organization that could claim hegemony over the activities of the laity.

Day broke from this fractured inheritance in two significant ways. First, a socialist both before and after her conversion, she sought to integrate her Catholicism and her Americanism on the level of the person. In many ways she stressed the convergence, not the separation, between nature (socialism) and grace (the Catholic faith). "You keep talking about secular idealism," she said in 1970, "but I don't draw that distinction in my mind—between secular idealism and an idealism in the service of God."[8] In terms reminiscent of Hecker's "renunciation," but from a completely different tradition, she sought to see the world as the place where God's grace operated. In her mind Peter Maurin knew what he meant.

> He meant it was time for the laity to be in the vanguard, to live in the midst of the battle, to live in the world which God so loved that He sent His only begotten Son to show us how to live and to die, to meet that last great enemy, Death. We were to explore the paths of what was possible, to find concordances with our opponents, to seek for the common good, to try to work with all men of goodwill, and to trust all men too, and to believe that goodwill, and to forgive our own failures and those of others seventy times seventy times. *We* could venture where priest and prelate could not or ought not, in political and economic fields. We could make radical mistakes without too great harm, we could retrace our steps, start over again in this attempt to build a new society within the shell of the old, as Peter and the old radicals (those who went to the roots of things) used to say.[9]

A convert, Day found in Catholicism the fulfillment of her personal quest. Her spirituality, then, unlike Ryan's, searched for convergence and unity. Beginning with the idea of personal quest, Day's spirituality was marked by a deep and profound Catholic humanism that acknowledged the role of the individual conscience, the operation of grace in nature, and God's love in everything.

Second, Ryan's juxtaposition of Catholicism and Americanism allowed the church to maintain its independence while at the same time adjusting to the values of American society. Coming from her personalist and communitarian convictions, Day critiqued the results of this separate but parallel rapprochement. On the side of the state, she redefined citizenship in terms of respectful but persistent protest

against the dominant economic, political, and social structures of the
time. On the side of the church, she severely questioned its social
position. Fond of quoting Romano Guardini's "the Church is the Cross
on which Christ was crucified," she carried the following convictions
from the beginning of her conversion until her death:

> When I see the Church taking the side of the powerful and forgetting the
> weak, and when I see bishops living in luxury and the poor being ignored
> or thrown crumbs, I know that Jesus is being insulted, as He once was,
> and sent to his death, as He once was. The church doesn't only belong
> to officials and bureaucrats; it belongs to all its people, and especially
> its most humble men and women and children, the ones He would have
> wanted to go see and help, Jesus Christ. I am embarrassed—I am sick-
> ened—when I see Catholics using their religion as a social ornament.
> Peter [Maurin] used to tell me that a good Catholic should pray for the
> Church as if it is a terrible sinner, in bad need of lots of prayers. I re-
> member being surprised for a second to hear him say that; he was such
> a *devout* Catholic. But then I realized that it was precisely *because* he
> was so devout that he said what he said.[10]

Such a statement, combining as it did loyalty and criticism, could
not have been made by someone living within the fractured inheritance of early twentieth-century Catholicism. On the one hand, Day's
convictions clearly received from that inheritance a complete faith
in the spiritual integrity and immutable truths of the church, truths
mediated through hierarchical structures demanding obedience. But
on the other hand, the criticism implied a different understanding of
the Christian life and of the church. In one of her conversations, Day
told the following story:

> But my friend kept pushing me. "Jesus wanted people to love others, to
> give of themselves to others, not to fall in love with buildings and altars
> and prelates and popes, and not to give their time and money and faith
> to all that." I told him right, absolutely right. But he said I can't have
> it both ways; I can't agree with him and with what "they" tell me in
> church. Well, I told him I can. I said I can go to church and pray to God,
> and when I pray I can say anything I want, and He is listening, and no
> one else. Once I asked a priest in confession if I was being out of line by
> thinking thoughts like the one my friend had, while sitting here in church.
> He laughed, and said he was afraid too many people don't have any
> thoughts in church; they just go through the motions. I told him I feel
> like crying sometimes, or I flush with anger: to be in church isn't to be
> calmed down as some people say they get when they are at Mass. I'm
> worked up. I'm excited by being so close to Jesus, but the closer I get,
> the more I worry about what He wants of us, what He would have us do
> before we die.[11]

In other words, without reforming the church, Day dissolved the fractured inheritance of Catholicism and social reform and integrated them in her person by challenging both church and state to be radical. This was, she knew, her vocation.

Day began to understand more fully the depths of this call to personal integrity in God during a course of retreats with which she first became acquainted in the late 1930s. Father Pacifique Roy (d. 1954), a Josephite, came to her breakfast table at the Worker house in New York and spoke about the spiritual teachings of a French Canadian Jesuit, Father Onesimus Lacouture (1881–1951). Roy "began talking of the love of God, how by our baptism we had been made sons of God and what that entailed for us, what responsibilities it laid upon us." His listeners, as Day would later relate, began from that time to recognize more deeply their own worth and saw in his teaching a "retreat which could be preached to the man on the breadline, to the worker, the scholar, to young and old, the educated and uneducated. It was the good news."[12] Inquiring how she could learn more, Day was next sent to a priest of the diocese of Pittsburgh, John J. Hugo (1911–1985). She made her first retreat under Hugo in July 1941, continued making them regularly for the next several years, and then periodically returned to them until her last one in 1976. This annual experience, with its unique challenge of renunciation and uncompromising love, gave her the spiritual sustenance for which she longed. "Who has not experienced that 'being in love,'" she wrote,

> which suddenly intensified all joys, transformed one's surroundings, made all work interesting and full of meaning, made all things new, so that one saw the loved one as God sees him (and as we ought always to see all men).
>
> O, those first days of our conversion—and those first days of the retreat which was a second conversion for so many—how filled with the keenest happiness they were for us all. We were companions indeed, those who made the retreat.[13]

Peter Maurin had given Dorothy Day a social vision; the retreat presented her with a picture of supernatural holiness.

Referring to her experience at different times as the "Scriptural," "Thomistic," "Pauline," or "Little Way" retreat, Day recognized from the very beginning its divisive impact on its participants. In 1947 she recalled that Pacifique Roy had disrupted a 1940 retreat given by Paul Hanley Furfey (1896–), an early admirer of Day's and at that time one of the most respected proponents of an evangelical "fire on the earth." Roy gave conferences on the love of God between the scheduled talks by Furfey. He criticized the lack of silence and the money wasted on cigarettes. Charges of a new rigorism or Jansenism broke out among those who attended. A year later, when Day made her first retreat under John Hugo, more serious controversies arose over pacifism, true leadership, and the use of "spiritual weapons" in the struggle with the world. Many objected to the retreat's "emphasis on self." By 1941 Lacouture was removed from his work, Hugo was discouraged from giving the retreat, and other priests who had promoted it were exiled. The historical evidence and details surrounding the controversy and Day's understanding of the issues are still being discovered, and at the present time no certain judgment is possible.[14]

But despite these uncertain elements, over and over again in her writings Day testified to the one great gift that the retreat had given to her. It affirmed her vocation as an avenue to heroic sanctity. In 1951 she stressed the essential continuity between Maurin's teachings and those of Lacouture: "Both men taught personal responsibility and the dignity of man. Both men recognized the dignity of the laity, the capacity of the layman for sacrifice, for sanctity." Again, in 1972, she wrote that Hugo's retreat "paid lay people the compliment of believing them to be capable of *growing* in the spiritual life."[15] Hugo's conferences blazed with a spiritual fervor that revealed to Day the evangelical possibilities in her own life. The extensive use of Scripture reaffirmed her own practice of reading the Word and also illuminated the text in a way she had not discovered on her own. The retreat explicitly attacked a type of institutional, "bourgeois Catholicism" that focused on the formation of Catholic societies, organizations, activities, committees, and recommendations to various groups. Hugo contrasted two types of life. Minimum Christianity avoided the negative values of mortification, self-denial, detachment, and penance, tried to attract people by concentrating on the natural virtues of courtesy, justice, purity, and temperance. It contented itself with the avoidance of mortal sin. Positive Christianity, on the other hand, based itself on the total love of God, renunciation, and the literal following of the Gospel maxim: "Be ye perfect as your Heavenly Father is perfect." The criticism of the dangers of Catholic Action and the description of a better way appealed to Day's radical nature.[16]

Hugo's description of the primacy of the inner life and union with Christ validated Day's own experience. His use of literature to illustrate his points and his focus on God's love in the Incarnation "so aroused our love in turn that a sense of the sacramentality of life was restored for us." Last, the retreat placed at the center of life the doctrine of sacrificial love come to completion on the cross of Christ. Pacifique Roy, Day wrote in *Loaves and Fishes*,

> made us know what love meant, and what the inevitable suffering of love meant. He taught us that when there were hatreds and rivalries among us, and bitterness and resentments, we were undergoing purifications,

prunings, in order to bear a greater fruit of love. He made us feel the power of love, he made us keep our faith in the power of love.[17]

In short, the retreat revealed to Day the depths of the universal call to sanctity and showed her that her thirst for sanctity could be practicably lived out in the world. "I wanted to be poor, chaste, and obedient," she noted of her conversion to Catholicism. "I wanted to die in order to live, to put off the old man and put on Christ."[18] Hugo's retreats on the radical nature of voluntary poverty, chastity, and obedience, enabled her to follow her deepest personal instincts. As Day later noted, it was a "little way," one modeled on Thérèse de Lisieux, and available to anyone. It was the way of love. Within the Catholicism of her time, this lay vocation to sanctity moved beyond the ecclesiological identification of heroic sanctity with religious vows. It represented a democratization of the spiritual life, and, along with her pursuit of integration, pointed to a new synthesis of a Catholic and American identity.[19]

CHAPTER
17
James Keller
To Light One Candle

*W*hile the founder of the *Catholic Worker* shared her "little way" with the city's poor and homeless, another person, more comfortable with New York's rich and famous, tried to change the world. Born in 1900, James Keller possessed a keen sense of his own unique call from the time of his youth. He responded to the words of the Gospel, "You have not chosen me, but I have chosen you," by entering the minor seminary in Menlo Park, California. In the fall of 1918, he heard one of the founders of the Catholic Foreign Missionary Society of America, James Anthony Walsh, describe plans for the conversion of China. Inspired by Walsh's vision and attracted by the exploits described in the missionary magazine, *The Field Afar*, Keller joined Maryknoll in 1921. He completed his theological studies at the Catholic University of America and was ordained in 1925. For the next twenty years Keller was one of the major American promoters of the foreign missions, first as a fund-raiser on the West Coast, and then, after 1931, in New York. As associate national director of the Society for the Propagation of the Faith, Keller edited its magazine, *Catholic Missions*, and helped revitalize the organization. He spent some time in the late 1920s and 1930s traveling in Asia and Europe but hoped above all that "Maryknoll would be able to take some active interest in the enormous work to be done in this country in saving the Christian tradition that seems to be fast disintegrating with the breakdown of Protestantism."[1]

Keller presented an overall vision for the "rechristianization" program in a 1945 article, "What About the Hundred Million?" Noting the experience of Catholic indifference in the face of fascism, the rampant spread of communism, and the undermining of the American social fabric by skepticism and atheism, the missionary called on priests and laity to leaven "this great mass of unbelievers in our land." He proposed plans to train priests who were "filled with the spirit of Christ" and the "methods of missionary penetration." He asked the laity to penetrate, as leaven in dough, the fields of education, communications, local community life, labor, and government, to restore public life to the fundamental Christian truths on which America was built. While calling his program "nothing more than Catholic Action," Keller stressed individual initiative and opened his appeal to non-Catholic participation. He also coined a name for the movement: the Christophers, people bearing Christ into the marketplace.[2]

Keller's ideas caused an immediate sensation. The first three printings of "What About the Hundred Million?" sold 37,000 copies. The Maryknoller furthered his argument in an article and pamphlet appealing to the Catholic populace. "*You* can be a Christopher," Keller challenged his readers:

> For the next twenty or thirty years, maybe longer, this nation will play the leading role in world affairs. Which way will it lead the world? If the Christian principles that make our country possible are strong and virile in the Hundred Million we may lead the world to Christ.
>
> The answer is in our hands and in the hands of people like us. It is a terrible challenge. But we must face the facts. There is no other way than the way of Christ. "I am the way and the truth and the life" (John 14:6). If we but strike a spark, that spark, in the Providence of God, may burst into a flame.[3]

The pamphlet received such an immense response (about 10,000 orders in six months) that Keller began the bimonthly *Christopher News Notes* in May 1946. Their purpose was to make isolated individuals aware of how much "leavening" was going on around them. The *Christopher News Notes* rose in circulation from 4,000 in 1946 to 800,000 by 1954. In 1985, nine years after Keller's death, the small pamphlets still boasted of a circulation of 650,000 in 150 different nations. Keller synthesized much of this approach in his November 1948 book, *You Can Change the World: The Christopher Approach.* One hundred fifty thousand copies were sold before March 1949. In the following years other best sellers extended the same message: *Careers That Change Your World* (1950) and *Government Is Your Business* (1951).[4]

Keller wanted more than just literary work, however. Realizing that the communists had successfully used mass meetings to focus attention on their objectives, he organized annual May Day celebrations. These rallies became huge demonstrations of American Catholic solidarity and indicated the mood of the times. The suggested program for the first rally in New York (1947) captured the fundamental spirit:

1. The Star Spangled Banner
2. Reading of Prepared Prayer
3. Talk on Basic Principles of Peace
4. Recitation of Archbishop Carroll's Prayer for Civil Authorities
5. Holy God [a Catholic hymn]

Although explicitly designed to show the united struggle against communism, the May Day celebrations achieved a twofold missionary result for Keller: "(1) millions of American Catholics prayed for millions of human beings in lands controlled by the Reds; (2) countless other millions in the U.S.A. and over the world had their attention drawn in passing at least to *spiritual values*." The numbers of people attending those "loyalty days" from 1947 to 1951 indicated that Keller had indeed united Americanism and Catholicism in such a way as to affect the faith of millions.[5]

During the course of the 1950s the work continued. Keller started Christopher Career Guidance Schools, an idea that proved unsuccessful; annual Christopher Awards for essays and books of outstanding merit; and study clubs. He gave retreats to men and women in Hollywood and entered the film industry. His weekly television programs, begun in 1952, were carried by over two hundred stations by 1954. The thirty-minute programs wedded God and the democratic experiment in the new field of mass communications. One-minute radio spots, "Christopher Thoughts for Today," appeared in 1957. In the following years Keller gave increasing attention to the development of the lay apostolate through study clubs and leadership courses. Living into the postconciliar period, he retired in 1970 and died on February 7, 1977.[6]

What he referred to as a "missionary method" lay at the heart of Keller's visionary work. The Maryknoller believed that the technique of going into the marketplace and there giving silent and unobtrusive witness to the truths of the gospel was the one that Christ himself had used. "Love thy neighbor," "Be ye wise as serpents," and "Go ye into the highways," were three gospel texts teaching modern Christians how to work. Often referring to Christianity's first entrance into pagan culture, Keller noted that the church had always adapted itself to native customs, working "to preserve and even further develop, all that is naturally good."[7] He explicitly described this technique of living the Christian life in the 1948 *Christopher News Notes:*

We are simply applying to the heart of America the same simple approach used by a Maryknoller in bringing Christ into the pagan city in China. Instead of sitting in the outskirts of the city, complaining or criticizing, he goes in—as Christ said to do—and puts into literal effect an old Chinese proverb: "It is better to light one candle than to curse the darkness." Even if only one missioner goes into the city, it is better than none at all. Even if he makes no apparent progress, or is persecuted and imprisoned, nevertheless he is there.[8]

As he implied in this description, Keller learned the method from James Anthony Walsh, who taught him very simply that the individual missionary was a bearer of Christ. All that was demanded was generosity "and a ready willingness to use the opportunities—or meet the difficulties which will inevitably present themselves." Taking his cue from Walsh and Thomas Price, Keller also believed that foreign and domestic mission work were inseparable. The world was one, and eventually the conversion of the United States *could have tremendous possibilities for the Christianization of China.*[9] One of Keller's supporters explained his approach by referring to James E. Walsh, later a bishop and the first of the society's missioners in China. "After many years of actual missionary experience in the fields of China," she wrote,

Walsh surprised the souls of his idealistic missioners-in-the-making, by requiring the cultivation of these low-sounding natural virtues: Accessibility, Adaptability, and Affability. The most seasoned and spiritual among us "swear by the natural" as the only means to the supernatural. The motive is what sublimates it.[10]

Keller believed this approach was ideally suited for spreading the gospel in the "home missions," the city streets and government agencies of modern America. The Christopher, he argued, was simply *there*, performing simple tasks, asking no favors, seeking no privileges, trying only to implant the fundamentals of life, and doing all of this for Christ. "And startling as it may seem, even a pagan in the darkest Africa or a Communist in the heart of America who learns even one of Christ's truths—and tries to spread that truth in the lifestream of his land—is beginning to be a Christopher, whether or not he realizes it. The more he does for Christ, the closer he draws to Christ."[11]

Several elements in Keller's own experience confirmed this "missionary method" as the true one in the modern world. A deep sense of the personal presence of God played a large role in the formation of his attitude. A classmate recalled that Keller believed in "prayer without ostentation." Abbot Columba Marmion (1888–1923), whose Christocentric spiritual theology made a deep impact on Keller's generation, and John Henry Newman (1801–1890) provided the guidelines. As Newman wrote, "At the foot of the cross, in your studies, in all your occupations, amid all distractions of daily life, strive hungrily, energetically, perseveringly, to commune with God." This piety emphasized self-restraint, discipline, and the Ignatian principle of *Age quod agis* ("Do what you are doing"). In his autobiography Keller noted how he learned the Sulpician method of meditation on Our Lord's life, designed as it was to "lead us to converse intimately with Him, to become more like Him and ultimately to act in a way that would make us more willing to be His representative in the world." Like many of his generation, he recited the breviary and made visits to the Blessed Sacrament and the daily stations of the cross. On his trip to Asia in 1928, the Maryknoller rode a rickshaw to a small corner of Singapore, where a man showed him a statue of Thérèse de Lisieux. The man commented: "She loved all people—everybody. And that is the reason for the shrine." Keller took this to heart, read the Little Flower's *Story of a Soul* repeatedly, and possessed a great devotion to the saint of the missions. "Few human beings," he wrote of Thérèse, "had such a universal sense of society. It was herself and the world, as though she regarded herself as the least of creatures. Her world was not bounded by convent walls. Her world was the whole world, and her heart went out to it." Here was an example the missionary longed to imitate.[12]

Keller's personal qualities and social background shaped his message almost as much as his piety. A representative of the individualistic middle-class culture, he learned efficiency from James Anthony Walsh, but on his own "came to the conclusion that all that was necessary to success, outside the grace of God, was to systematize efforts and follow details." Totally dedicated to work, he had little time for friendship. After moving to New York, Keller studied office procedures and the business manuals of major corporations (Chrysler, General Motors). He tried to improve his speaking ability by taking voice lessons. Modeled after one of the "state of the art" commercial magazines, *Catholic Missions*, under his editorship, took on a flair for the dramatic photo and catchy phrase. For example, in an ad entitled, "You're not talking to me!," with a picture of a beautifully coiffed and manicured woman, Keller ran the caption: "Oh, yes we are. You're *just* the one we're talking to! For if *you* won't listen to us, who will?" The magazine used Pan American Airways to illustrate its concept of "one world," and referred to Standard Oil as an example of distribution and efficiency that the Propagation of the Faith might imitate.[13]

It is partially in this mass-market context that Keller's formula for his very popular book on prayer, *Three Minutes a Day—Christopher Thoughts for Daily Living*, should be examined. Through these simple meditative exercises he wanted to establish "a pattern for a brief daily meditation that would help the average person live a more purposeful life." The formula, he said, should stress human and divine values and stimulate the reader to active participation in shaping the modern world. Each excerpt should be composed of a human-interest story, a supernatural application, an appropriate passage from the Bible, and a short simple prayer. Keller presented two basic rules:

1. Don't theologize too early in the story. And when you do, be chatty.
2. Hit for something in the Gospels. Don't let them know, but aim and tie up with Gospels.[14] '

By 1963 five volumes of this series on prayer had sold 1 million copies. The missionary transferred the idea into another medium with his radio spots. James Keller's techniques reflected the entry of American Catholics into the economic mainstream.

The worldwide struggle against communism also impressed Keller. On his trip to Asia he experienced a great contrast between the attitudes of Christian missionaries and the growing numbers of Communist party workers. The latter saw their crusade in global terms. They stressed personal responsibility, daring, self-sacrifice, participation in society, and sense of purpose. Keller compared their techniques and schools of propaganda at the University of Moscow and the Jefferson School of Social Science in New York to the methods of the early church. The Jefferson School of Social Science alone was reported to have trained 50,000 people in its first five years. The Maryknoller cited the example of these communist organizations many times in his writings. In the context of the Korean war, he chided his readers: "Doing nothing more than condemning Communists accomplishes little. At least the Communists are on the job. The Lord Himself told the *children of light* to learn from the *children of darkness*. Communism's only strength, outside the Devil, is our weakness." In the fight against totalitarianism, Keller also held out as an example the people of Nazi Germany who wanted good schools but had not troubled themselves to work for them. "Along came Hitler and the Nazis, who saw the far-reaching influence of the schools. They didn't mind the small pay, the hard work, the little glamour that is the lot of the teacher. They gladly made the sacrifice for their cause."[15] Such examples carried great appeal during the Cold War, and although Keller's anticommunism declined after the McCarthy hearings in the early 1950s, his own sense of urgency and techniques for the "missionary method" took a great deal from his adversaries. The Christophers, like the communists, tried to penetrate every structure of society.

Keller combined personal piety, mass-market techniques, and

anticommunism into two fundamental beliefs that supported his missionary program. First, when traveling in Europe, he learned that the best way to combat totalitarianism was to concentrate on the fundamental rights of each individual as a unique child of God. In 1936 *Catholic Missions* carried a picture of a single lit candle, and on the opposite page was the caption, "Why Help the Missions." Keller commented in the following way:

> Every human being, regardless of creed or color, is made to the image and likeness of God and possesses a soul more precious than all the world and has only one purpose here: to prepare his soul for eternity by knowing, loving, and serving his Maker in this life. To help each and every soul, God sent His Divine Son to redeem us and give us both a plan and unlimited assistance to attain eternal salvation. We have already received the gift of faith but nearly two thirds of mankind has not. God has left it in our hands to see that they do.[16]

Keller connected this sense of the image and likeness of God in each individual to the individual's priestly vocation. It implied a harmony between nature and grace in the classic Thomistic sense, a harmony brought to spiritual fulfillment in baptism. The Maryknoller formulated this conviction in the context of a revival of medieval studies. When commenting on his training at the Catholic University, he noted that "recent historians have attributed our modern political system, our scientific thought and our art to the development of principles formulated during this period of vision, beauty, and vigor in which the people succeeded remarkably well in blending the divine with human affairs." Visiting Notre Dame Cathedral in Paris, he reflected on the sheer wonder of "thousands upon thousands" of persons "bringing God's beauty, love and truth into every phase of our modern life." *You Can Change the World* characterized communists as those with a militant hatred of basic truths. Among the basic truths Keller listed: Each human being is a child of God, created in his image and likeness; fundamental rights come from God not the state; the chief purpose of the state is to *protect* God-given rights. "We confine ourselves to the broad pursuit of major principles," he wrote, "and rely on the refreshing resourcefulness God has placed in every individual to do the rest. This simple freedom allows greater originality, more imagination, enterprise, and daring, and more enduring dynamism." The Christopher, he described, "worked on the side of the fundamental goodness which the Creator of all has embedded deep in the heart and soul of each and every human being."[17]

Immersed in a way of thinking that harmonized the Catholic tradition and constitutional principles, Keller identified Christianity and the American way of life. This identification was the second major belief shaping his work. His 1945 program for the Christophers listed five fundamental Christian ideals at the base of American civilization: the existence of a personal God; the divinity of Christ; the ten commandments; the sacredness of the individual; and the sanctity of marriage and home. Keller elaborated on these connections in his major works from 1948 to 1960, and extended the convergence between American civilization and Christianity to include the right to private property, respect for domestic, civil, and religious authority, and judgment after death. Had not the Declaration of Independence contained specific references to the dependence of the nation on God? Was not the eye of God printed on every dollar bill?

Keller argued that from the perspective of the communists, America and religion were the two greatest enemies; no distinction need be made between Catholics and Protestants. At the crossroads of civilization, people should come together in an unselfish offensive against paganism: "If a person is not a creature of God and the noblest act of God, with rights from Him," Keller wrote, "then he is just a clod of earth or the merest tool of the almighty state. He must be one or the other. He cannot be both." Throughout his writings, the home missionary referred to Protestants and Catholics who felt similarly, among whom were Walter Lippmann, John Courtney Murray, Arthur Schlesinger, Jr., and Fulton Oursler. "As Americans," he concluded in *Government is Your Business*, "we have no excuse for failing to have the best government in the world. It was founded upon Divine Truth, and we pay more for it than any people ever paid for government. *God does not long bless those who are negligent or wasteful.*"[18]

James Keller's wedding of Christianity and Americanism did not go unchallenged in some segments of the Catholic community. Certainly Dorothy Day objected to his style, and Keller considered her *Catholic Worker* a critic of his enterprise.[19] The most penetrating attack came from Carol Jackson (1911–   ), the editor of *Integrity* magazine. Writing as "Peter Michaels," she likened Keller to Dale Carnegie and described *You Can Change the World* as filled with "pious slogans" and "modern clichés." Although Jackson agreed that the laity should be apostolic, she argued that Keller avoided presenting the "fullness of the doctrine that we are *other* Christs." He clung to the "natural level" of goodness, placed undue hope in people's abilities, and ignored the frequentation of the sacraments. His plan, in short, was naive. Above all, the Maryknoller ignored any lay apostolate other than the Christophers. "Now it happens that holiness and prayer and sacrifice and souls' struggles have gone into the understanding and launching of the modern lay apostolate. Yet Catholic Action, the Legion of Mary, Friendship House, the Catholic Worker, and other organizations might just as well have never existed for all that Keller pays any attention to them." Father Keller, Jackson finished, "has suddenly found the whole thing is easy and no organization is necessary. Whoever has worked in the modern situation has discovered the necessity of organization, which also has strong papal support." Father Leonard Feeney, S.J. (1897–1978), also criticized the Christopher program. For both Jackson and Feeney, the major difficulties surrounded Keller's disparagement of Catholic Action and his "invitation to all to join him regardless of religious confession."[20]

Eventually, Keller received an inquiry from the Vatican through the apostolic delegate, Archbishop Amleto Cicognani. He responded by submitting his ideas to censors of the archdiocese of New York in this summary form:

> As true followers of Christ, we have a fourfold obligation:
>
> 1. to those who are members of the Catholic Church;
> 2. to those who are interested in entering the Church;
> 3. to those who have no desire or who refuse to become Catholics;
> 4. to those who hate the Church and fight against it.
>
> Most Catholics show a laudable interest in the first two groups. But much remains to be done with regard to the other two. . . . If we succeed in nothing more than getting them to be one degree more disposed towards Christ, to offer one prayer or do one small deed for the love of God, it is an important step in the right direction.[21]

Negotiations continued for some time with Keller claiming the support of the Dominican theologian Walter Farrell (1902–1951) and the Vatican undersecretary of the Congregation of the Sacraments. Finally, with the approval of the censors and his Maryknoll superiors, a statement identifying the Christophers as a Catholic movement was released. "By the very fact that it is Catholic," the statement read, "it is deeply concerned, for time and for eternity, with the welfare of all men—even those whose background makes them hostile to religion. In loving solicitude we are bound to include all and exclude none. Each is a child of God through creation and is a potential citizen of heaven. Each, doing even one thing for Him, can start to be a Christopher, a Christbearer."[22]

Although the joint statement quieted fears for Keller's orthodoxy and at the same time vindicated his missionary technique, the Maryknoller continued to labor under the shadow of the controversy. He declined to participate in interfaith groups, reported to Cardinal Francis Spellman (1889–1967) on the success of his work, wrote a position paper supporting his missionary method with statements from the popes, and in later years carefully described the Catholic lay apostle as guided by the hierarchy. Such tactics enabled him to make peace with the aggressive position of the dominant approach of Catholic Action. Still, despite these conciliatory gestures, he published his last book, *Change the World from Your Parish*, as an explicit defense of the fundamental principles of his missionary method.[23]

In conclusion, several significant features of James Keller's vision of the Christian life should be noted. A second-generation product of a fractured inheritance that promoted the assimilation of Catholics into American life, he reflected that inheritance while at the same time changing it. Confronted with the totalitarian state that both Virgil Michel and Dorothy Day had battled, the Maryknoller shared with them an emphasis on personal responsibility, the dignity of the individual, and the integration of social reform and spirituality. Also a product, as they were not, of Madison Avenue, he departed from his contemporaries in his aggressive adoption of mass-market techniques and acceptance of economic individualism. The result was, on the one hand, an integration of spirituality and social reform on the basis of a common Christianity, and, on the other, a privatization of a Catholic spiritual life. For example, in *You Can Change the World*, Keller presented a short portrayal of life that included the following signs of growth in Christian values: expanding horizons; increased power; sense of proportion in taking others more seriously and oneself less seriously; learning how to disagree without being disagreeable; the development of an ever-increasing imagination and enterprise, which would be a gift of God; keenness of observation; capacity for work; and real *joy* of living. In the same work he suggested the following daily schedule for Catholics: morning prayer; meditation; mass and reception of communion; grace at meals; recitation of the rosary and Angelus; reading of a spiritual book for five minutes; night prayers; examination of conscience.[24] This juxtaposition clearly implied a fractured world, yet by his insistence on a common basis for the Christian life, Keller integrated Catholics much more into the demands of religious pluralism and set the stage for an emerging ecumenical consciousness.

Connected with this ecumenical insight was a democratization of the spiritual life and a movement away from the methods and presuppositions of Catholic Action. In 1960, on the eve of Vatican II, Keller released a special *Christopher News Notes* bulletin called "Christopher Tips for Lay Apostles." Its fourteenth point summarized the work of a lifetime and pointed to a Catholic world about to be born:

14. *Blend the divine and the human*—On February 20, 1946, Pope Pius XII said: "*She* [the Church] *must today, as never before, live her mission; she must reject more emphatically than ever that false and narrow concept of*

spirituality and her interior life which would confine her, blind and mute, in the retirement of the sanctuary." . . . Are you helping the Church to *"live her mission?"* Or by noninvolvement do you *"confine"* her to the *"sanctuary"*? . . . If the followers of Christ do not apply eternal truths to every human sphere, be it raising children, improving politics, writing TV scripts or upholding justice in labor-management relations—who will?[25]

CHAPTER
18
Thomas Merton
Contemplation for All

❦

$\mathcal{T}$he story of Thomas Merton, monk and writer, is well known. Born to a New Zealand artist father and an American mother in 1915, he grew up in the cosmopolitan world of postwar France and England. After the death of his parents, he immigrated to the United States in the same year, 1932, in which Dorothy Day met Peter Maurin. Merton received his B.A. and M.A. degrees from Columbia University and converted to Roman Catholicism in 1938. In 1941, after a painful vocational search, he entered Gethsemani Abbey, Kentucky, a Trappist monastery not far from Louisville. Reviewing his life in the monastery in 1962, Merton divided it into four major periods. First was the period from 1942 to 1944, his novitiate years and first exposure to the monastic spiritual tradition. The second, from 1944 to 1949, was a period of extensive study of philosophy and theology, translation of French books and articles, and preparation for the priesthood. During this period the young monk wrote his best-selling autobiography, *The Seven Storey Mountain* (1948) as well as *Seeds of Contemplation* (1949) and *The Waters of Siloe* (1949). During the third period, from his ordination in 1949 until the time he was made master of the choir novices in 1955, he prepared conferences for the monks studying for the priesthood and published *The Ascent to Truth* (1951), *The Sign of Jonas* (1953), and *No Man Is an Island* (1955). Merton's work showed increasing maturity in the fourth period, from 1956 onward, as he began to comment on American society, issues of war and peace, monastic renewal, liturgy, solitude, and world religions from the perspective of his own spiritual quest. The best-known books from this period included *The New Man* (1961), *Life and Holiness* (1963), *Conjectures of a Guilty Bystander* (1966), *Mystics and Zen Masters* (1967), and the posthumously published work on monastic renewal, *Contemplation in a World of Action* (1971). The scope of his work and its impact on the Catholic community in the United States has yet to be fully comprehended. For the purpose of this present analysis, Merton's significance can be seen in his focus on the unity of all vocations in the contemplative experience of God. It was this experience that made him, along with Michel, Day, and Keller, the herald of a new understanding and a forerunner of Vatican Council II.[1]

Just three years after his conversion, during Holy Week 1941, Merton made a retreat at Gethsemani. Obviously enamored of its peacefulness, simplicity, and spiritual depth, the young convert described the monastery as the "center of America." "Gethsemani," he wrote in his journal,

> holds the country together the way the underlying substrata of natural faith that goes with our whole being and can hardly be separated from it, keeps living on in a man who has "lost the faith"—who no longer believes in Being and yet himself *is*, in spite of his crazy denial that He who IS mercifully allowed him to *be*.

Merton continued the meditation by noting that the monastic vocation was rooted in the desire to love God by wanting to be like God. The abbey was full of cleanness, order, and stability; its church was tidy; its discipline was strict. Yet its fundamental purpose could hardly be encompassed by these external characteristics. The religious life, Merton wrote, "exists and thrives not in buildings or dead things or flowers or beasts but in the soul." A few days later, having shared the life of the monks in some detail, this visitor to the "center of America" compared the development of the life of the soul to a poet trying over a period of years adequately to translate his image or intuition of truth into words: "This image confronts the poet for years. He may work it out, once, simply, in one poem, and then work it over and over again in more complex poems, piece by piece, developing and complicating metaphors that are all part of one long, central metaphor."[2]

These reflections on the life of the soul and the quest for God were sandwiched into Merton's journal between much longer sections on his experiences in New York and at Saint Bonaventure's University, where he taught. When he returned to the university from Gethsemani, he recorded how he had been particularly impressed by a lecture that Baroness Catherine de Hueck (1900–1985) had given to the students attending the summer session. The Russian émigrée spoke about her work among the poor blacks in Harlem and the establishment of Friendship House. During the following months of 1941, Merton visited Harlem and became an evening patron of the house. In his subsequent letters to the baroness he grappled with the political excesses of Catholic Action as reflected in the Spanish Civil War or in the policies of the medieval papacy, and speculated about the true foundation for a "lay vocation." Merton also expressed an intuition that the poor, the monastery, the hermitage, and the life of children were somehow interconnected in the pursuit of holiness. It was in these places, he believed, that "angels appeared," and he clearly wanted to find a place where all these experiences could be united.[3]

For a few months between his retreat at Gethsemani and entrance into the monastery in December, Merton considered joining Friendship House. He warned the baroness that she was "getting no bargain." The life of "*real* poverty, without security," completely dependent on God, inspired him. "Harlem is where Christ is, where the Blessed Mother is more likely to appear than anywhere—except perhaps a Trappist monastery." He believed that the same infinite source of life nourished both the work in Harlem and the monastery. They were two dimensions of the one Mystical Body of Christ. Finally, he decided for the Trappists. "I simply long with my whole existence," he concluded in his letter to the baroness before his entrance into Gethsemani,

> to be completely consecrated to God in every gesture, every breath and every movement of my body and mind, to the exclusion of absolutely everything except Him: and the way I desire this, by His grace, is the way it is among the Trappists. F.H. [Friendship House] made sense to me, but I was not eaten up with this kind of longing for the lay apostolate that I seem to have for a contemplative community and a life of prayer and penance.[4]

Once he entered Gethsemani, Merton labored, like the poet in his description, to unveil the central insights of his vocation that he had expressed in his journal and in the letters to Catherine de Hueck. In 1941 he intuited a profound connection between the concerns of the baroness in Harlem and the *opus Dei* of the monks in Kentucky. Both belonged to the same Body of Christ, and Gethsemani lay at the center of America precisely because it embodied for him the life in which all things became one: God. He entered the monastery, just as Dorothy Day had been drawn to the poor, to come in contact with the deepest wellsprings of the world and of humanity itself: love.

Merton analyzed this central vocational insight, which he expressed in the term "contemplation," in his "Meditatio Pauperis in Solitudine," the concluding part of *Seven Storey Mountain*. "America," he wrote, "is discovering the contemplative life," and in that context he wanted to examine the age-old distinction between action and contemplation. He turned to Thomas Aquinas. The Dominican doctor, according to Merton, demonstrated that "contemplative life establishes a man at the very heart of all spiritual fecundity." Rather than dichotomizing action and contemplation, Aquinas further noted that the highest rank in religion belonged to those leading a mixed life, one in which "love is *so much more vehement, so much more abundant* that it has to pour itself out in teaching and preaching." Starting from these premises, Merton decided that twentieth-century monks, in order to reach the highest rank, had to pass on the fruits of their contemplation to the world, and those working in the world needed to develop a deep interior life. In either case, there was a profound coming together around the vocation of contemplation.

The Trappist turned to the tradition of Saints Francis and Bonaventure to offer a specific example. The highest of all vocations, he argued, was expressed in Francis's reception of the stigmata, the perfect act of contemplation.

> It is the vocation to transforming union, to the height of the mystical life of mystical experience, to the very transformation into Christ that Christ living in us and directing all our actions might Himself draw men to desire and seek that same exalted union because of the joy and the sanctity and the supernatural vitality radiated by our example—rather because of the secret influence of Christ living within us in complete possession of our souls.[5]

This vocation, Merton noted, made no distinctions, no divisions between people. Christ had imprinted his image on Francis of Assisi not to draw some men, nor to attract simply a few monks, but to lead "*all* truly spiritual men to the perfection of contemplation which is nothing else but the perfection of love." "This means, in practice," he concluded,

> that there is only one vocation. Whether you teach or live in the cloister or nurse the sick, whether you are in religion or out of it, married or single, no matter who you are or what you are, you are called to the summit of perfection: you are called to a deep interior life perhaps even to mystical prayer, and to pass the fruits of your contemplation on to others. And if you cannot do so by word, then by example.[6]

In succeeding years Merton tried to make accessible to others, through the written word and his own example, the one vocation to transforming union in Christ. Several examples can be given. *Seeds of Contemplation*, although written by a monk and focused on such traditional monastic themes as solitude, freedom under obedience, detachment, renunciation, and inward destitution, had "no other end or ideal in view than what should be the ordinary fulfillment of the Christian life of grace, and therefore everything that is said here can be applied to anyone, not only in the monastery but also in the world." In this work Merton presented fruits of his own life with God that would eventually lead him to embrace the whole world. "Everything that is, is Holy," he wrote; "Go into the desert not to escape other men but in order to find them in God"; "Love comes out of God and gathers us to God in order to pour itself back into God through all of us and bring us all back to Him on the tide of His own infinite mercy." In 1955 *No Man Is an Island* elaborated on these views, and Merton significantly unified solitude, humility, self-denial, action and contemplation, the sacraments, the monastic life, family, war and peace in "the central reality which is God's love loving and acting in those whom He has incorporated in His Christ." In the 1960s, Merton directed *Life and Holiness* to those engaged in "active life" and tried to strengthen their sense of grace and interiority. The same period saw numerous essays on the relationships between the monastic life and the problems of the world. "It is not a question of either-or," he wrote, "but of all-in-one. It is not a matter of exclusivism and 'purity' but of wholeness, wholeheartedness, unity and Master Eckhart's *Gleichheit* (equality) which finds the same ground of love in everything." Finally, he presented the Christological center of the one vocation in *The New Man.* "What is this life?" he asked.

> It is eternal life, mystical life in the knowledge of "Thee, the one true God, and Jesus Christ Whom Thou has sent." Much more, it is the knowledge promised by Christ to the Apostles "in that day" when they would receive His Spirit. "In that day you will know that I am in my Father and you in me and I in you."[7]

There can be little doubt that Merton struggled to express this vocation of love, and the challenge led him constantly to proclaim the "death" of oneself and the birth of a new, more integrated person. His early works tended to focus on some of the external elements of the monastic vocation: its discipline, regularity, order. His *Secular Journal,* covering his life before entrance into the monastery, *The Sign of Jonas,* a spiritual diary from the early 1950s, and *Conjectures of a Guilty Bystander* reflect a progressive development and broadening to embrace God, himself, others, and the world. Studies of his theology of prayer note the movement from alignment of contemplation with the act of justice to contemplation as personal transformation through self-transcendence in God. Certainly, Merton's own inner torment over self-love, his struggle with guilt, and search for some human companionship indicate a restless quest for fulfillment.[8] Yet throughout all of this development, he continually broke from the fractured in-

heritance of the early twentieth century and attempted to integrate
the often dichotomized forces of nature and grace, action and contemplation, the world and the church. The focal point of the whole
discussion, as it had been for Michel, Day, and Keller, was the person,
and his or her transformation in Christ. For Merton, every single thing
that existed was one in the all-consuming act of God's love. Seen from
the perspective of the dominant ecclesiastical structures, such an understanding of the spiritual life implied a democratization of far-
reaching consequences. The Trappist monk, precisely because of the
symbolic clarity of his renunciation of the world and pursuit of love
in God, prophesied a postconciliar Christian vision.

Epilogue

❧

$\mathcal{V}$irgil Michel, Dorothy Day, James Keller, and Thomas Merton anticipated a new vision and practice of Catholic spiritual life in many different ways. First, on the level of the person, each of them emphasized the harmony that could exist between nature and grace, reason and faith. Reacting strongly to the forces of the totalitarian state and an ecclesiastical emphasis on juridical structures, they turned inward, combining the strains of interiority latent in the more objective Thomistic tradition with the subjective emphasis on will and the affections in Augustinianism. The personalist element so evident in Michel and Day received its theological complement in Keller's and Merton's return to the biblical and patristic teachings on men and women as the image of God. By placing the person at the center of their synthesis, they shifted the focus of the spiritual life away from institutional expressions towards the creation of the "new man in Christ."

Socially, the acknowledgment of the dignity of the person and the natural "seeds of grace" embedded in humanity allowed Michel, Day, Keller, and Merton to stress the universal elements of Catholic self-definition. The founder of the liturgical movement argued explicitly for stronger bonds between Catholics and Protestants; Day's approach moved beyond the sectarian emphasis of Catholic Action; Keller's missionary mentality attempted to embrace the world, and Merton, in his later years, moved toward a reconciliation of East and West. A corollary to this search for harmony between religious traditions was an attempt in the context of secularism to apply Christian principles to the understanding of massive social problems. The economic issues of capital and labor, the effects of industrialization on the life of the poor, the anonymity of the modern person in the face of mass-market techniques, the world situation created by Hiroshima and the

Holocaust, and the dangers of the Cold War—all of these issues and many others, in the minds of these forerunners, played a decisive role in the formation and development of Catholic spiritual life.

Ecclesiologically, each of these people worked to reestablish the broken bonds of community. Michel, Day, and Merton reacted strongly to the individualism implicit in the fractured inheritance. They turned away from the juridical categories of the perfect society and toward the values of spiritual interdependence and complementarity expressed in Paul's teaching on the Mystical Body of Christ. Even James Keller, the most individualistic of the four, clearly believed that "lighting one candle" would affect the lives of thousands of others. In this area above all, the forerunners of Vatican II democratized the spiritual life and dissolved the barriers dividing clergy, religious, and laity into separate worlds.

Fourth, from Michel's and Day's critique of minimum Christianity, through Keller's rejection of lukewarm religiosity, to Merton's rejection of an externalized monasticism, these reformers departed from the purgative way tradition that had so dominated Catholic life in the United States. While accepting the values of obedience and discipline, they argued for a more affective, interior sense of prayer, a unity between action and contemplation, the role of conscience in the spiritual life, and the primacy of love. Each person, in his or her own way, focused on the illumination that came with a personal experience of God. They moved toward a Christocentric humanism that found Christ in the embrace of the brother and sister.

Michel, Day, Keller, and Merton, albeit in dramatically different ways, also attempted to unite the fractured elements of the American and Catholic identities. Michel argued for a convergence between Catholicism and true democracy in the sacrificial action of the Mass; Day, for a return to unity based on the radical call of the gospel; Keller, in the context of anticommunism, almost equated Christianity and the American way of life; Merton turned to the critical tradition of American romanticism in his identification of Gethsemani as the "center of America." The focus of each forerunner on the dignity of the person and creative action of God in the world encouraged the acceptance of those elements in American culture that harmonized with their vision of Catholicism.

Finally, in their quest to spread "fire on the earth," each of these people initiated a reform of Catholic life from within the structures of the fractured inheritance. Michel promoted the priesthood of the faithful and the reform of asceticism while immersed within the daily routine and boundaries of a Benedictine abbey; Day combined the nonsectarian approach of the Houses of Hospitality with a devout allegiance to ecclesiastical authority; Keller united a very privatized

Catholic piety with a universal missionary outlook; and Merton, practicing the contemplative tradition in the context of one of the church's most disciplined and rigorous religious orders, found universality in the heart of his Catholic identity. It was precisely this strength of the institutional church with its doctrinal integrity, well-defined structures, and specific ritual expressions that provided the self-identity necessary for the reformers' advocacy of a spiritual and social revitalization. Secure in their own Catholicism, they could reach out to promote integration and democratization within the context of American society and their mission to the world. In a paradoxical way, the reform could occur only because its opposite held sway.

When the Second Vatican Council met, it brought to fruition the seeds of the spiritual renewal that had been sown by Michel, Day, Keller, and Merton. The Council also marked a shift in the history of Catholic spiritual life in the United States. No longer privileged to share in the security of the fractured Catholic identity, the postconciliar generation now had to combine in a new way the church with the world, faith with doubt, contemplation with action, and the spirit with institutional and human frailty. The discernment of these events must necessarily elude the historian. Suffice it to say that the Catholic community today is not attempting anything that previous generations have not also had to accomplish. The task is simply to respond within the context of history to the invitation that has been issued to the Catholic community in the United States since the days of John Carroll: "Come to him, a living stone, rejected by men but approved nonetheless, and precious in God's eyes. You too are living stones, built as an edifice of the Spirit, into a holy priesthood, offering spiritual sacrifices acceptable to God, through Jesus Christ."

Notes

Part I   An Enlightenment Synthesis, 1776–1815

1. *Ex hac apostolicae* is printed in John Tracy Ellis, ed., *Documents of American Catholic History* (Chicago, 1967), 1:163–67. Carroll's comments are taken from "Sermon on Occasion of Possessing His Pro-Cathedral," in Thomas O'Brien Hanley, S.J., ed., *The John Carroll Papers*, vol. 1, *1755–1791* (Notre Dame, Ind., 1976), p. 477. Carroll to Charles Plowden, November 13, 1795, in Hanley, ed., *The John Carroll Papers*, vol. 2, *1792–1806*, p. 158. On Carroll's dealings with Latrobe,

see Annabelle M. Melville, *John Carroll of Baltimore: Founder of the American Catholic Hierarchy* (New York, 1955), pp. 268–69. Maréchal's remark can be found in his "Report to Propaganda," October 16, 1818, printed in Ellis, *Documents*, p. 204.

Chapter 1   Religious Pluralism

1. "The Last Judgment," in Hanley, ed., *The John Carroll Papers*, vol. 3, *1807–1815*, pp. 390–93.
2. For Carroll's use of terms see Hanley, *Papers* 3:407, 375, 392, 426, and *Pastoral Letters of Archbishop Carroll to the Congregation of Trinity Church, in Philadelphia, 1797; And of Archbishop Marechal to the Congregation of Norfolk, Virginia, 1819* (Baltimore: Joseph Robinson, 1820), 15.
3. Carroll to Plowden, October 12, 1791, Hanley, *Papers* 1:522–24; Carroll to Berington, July 10, 1784, Hanley, *Papers* 1:147–49; for Berington's remarks, see his *The State and the Behaviour of English Catholics from the Reformation to the Year 1780 with a View of Their Present Number, Wealth, Character, etc.* (London: R. Faulder, 1780), p. 187; John Fletcher, *Reflections on the Spirit etc., etc. of Religious Controversy* (London: Deathing, Brown & Keating, 1804), p. ii; for Carroll's reliance on these English apologists, see Joseph P. Chinnici, "American Catholics and Religious Pluralism, 1775–1820," *Journal of Ecumenical Studies* 16 (Fall 1979): 727–46; a "system of piety and humility" is taken from Fletcher, *Reflections*, p. 38.
4. Thomas O'Brien Hanley, "The Emergence of Pluralism in the United States," *Theological Studies* 23 (June 1962):207–32; "Reluctant Witness to Pluralism in Early America," ibid. 26 (September 1965):375–92.
5. Hanley, "Infidelity," *Papers* 3:385.
6. The "language of a republican" is found in Carroll to Plowden, February 10, 1782, Hanley, *Papers* 1:65; Carroll to Arthur O'Leary, 1787, Hanley, *Papers* 1:224–26. For the colonial Maryland tradition, see Gerald P. Fogarty, S.J., "Property and Religious Liberty in Colonial Maryland Catholic Thought," *Catholic Historical Review* 72 (October 1986):573–600.
7. *An Introduction to the Devout Life*, which circulated among the Maryland colonists, was first published in the United States in 1806, and permeated the writings of Carroll's favorite English apologists and devotional writers, Joseph Berington, James Archer, John Fletcher, and Richard Challoner.
8. For early education, see Hanley, "Young Mr. Carroll and Montesquieu," *Maryland Historical Magazine* 58 (December 1963):394–418; publishing information can be found in Joseph M. Finotti, *Bibliographia Catholica Americana: A List of Works Written by Catholic Authors, and Published in the United States*, pt. 1, *1784–1820* (New York: The Catholic Publication House, 1872). On the English devotional writers, Sister Marion Norman, I.B.V.M., "John Gother and the English Way of Spirituality," *Recusant History* 11 (1971–72):306–319, and Richard Luckett, "Bishop Challoner: The Devotionary Writer," in Eamon Duffy, ed., *Challoner and His Times: A Catholic Bishop in Georgian England*

(London, 1986), pp. 71–89. Carroll spoke of Chesterfield in a letter to Charles Plowden, March 1, 1788, Hanley, *Papers* 1:275.

9. Carroll to Robert Plowden, July 7, 1797, Hanley, *Papers* 2:219.

10. *Catechism on the Foundations of the Christian Faith. For the Use of Both the Young and the Old* (New York: Office of the Economical School), p. 23; Charles Butler's *Life of Fenelon* was published in 1811. Works of the Frenchman that appeared during Carroll's lifetime include: *The Adventures of Telemachus* (1796, 1797, 1806); *Extracts from the Writings of Francis Fenelon, Archbishop of Cambray* (1804); *Treatise on the Education of Daughters* (1806); *Dialogues Concerning Eloquence in General and Particularly that Kind which is Proper for the Pulpit* (1810); *Pious Reflections* (1814).

11. For Carroll's friendships, see Melville, *John Carroll, passim.*

12. Sister Marion Norman, "John Gother," p. 311; J. D. Crichton, "Recusant Writers on the Priesthood of the Laity," *The Clergy Review* 71 (December 1984):455–57; *The Catholic Laity's Directory to the Church Services with an Almanac for the Year 1817* (New York: M. Field, 1817), pp. 22–23, here p. 22.

13. Twenty-five editions of fifteen of his works were published prior to 1818. Such works as the *Garden of the Soul* (1773, 1792, 1809), *Think Well On't* (1791, 1800, 1809), and his translation of the *Imitation of Christ* (1800, 1808, 1809) nourished the daily faith of the Catholic and Protestant communities.

14. Finotti, *Bibliographia Catholica Americana;* Luckett, "Bishop Challoner."

15. Georgetown University, Special Collections, has Carroll's copy of Giovanni Pietro Maffei, *De vita et morib. Ignatii, Loiolae: Qui Societatem Jesu fundavit* (Rome: Franciscum Zannettum, 1585); Carroll to John Grassi, September 24, 1813, Hanley, *Papers* 3:231; Carroll to Robert Plowden, August 14, 1804, Hanley, *Papers* 2:448; on Alfonso Rodríguez, see Armand de Vassal, "Un Maître de la vie spirituelle. Le Père Alphonse Rodriguez," *Etudes* 150 (January–March 1917):297–321, and for use in the colonies, Thomas Hughes, *History of the Society of Jesus in North America, Colonial and Federal*, vol. 2, *1645–1773* (New York: Longmans, Green and Co., 1917), pp. 515ff; L. P. Vincent Huby, S. J., *The Spiritual Retreat of the Reverend Father Vincent Huby of the Society of Jesus* (Philadelphia: Matthew Carey, 1795).

Chapter 2   Nature and Grace

1. "Faith," Hanley, *Papers* 3:386–87.

2. Carroll's view probably derived from the eighteenth-century natural-law tradition of Louis Thomassin (1619–95) and Montesquieu. Carroll also appealed to Augustine, Aquinas, and the Council of Trent. For Thomassin, see Pierre Clair, "L'idée de nature chez le Père Thomassin," *Revue des etudes augustiniennes* 18 (1972):261–86.

3. Carroll's interpretation of *extra ecclesiam* can be found in "An Address to the Roman Catholics of the United States of America By a Catholic Clergyman" (1784), Hanley, *Papers* 1:88–91.

4. "Faith and Infidelity," Hanley, *Papers* 3:376, 379–80.

5. Fletcher, *Reflections*, pp. 165–66.

6. *Catechism*, pp. 26–38.
7. "Duties of Parents," Hanley, *Papers* 3:447–50, here 447.
8. See Henri de Lubac, *Augustinianism and Modern Theology* (London: Geoffrey Chapman, 1969), trans. Lancelot Sheppard; idem, *The Mystery of the Supernatural* (New York: Herder and Herder, 1967), trans. Rosemary Sheed; Bernard Plongeron, *Théologie et politique au siècle des lumières (1770–1820)* (Geneva: Librairie Droz, 1973); René Taveneaux, *Jansénisme et politique* (Paris: Armand Colin, 1965).
9. Carroll to Hyacinth Gerdil, December 1795, Hanley, *Papers* 2:160.
10. Carroll to Berington, July 10, 1784, Hanley, *Papers* 1:147–49; for Carroll's discussion of his plans, see Robert Plowden, *A Letter to a Roman Catholic Clergyman upon Theological Inaccuracy* (London: J. P. Coghlan, 1795), p. 151; Robert Plowden to Carroll, March 10, 1799, Archives of the Archdiocese of Baltimore, 6S7; "Provincial Council Resolutions," in Hanley, *Papers* 3:133, no. 9.
11. Stephen Dubisson to Maréchal, August 30, 1821, AAB, 16B1; Francis Patrick Kenrick to Propaganda Fide, June 10, 1829, and Bishop Rosati to Propaganda, as cited in Rev. Thomas F. Casey, *The Sacred Congregation de Propaganda Fide and the Revisions of the First Provincial Council of Baltimore (1829–1830)* (Rome: Gregorian University, 1957), p. 45, n. 14; p. 133, n. 47.
12. P. Babade to Propaganda, November 21, 1806, Archives of the Sacred Congregation of the Propagation of the Faith, Atti della Congregatione Particolare de 4 Marzo, 1808, America Settentrionale, 145, f. 103rv, 104r, 105r, here 105r.
13. Carroll to Francis Beeston, November 16, 1791, Hanley, *Papers* 1:545–46; Carroll to Leonardo Antonelli, March 1, 1785, Hanley, *Papers* 1:181; Carroll to Monsignor Bracadoro, February 10, 1802, Hanley, *Papers* 2:375; Carroll to Stefano Borgia, February 14, 1804, ibid. 434; for regulations of the First Diocesan Synod, see Hanley, *Papers* 1:529–31; "Matrimony," Hanley, *Papers* 3:430. For personal background, see Robert F. McNamara, "John Carroll and Interfaith Marriages: The Case of the Belle Vue Carrolls," in Nelson H. Minnich, Robert B. Eno, S.S., and Robert F. Trisco, eds., *Studies in Catholic History in Honor of John Tracy Ellis* (Wilmington, Del., 1985), pp. 27–59.
14. "Matrimony," Hanley, *Papers* 1:432; ibid. p. 425.
15. "Matrimony," Hanley, *Papers* 3:426–29, with long quotation from p. 428.

Chapter 3   "Spiritual Matters"

1. Carroll to Charles Plowden, April 22, 1790, Hanley, *Papers* 1:56.
2. For evolution of *spiritualitas*, see Jean Leclerq, O.S.B., "Spiritualitas," *Studi Medievali* 1 (1953):279–96.
3. Carroll to Charles Plowden, February 28, 1779, Hanley, *Papers* 1:53.
4. "Constitution of the Clergy," June 27, 1783 to October 11, 1784, in Hanley, *Papers* 1:71–77, here art. 19; to Pope Pius VI, 1783, ibid. 1:69.
5. Carroll to Berington, July 10, 1784, Hanley, *Papers* 1:148; Carroll to Dominick Lynch and Thomas Stoughton, January 24, 1786, ibid. 203–206.
6. For a presentation of Carroll's ecclesiology emphasizing his juridical

relationships, see James Hennesey, S.J., "An Eighteenth Century Bishop: John Carroll of Baltimore," *Archivum Historiae Pontificae* 16 (1978):171–204.

7. *Pastoral Letters of Archbishop Carroll . . . and Ambrose Maréchal,* pp. 9, 13, 14; "Holy Orders," Hanley, *Papers* 3:410.

8. "Eucharist: The Old Law and the New," Hanley, *Papers* 3:405.

9. "Charity," Hanley, *Papers* 3:436–43.

10. "Holy Orders," Hanley, *Papers* 3:408–13, here 409; 413–15, here 415.

11. *Pastoral Letters of Archbishop Carroll . . . and Ambrose Maréchal,* pp. 6, 9, 16, 6, 8, 10; Hanley, *Papers* 3:414, 416, 417.

12. The sermon is printed in full in Peter Guilday, *The Life and Times of John Carroll, Archbishop of Baltimore, 1735–1815* (New York, 1922), 2:434–41. Cf. Robert Emmett Curran, S.J., " 'The Finger of God Is Here': The Advent of the Miraculous in the Nineteenth-Century American Catholic Community," *Catholic Historical Review* 73 (January 1987):41–61, for a discussion of the two traditions of Jesuit piety.

Chapter 4   The Sentiments and Affections of Jesus Christ

1. Carroll to Leonardo Antonelli, March 1, 1785, Hanley, *Papers* 1:180; "Confirmation," Hanley, *Papers* 3:420.

2. "First Diocesan Synod," Hanley, *Papers* 1:531 (art. 17); "The Sabbath," Hanley, *Papers* 3:393–94; for an exposition of the liturgical calendar and celebrations during the Carroll era, see John A. Gurrieri, "Holy Days in America," *Worship* 54 (September 1980):417–46, and "Catholic Sunday in America: Its Shape and Early History," in Mark Searle, ed., *Sunday Morning: A Time for Worship*" (Collegeville, Minn., 1982), pp. 75–95.

3. For the English tradition, see J. D. Crichton, "Recusant Writers on the Priesthood of the Laity," and Joseph A. Agonito, "The Significance of Good Preaching: The Episcopacy of John Carroll," *American Ecclesiastical Review* 167 (December 1973):697–704; *The Office of Holy Week, According to the Roman Missal and Breviary, Containing the Morning and Evening Service, from Palm Sunday, to Tuesday in Easter Week; in Latin and English* (Baltimore, 1810), "Preface."

4. Carroll to Matthew Carey, January 30, 1789, Hanley, *Papers* 1:348–49; March 19, 1789, ibid., p. 350; April 8, 1789, ibid., p. 355; September 10, 1789, ibid., 380–81; "An Address to Roman Catholics on Wharton," Hanley, *Papers* 1:137–41.

5. "First Diocesan Synod," Hanley, *Papers* 1:528 (art. 5), 529 (art. 10), 534 (art. 24), 531 (art. 17); "Provincial Council Resolutions," ibid. 3:134 (art. 18); for Jesuit emphasis see V. F. Alfonso Rodríguez, *The Practice of Christian and Religious Perfection,* translated from the French (Philadelphia, 1831), vol. 2, treatise 8.

6. "Faith and Infidelity," Hanley, *Papers* 3:376–77; "Penance," ibid., pp. 435–36; "Lenten pastoral," ibid., 2:10–13; "Charity: The Neighbor," ibid., 3:445; "Death," ibid., pp. 456–57; for a general treatment, see John McManners, *Death and the Enlightenment* (Oxford, 1981).

7. Cf. Mr. Fournier to John Carroll, August 28, 1797, AAB, "Badin," 10B4–4S6; Badin to Carroll, 1804, ibid., Sp AL11; Badin to Carroll, March

10, 1808, ibid., 1I6; Badin to Carroll, August 29, 1808, ibid., 1I10; Badin to Carroll, June 9, 1802, ibid.

8. Badin to Carroll, February 20, 1799, ibid., 1E12; Wilson to Carroll, August 25, 1806, ibid., 8B–L6; same to same, July 25, 1806, ibid., 8B–L5.

9. "Biographical Sketch of Francis Beeston" (1810), Hanley, *Papers* 3:109.

10. "Charity," Hanley, *Papers* 3:438.

11. Rodríguez, *The Practice of Christian and Religious Perfection*, bk. 7, chap. 3, pp. 188–89; Carroll referred to the sections on humility and obedience from Rodríguez in a letter to John Grassi, November 22, 1813, Hanley, *Papers* 3:242–43.

12. Carroll to Thomas Ellerker, January 23, 1772(?), Hanley, *Papers* 1:27–28; same to same, February 3, 1773, ibid., pp. 28–30; for practice in the colonies, see Hughes, *Society of Jesus* 2:518; Carroll to Leonardo Antonelli, June 17, 1793, Hanley, *Papers* 2:96; Carroll to Monsignor Bracadoro, February 10, 1802, ibid., p. 375; *Pious Guide to Prayer and Devotion, Containing Various Practices of Piety Calculated to Answer the Various Demands of the Different Devout Members of the Roman Catholic Church* (Georgetown, 1792), pp. 13–61 for "Devotion to the Sacred Heart."

13. *Pious Guide*, pp. 13–17.

14. Ibid., pp. 18–19, 21, 22, 27.

15. Ibid., p. 27.

16. *The Spiritual Retreat of Reverend Father Vincent Huby*, "Preface." The preface is printed in Hanley, *Papers* 2:135–36.

17. For Huby, see Henry Marsille, "Huby, Vincent," *Dictionnaire de spiritualité* 7:1, 842–51; the selection, also present in Carroll's edition, is from day 9, meditation 2, point 1, in *The Spiritual Retreat of Reverend Father Vincent Huby*, pp. 188–89.

18. Cf. Rodríguez, *The Practice of Christian and Religious Perfection*, vol. 2, treatise 8, chap. 8, p. 221; Carroll, "On the Assumption of Mary," Hanley, *Papers* 3:402–403; for Carroll's devotion to Mary, see Melville, *John Carroll*, p. 283.

19. Cf. "Charity," Hanley, *Papers* 3:436–43; "Charity: John the Apostle," ibid., pp. 443–44; "An Appeal for School Funds," ibid., pp. 463–65.

Part II   The Immigrant Vision, 1830–1866

1. Peter Guilday, ed., *The National Pastorals of the American Hierarchy 1792–1919* (Washington, D.C., 1923), "The Pastoral Letter of 1866," pp. 198–225, here p. 224.

Chapter 5   Christ, the Person, and the Church

1. The standard works on Spalding are J. L. Spalding, *The Life of the Most Rev. M. J. Spalding* (New York, n.d.); Thomas W. Spalding, *Martin John Spalding: American Churchman* (Washington, D.C., 1973); Adam A. Micek, *The Apologetics of Martin John Spalding* (Washington, D.C., 1951); Brother David Spalding, C.F.X., "Martin John Spalding, Leg-

islator," *Records of the American Catholic Historical Society of Philadelphia* 75 (September 1964):131–60; "Martin John Spalding's 'Dissertation on the American Civil War'," *Catholic Historical Review* 52 (1966–67):66–86.

2. M. J. Spalding, *Miscellanea: Comprising Reviews, Lectures, and Essays, on Historical, Theological, and Miscellaneous Subjects* (Baltimore, 1892), vols. 1–2, "The Catholic Doctrine of Satisfaction," pp. 419–20.

3. Cf. J. L. Spalding, *Life*, chap. 1, pp. 11–22; T. W. Spalding, *Martin John Spalding*, chap. 1, pp. 1–7.

4. Cf. John Martinus Spalding, *Theses ex universa theologia et jure publico ecclesiastico* (Rome, 1834), nos. 73 and *passim;* his later opinion is taken from M. J. Spalding, *Lectures on the Evidences of Catholicity* (Baltimore, 1865), p. 51.

5. *Theses ex universa theologia*, 106; M. J. Spalding, *Evidences*, p. 321; "The Influence of Catholicity on Civil Liberty" (1835), in idem, *Miscellanea*, pp. 131–32; Peter Guilday, *The National Pastorals of the American Hierarchy (1792–1919)*, "Pastoral Letter of 1866," pp. 205–207; for background, see James Hennesey, S.J., "The Baltimore Council of 1866: An American Syllabus," *Records* 76 (September 1965):157–73.

6. *General Regulations for the Organizing of Congregations and the Administering of the Temporalities of the Roman Catholic Churches, in the Diocese of Kentucky* (Bardstown, Ky., 1836), chaps. 1–3; for background on lay trusteeism and incorporation, see Patrick J. Dignan, *A History of the Legal Incorporation of Church Property in the United States, 1784–1832* (Washington, D.C., 1932); Patrick W. Carey, *People, Priests, and Prelates: Ecclesiastical Democracy and the Tensions of Trusteeism* (Notre Dame, Ind., 1987).

7. Spalding to Purcell, January 30, 1846, Archives of the University of Notre Dame.

8. M. J. Spalding, *Evidences*, especially chaps. 4, 6, 13.

9. "Influence of Catholicity," p. 131; M. J. Spalding, *Evidences*, p. 321; "Philadelphia Riots," in idem, *Miscellanea*, pp. 596–618.

10. M. J. Spalding, *Evidences*, p. 35; cf. M. J. Spalding, *Theses ex universa theologia*, 139–45.

11. Cf. Bruno Franz Liebermann, *Institutiones theologicae* (Brixae, 1830), pp. 91–123; for Spalding's familiarity with Liebermann see M. J. Spalding, *Evidences*, p. 384; for solidarity in sin, see "Influence of Catholicity," p. 133; quotation from "The Catholic Doctrine of Satisfaction," p. 418.

12. Cf. "Philadelphia Riots," pp. 611–12, where Spalding quotes from the Protestant "Olive Branch"; see Ray Allen Billington, *The Protestant Crusade 1800–1860: A Study of the Origins of American Nativism* (New York: Macmillan, 1938), for general background.

13. "Philadelphia Riots," pp. 604–605.

14. Ibid., p. 598.

15. Ibid., p. 602; cf. "Influence of Catholicity"; "On the Intolerant Spirit of the Times," in M. J. Spalding, *Miscellanea*, pp. xx–lx; "A Chapter on Mobs," ibid., pp. 619–34.

16. "Influence of Catholicity," pp. 133–35.

17. "Philadelphia Riots," p. 604; cf. "Our Colonial Blue Laws," in M. J. Spalding, *Miscellanea*, pp. 353–68, 369–80, and "Catholic and Protestant Countries," pp. 455–72, for the interpretation of Protestantism.

18. "Philadelphia Riots," pp. 604–605.
19. "The Catholic Doctrine of Satisfaction," p. 420; "The Charge of Idolatry—Honor and Invocation of Saints," in M. J. Spalding, *Miscellanea*, pp. 397–417.
20. "Philadelphia Riots," p. 604; cf. Spalding's many apologetic essays on the Middle Ages, *Miscellanea, passim;* for background, Philip Gleason, "Mass and Maypole Revisited: American Catholics and the Middle Ages," *Catholic Historical Review* 57 (July 1971):249–74.
21. The alienation theme has been a constant in immigration history from Oscar Handlin, *The Uprooted* (Boston, 1952), to, most recently, Kerby A. Miller, *Emigrants and Exiles: Ireland and the Irish Exodus to North America* (New York, 1985).
22. "The Catholic Doctrine of Satisfaction," p. 419; cf. Liebermann, *Institutiones theologicae* for a probable source of Spalding's views.
23. "The Catholic Doctrine of Satisfaction," pp. 421–22; cf. M. J. Spalding, *Evidences*, pp. 32–33 for similar argument. It could be that Spalding's emphasis on cooperation derived from his French mentor, John Baptist David, who was influenced by the eighteenth-century priest Bergier's *Dictionnaire de Théologie*. Bergier's work leaned toward a semi-Pelagian position. For David's approval of Bergier see David to John Baptist Purcell, April 2, 1834, Archives of the University of Notre Dame. The emphasis on both human weakness and human cooperation was an alliance forged in opposition to the Enlightenment.
24. "The Catholic Doctrine of Satisfaction," p. 435.
25. Ibid., pp. 429, 430–31. The tendency to attribute temporal ills to the guilt of sin was common. Cf. Fr. Joseph Tichetoli to Fr. Frederick Résé, December 1, 1832, Archives of the University of Notre Dame, on the cholera epidemic in New Orleans; also, John Baptist Purcell's pastoral during the 1849 cholera epidemic in Cincinnati that described the disease as due to the vengeance of God on "crimes of intemperance, *profane swearing*, desecration of the Sabbath, contempt of religion, dishonesty, and oppression and insensibly [sic] to the wants of the poor." Cited in Andrew H. Deye, "Archbishop John Baptist Purcell of Cincinnati, Pre–Civil War Years," (Ph.D. diss., University of Notre Dame, 1959), p. 313.
26. "Influence of Catholicity," p. 132; "The Intolerant Spirit of the Times," xx; "Chapter on Mobs," p. 621; "The Catholic Doctrine of Satisfaction," p. 429; ibid., p. 421.
27. John Baptist David, *A Spiritual Retreat of Eight Days* (Louisville, Ky., 1864), pp. 166, 168. Spalding edited David's retreats and wrote a substantial introduction. On David, see Sister Columba Fox, *The Life of the Right Reverend John Baptist Mary David (1761–1841)* (New York, 1925). Spalding's view can be found in his *Sketches of the Early Catholic Missions of Kentucky, 1787–1826* (Louisville, Ky., 1844), chap. 13 and *passim*.
28. David, *Spiritual Retreat*, pp. 174–75.
29. M. J. Spalding, "Introduction" to *Spiritual Retreat*, p. 45.
30. [John Baptist David], A Catholic Clergyman of Baltimore, *True Piety; or, The Day Well Spent, Being a Catholic Manual of Chosen Prayers, and Solid Instructions* (Baltimore, 1809); for the impact of *True Piety* and the opinions of others, see Joseph P. Chinnici, "Organization of the Spiritual Life: American Catholic Devotional Works, 1791–1866,"

Theological Studies 40 (June 1979): 229–55, here 236–45; Neumann's view is treated in Richard Andrew Boever, "The Spirituality of St. John Neumann, C.SS.R., Fourth Bishop of Philadelphia" (Ph.D. diss., Saint Louis University, 1983), chap. 2.

31. For Loretto, see Sister Antonella Hardy, *Rev. Charles Nerinckx (1761–1824) and Devotion to the Sacred Heart,* a small pamphlet published at Loretto Motherhouse, June 1928.
32. "Chapter on Mobs," pp. 620–21.
33. "The Catholic Doctrine of Satisfaction," p. 422.
34. Ibid., p. 434.
35. Ibid., p. 424.
36. Spalding, "Introduction" to David, *Spiritual Retreat,* pp. 43, 37.
37. David, *Spiritual Retreat,* p. 238.
38. Cf. J. L. Spalding, *Life,* pp. 145, 149, 220, 454–56.
39. "Chapter on Mobs," p. 621; cf. "Philadelphia Riots," p. 613.
40. M. J. Spalding, *Evidences,* pp. 196–97 on sinners in the church; p. 47; and p. 52 for quotation.
41. For other pertinent examples, see *The Catholic Laity's Directory to the Church Service with an Almanac for the Year 1817* (New York, 1817), p. 53; Lawrence Kehoe, *Complete Works of the Most Rev. John Hughes, D.D., Archbishop of New York. Comprising Sermons, Letters, Lectures, Speeches, etc., Carefully Compiled from the Best Sources* (New York, 1865), 2 vols.: "The Importance of Being in Communion with Christ's One, Holy, Catholic, and Apostolic Church," 2:577–636; "The Silence of Christ Before His Judges," 2:275–83; "The Last Words of the Saviour," 2:301–308.
42. M. J. Spalding, *Evidences,* p. 51.
43. David, *Spiritual Retreat,* p. 174.
44. M. J. Spalding, *Evidences,* p. 52.
45. For studies of these three people, see Joseph P. Chinnici, O.F.M., *Devotion to the Holy Spirit in American Catholicism* (New York, 1985), *passim.*
46. Rt. Rev. John Hennessy, "The Sanctity of the Church," *The Memorial Volume: A History of the Third Plenary Council of Baltimore* (Baltimore, 1885), pp. 224–44, with definition of "church," p. 229; long quote, p. 234; holiness of individual, p. 225.

Chapter 6   The Triumph of the Purgative Way

1. Hughes's sermon of August 15, 1858, and his circular letter are printed in Lawrence Kehoe, *Complete Works* 2:263–70. For further information cf. Margaret Carthy, O.S.U., *A Cathedral of Suitable Magnificence: St. Patrick's Cathedral, New York* (Wilmington, Del., 1984), chap. 2, pp. 25–47. .
2. The most important works on Hughes are John R. G. Hassard, *Life of the Most Reverend John Hughes, D.D.* (New York: Appleton & Co., 1866); Richard Shaw, *Dagger John: The Unquiet Life and Times of Archbishop John Hughes of New York* (New York, 1977); Henry J. Browne, "The Archdiocese of New York a Century Ago: A Memoir of Archbishop John Hughes, 1838–1858," *Historical Records and Studies,* 39–40 (1952):129–90; Thomas T. McAvoy, C.S.C., "Orestes A. Brownson and

Archbishop John Hughes in 1860," *Review of Politics* 24 (January 1962):19–48. For important autobiographical reflections, see "On the Emancipation of Irish Catholics," in Kehoe, *Complete Works* 1:29–40; "Letters on the Moral Causes Which Produced the Evil Spirit of the Times," ibid. 1:450–63.

3. "Sermon of Bishop Loughlin," in Kehoe, *Complete Works* 1:26–29, here 29.

4. Cf. "An Examination of the Reasons Alleged by a Protestant for Protesting Against the Doctrine of the Catholic Church; or, an Answer to Objections, under the Title of 'Protestantism and Popery,' Made by an Anonymous Writer," in Kehoe, *Complete Works* 2:633–37; John Hughes, *Controversy Between Rev. Messrs. Hughes and Breckinridge, on the Subject, "Is the Protestant Religion the Religion of Christ?"* (Philadelphia, 1834), with definition of *church* on p. 45; "A Review of the Charge Delivered May 22, 1833, by the Right Rev. Bishop Onderdonk, on the Rule of Faith," in Kehoe, *Complete Works* 2:667–84. For background, see John B. Purcell, *A Debate on the Roman Catholic Religion: Held in the Sycamore-Street Meeting House, Cincinnati, from the 13th to the 25th of January, 1837, between Alexander Campbell, of Bethany, Virginia, and the Rt. Rev. John B. Purcell, Bishop of Cincinnati* (Cincinnati: H. S. Bosworth, 1861), in which Purcell with more sophistication takes a position similar to that of Hughes; and Robert Gorman, *Catholic Apologetical Literature in the United States* (Washington, D.C., 1939).

5. Cf. especially Hughes's sermons delivered in later life: "Triumph of the Catholic Church," in Kehoe, *Complete Works* 2:236–46; "The Unity, the Universality, and Visibility of the Church," ibid., pp. 325–32; "The Visibility of the Church of God," ibid., pp. 332–43.

6. Cf. Kehoe, *Complete Works* 2:549–632 for Hughes's view of trusteeism, and p. 551 for "scenes of strife." Background can be obtained in Patrick Carey, "Two Episcopal Views of Lay-Clerical Conflicts: 1785–1860," *Records of the American Catholic Historical Society of Philadelphia* 87 (March–December 1976):85–98; Carey, "The Laity's Understanding of the Trustee System, 1785–1855," *Catholic Historical Review* 64 (July 1978):357–76; Robert F. McNamara, "Trusteeism in the Atlantic States, 1785–1863," ibid., 30 (July 1944):135–44.

7. John Hughes to Simon Gabriel Bruté, May 7, 1827, Catholic University of America, Hughes Papers, reel 1, from Vincennes archives.

8. Hughes to Henry Conwell, January 29, 1829, ibid., from archives of Propaganda Fide.

9. "Pastoral of Bishop Hughes," in Kehoe, *Complete Works* 1:314–27.

10. Ibid., p. 325.

11. "Bishop Hughes' Apology for his Pastoral Letter," ibid., pp. 327–35, and "Letter of Rt. Rev. Bishop Hughes to David Hale, Esq.," pp. 335–50, here 341, for long quotation. Hughes definitely linked the ecclesiastical system of lay control with forms of Protestantism but declined to make the connection between that system and American republican principles. Elsewhere he argued that "the Church herself, in all her own forms of government, was, as she still is, a model of modified and admirably well-regulated democratic jurisprudence." See "The Mixture of Civil, and Ecclesiastical Power in the Middle Ages," ibid., pp. 417–37, here 431.

12. "Papal Intermeddling," *Church Review* 15 (October 1863):435–50; for Hughes's recognition of his departure from Carroll, see Kehoe, *Complete Works* 2:550–51; his response to the Public School Society is treated in Joseph J. McCadden, "Bishop Hughes versus the Public School Society of New York," *Catholic Historical Review* 50 (July 1964):188–207; on Bedini, see Shaw, *Dagger John*, pp. 277–88.

13. "To the Leopoldine Society," in Kehoe, *Complete Works* 2:459–64; cf. Browne, "The Archdiocese of New York a Century Ago," pp. 157–58.

14. Browne, "The Archdiocese of New York a Century Ago," p. 168; for statistical information and a description of the social structure, see Jay P. Dolan, *The Immigrant Church: New York's Irish and German Catholics, 1815–1865* (Baltimore, 1975).

15. Rev. Augustus J. Thébaud, S.J., *Forty Years in the United States of America (1839–1885)*, ed. Charles George Herbermann (New York, 1904), p. 181.

16. James Parton, "Our Roman Catholic Brethren," *Atlantic Monthly* 21 (April 1868):432–51; (May 1868):556–74, with quotation from p. 565.

17. Thébaud, *Forty Years in the United States*, pp. 102–18; for background, see Thomas L. Haskell, "Capitalism and the Origins of the Humanitarian Sensibility," pt. 1, *American Historical Review* 90 (April 1985):339–61; pt. 2 (June 1985):547–66; Joseph P. Chinnici, O.F.M., "Spiritual Capitalism and the Culture of American Catholicism," *U.S. Catholic Historian* 5 (1986):131–61.

18. Thébaud, *Forty Years in the United States*, p. 181.

19. Hughes, "Influence of Christianity upon Civilization," in Kehoe, *Complete Works* 1:351–70, here 369.

20. Cf. "Influence of Christianity upon Civilization"; "The Influence of Christianity on Social Servitude," in Kehoe, *Complete Works* 1:371–85; "The Mixture of Civil and Ecclesiastical Power in the Middle Ages"; "The Importance of a Christian Basis for the Science of Political Economy," ibid., pp. 513–34; Introduction to *An Inquiry into the Merits of the Reformed Doctrine of "Imputation"; or, the Cardinal Point of Controversy between the Church of Rome and the Protestant High Church: Together with Miscellaneous Essays on the Catholic Faith* (Vanbrugh Livingston, N.Y., 1843).

21. "The Influence of Christianity on Social Servitude," p. 371; quotation from p. 385; cf. "Introduction" to *An Inquiry*, p. vii.

22. The argument is presented in detail in "The Importance of a Christian Basis for the Science of Political Economy," in Kehoe, *Complete Works*, vol. 1.

23. Cf. "Influence of Christianity upon Civilization," p. 351, for definition of "society"; comments on Fourier and transcendentalism can be found in "The Importance of a Christian Basis for the Science of Political Economy," p. 525, and later, in the Introduction to Antoine Martinet, *Religion in Society or the Solution of Great Problems; Placed Within the Reach of Every Mind* (New York, 1850), reprinted in Kehoe, *Complete Works* 2:787–90; quotation from the Introduction to *An Inquiry*, p. viii.

24. Cf. Introduction to *An Inquiry*, pp. xvi–xvii; similar presentations of Justification can be found in "An Examination of the Reasons Alleged by a Protestant for Protesting against the Doctrine of the Catholic Church," in Kehoe, *Complete Works* 2:647–51; "Importance of a Chris-

tian Basis," ibid. 1:526. Hughes consistently emphasized human cooperation in justification, a position that he partially derived from his Counter Reformation theology.

25. For examples see Kehoe, *Complete Works* 1:357, 376, 561, 788.

26. Hughes's arguments based on "fallen human nature" follow the standard approach of the Catholic apologists reacting to the excesses of the French Revolution. For his consistent application of the perspective see: "On the Emancipation of Irish Catholics," in Kehoe, *Complete Works* 1:29–40; "Life and Times of Pius VII," pp. 299–312; "The Influence of Christianity on Social Servitude"; "Christianity, the Only Source of Moral, Social and Political Regeneration," pp. 558–73; "The Church and the World, Since the Election of Pius IX to the Chair of Saint Peter," ibid. 2:69–87; "On Reason and Faith," pp. 325–32.

27. "A Christian Basis for the Science of Political Economy," pp. 515–16; cf. pp. 526–27.

28. Ibid., p. 528.

29. Ibid., p. 525; cf. pp. 526–27.

30. "Reason and Faith," in Kehoe, *Complete Works* 2:328.

31. "A Christian Basis for the Science of Political Economy," ibid., p. 527.

32. Sermon on the Occasion of the Dedication of St. Stephen's Church," in Kehoe, *Complete Works* 2:223–28, with quotation from p. 225.

33. "A Christian Basis for the Science of Political Economy," p. 527, argument from pp. 518–19.

34. Rev. S. V. Ryan, "The Observation of Feasts," *The Memorial Volume: A History of the Third Plenary Council of Baltimore* (Baltimore, 1885), pp. 122–41. Also cf. John Gilmary Shea, "The Church and Her Holydays," *American Catholic Quarterly Review* 11 (July 1886):462–75; John A. Gurrieri, "Holy Days in America," *Worship* 54 (September 1980):417–46 for general background.

35. *A Manual of Catholic Devotions, for the Use of the Faithful, Who Desire to Live Piously and Die Happily* (Baltimore: John Murphy, 1859), p. 62.

36. Almost all of the prayer books I have surveyed that were in use in nineteenth-century America took a similar approach to meditation. Cf., for example, *Pious Guide to Prayer and Devotion*, pp. 4, 68–69; *True Piety* (1809), pp. 58–67, with example of meditation from F. Bonhours, pp. 223–69; *The Ursuline Manual; or A Collection of Prayers, Spiritual Exercises, etc.* . . . , (New York, 1844), pp. 289–91. For background on this interpretation, see William J. Bouwsma, "Anxiety and the Formation of Early Modern Culture," in Barbara C. Malament, ed., *After the Reformation: Essays in Honor of J. H. Hexter* (Philadelphia, 1980), pp. 215–46; Jacques LeGoff, "Merchant's Time and Church's Time in the Middle Ages," in Goff, *Time, Work and Culture in the Middle Ages* (Chicago, 1980), pp. 29–42, trans. Arthur Goldhammer; Keith Thomas, "Work and Leisure in Pre-Industrial Society: Conference Paper," *Past and Present* 29 (December 1964):50–62.

37. "Influence of Catholic Prayer on Civilization," *Brownson's Quarterly Review*, ser. 2, vol. 2 (July 1848):345–80, at 379. The article was an English translation of a paper by Father Louis Taparelli d'Azeglio, S.J.

38. For an analysis of the popular dimensions of this attitude, see Ann Taves, *The Household of Faith: Roman Catholic Devotions in Mid-*

Nineteenth Century America (Notre Dame, Ind., 1986); Paul R. Messbarger, *Fiction with a Parochial Purpose: Social Uses of American Catholic Literature, 1884–1900* (Boston, 1971).

39. Hughes, "A Christian Basis for the Science of Political Economy," pp. 533–34.
40. Jay P. Dolan, *Catholic Revivalism: The American Experience 1830–1900* (Notre Dame, Ind., 1978), pp. 156–65.
41. Rev. E. J. Remler, C.M., *Supernatural Merit: Your Treasure in Heaven* (Saint Louis, Mo., 1922), p. xiv; for another example, see Bernard J. Otten, S.J., *The Business of Salvation* (Saint Louis, Mo., 1916).
42. F. P. Kenrick, "Prayer Books," *Brownson's Quarterly Review*, New York ser. 2 (April 1857):184–90, quotation from p. 185.
43. Michael Muller, C.SS.R., *Prayer the Key of Salvation* (Baltimore, 1868), 146–47.
44. Spalding also drew on his retreat notes from his student days at Propaganda to prepare the "Introduction." For his sourcebook, see *Manresa: Or the Spiritual Exercises of St. Ignatius* (New York, n.d.), pp. xv–xvi. Some idea of the tradition in which Spalding was educated can be found in his *Sketches of the Life, Times, and Character of the Rt. Rev. Benedict Joseph Flaget, First Bishop of Louisville* (Louisville, Ky., 1852), in which he translates part of a French life of Flaget, emphasizing his "spirit of prayer," 367–73; and *Evidences*, pp. 26–30, in which he quotes Fénelon on prayer. For general background to the Sulpician school see Justus George Lawler, "Religious Life, Fundamentals and Accidentals," *Worship* 27 (September 1953):437–51.
45. Cf. Spalding's "The Catholic Doctrine of Satisfaction."
46. For the best brief account, see Jay P. Dolan, "American Catholics and Revival Religion, 1850–1900," *Horizons* 3 (Spring 1976):39–57, and his longer treatment, *Catholic Revivalism*.

Chapter 7   The Golden Chain Binding Heaven and Earth

1. On Neumann's experience see Rev. John A. Berger, C.SS.R., *Life of Right Rev. John N. Neumann, D.D., of the Congregation of the Most Holy Redeemer. Fourth Bishop of Philadelphia*, trans. Rev. Eugene Grimm (New York, 1884), p. 374. For colonial practice, see John LaFarge, S.J., "Our Pioneer Adorers of the Blessed Sacrament," *Emmanuel* 35 (August 1929):176–79. Title VI.2 of the legislation of the Second Plenary Council of Baltimore can be found in *Acta et Decreta Sacrorum Conciliorum Recentiorum, Collectio Lacensis*, 3 (Freiburg im Breisgau, 1875). Samples of synodal legislation would be *Constitutiones Synodi Hartfordiensis*, vol. 2 (Hartford, Conn., 1878), 40, and *Synodus Diocesina Baltimorensis Nona Quae Antecendentium Etiam Complectitur Constitutiones* (Baltimore, 1886), 45. For general context, see Ann Taves, "Context and Meaning: Roman Catholic Devotion to the Blessed Sacrament in Mid-Nineteenth Century America," *Church History* 54 (December 1985):482–95.
2. Cf. Alfred C. Rush, C.SS.R., *The Autobiography of St. John Neumann, C.SS.R., Fourth Bishop of Philadelphia* (Boston, 1977), pp. 23, 39 for quotations and *passim* for information. The better biographical studies of Neumann are Berger, *Life of Neumann*; Joseph Wüst, C.SS.R., "John

N. Neumann, a Saintly Bishop," *Catholic World* 56 (December 1892):322–38; John F. Byrne, C.SS.R., "The Venerable Bishop Neumann," *The Redemptorist Centenaries* (Philadelphia, 1932), pp. 288–316; Michael J. Curley, C.SS.R., *Venerable John Neumann, C.SS.R.* (Washington, D.C., 1952), the standard work; Alfred C. Rush, C.SS.R., and Thomas J. Donaghy, F.S.C., "The Saintly John Neumann and his Coadjutor, Archbishop Wood," in James F. Connelly, ed., *The History of the Archdiocese of Philadelphia* (Philadelphia, 1976), pp. 209–70.

3. To compare Neumann with Hughes and Spalding, cf. on nativism, Curley, *Venerable John Neumann*, 95–96, and the chapter on bigotry; on trusteeism, ibid., *passim*, and Alfred C. Ruch, ed., "The Letters of Saint John N. Neumann to Archbishop Francis P. Kenrick, 1852–1859," *Spicilegium Historicum Congregationis SSmi. Redemptoris* 28 (1980):47–123, *passim;* on finances, Curley, *Venerable John Neumann*, pp. 71, 99, 190ff.; on his calling to the German immigrants, Alfred C. Rush, "The American Indians and the German Immigrants in the Missionary Plans and Work of St. John Neumann, 1832–1840," *Spicilegium* 25 (1977):118–29. For general background that places Neumann's spirituality in this context, see the superficial but indicative dissertation by Richard Andrew Boever, "The Spirituality of St. John Neumann, C.SS.R., Fourth Bishop of Philadelphia" (Ph.D. diss., St. Louis University, 1983).

4. The French portion of Neumann's spiritual journal is translated in William Nayden, "John N. Neumann's *Spiritual Journal*," 1 (October 1–December 31, 1834), *Spicilegium* 25 (1977):321–418; 2 (January 1–February 28, 1835), ibid. 26 (1978):9–74; 3 (March 1–May 4, 1835), ibid. 291–352; 4 (May 5, 1835–July 21, 1838), ibid. 27 (1979):81–152.

5. Cf. Augustinus Kurt Huber, "John N. Neumann's Student Years in Prague, 1833–1835," trans. Raymond H. Schmandt, *Records of the American Catholic Historical Society of Philadelphia* 89 (March–December 1978):3–32; for personal background, see Rush, *Autobiography*, 23; for his later use of Canisius, see Mary Charles Bryce, "An Accomplished Catechist: John Nepomucene Neumann," *Living Light* 14 (Fall 1977):327–37; for the use of the various writers, see Nayden, *"Spiritual Journal," passim.*

6. For specific examples, see Nayden, *"Spiritual Journal,"* under November 5, 1834; March 10, 1835; November 18, 1834; November 7, 1834; November 28, 1834; October 2, 1834; and October 22, 1834, for use of Croiset. On the latter, see Paul Mech, "Jean Croiset," in *Dictionnaire de Spiritualité* 2:2558–60. All of this evidence would indicate that it would be impossible to interpret the use of de Sales, Teresa of Avila, or à Kempis in the nineteenth century in the same way as was done in the eighteenth century. Social and theological presuppositions conditioned the reading of classic texts.

7. Cf. Nayden, *"Spiritual Journal"* (December 1, 1834), for long quotation, and *passim* for Neumann's self-perception. For a brief analysis, see Boever, "The Spirituality of St. John Neumann," pp. 56–78.

8. Nayden, *"Spiritual Journal"* (January 29, 1835).

9. For Neumann's asceticism, see Nayden, *"Spiritual Journal"* (October 4, 1834; April 4, 1835), and *passim;* Curley, *Venerable John Neumann*, pp. 45, 49, 76, 89–90, 110, 229, etc; Rush, *Autobiography*, pp. 41, 44; Wüst, "John N. Neumann," p. 329.

10. Cf. Nayden, *"Spiritual Journal,"* November 1, 1834; October 8, 1834; October 5, 1834; November 1, 1834; January 2, 1835; April 11, 1835; n.d., 151 in pt. 4.

11. Ibid., October 6, 1834; cf. Berger, *Life of Neumann,* p. 387, and Boever, "Spirituality of St. John Neumann," pp. 146–50.

12. Cf. Boever, "Spirituality of St. John Neumann," p. 22, and pp. 101–28 for ecclesiology; Nayden, *"Spiritual Journal"* (January 4, 1835).

13. For Neumann's years as a bishop, see Rush, *Autobiography,* pp. 53–66; Rush, "The Letters of Saint John Neumann to Archbishop Francis P. Kenrick"; Curley, *Venerable John Neumann, passim.*

14. As cited in Alfred Rush, C.SS.R., "The Second Vatican Council, 1962–1965, and Bishop Neumann," *Records* 85 (1974):3–4, 123–28. See also Pope Paul VI, "St. John Neumann: Canonization Homily," *Catholic Almanac,* (Huntingdon, Ind., 1978), pp. 106–107; Nicola Ferrante, C.SS.R., "The Cause of the Beatification and Canonization of St. John Nepomucene Neumann, C.SS.R.," *The Province Story* (Brooklyn, N.Y., October 1977), pp. 36–66.

15. Berger, *Life of Neumann,* p. 451, cf. pp. 450–57.

16. For general background, see Sheridan Gilley, "Supernaturalized Culture: Catholic Attitudes and Latin Lands 1840–1860," in Derek Baker, ed., *The Materials, Sources, and Methods of Ecclesiastical History,* Studies in Church History, 11 (Oxford, 1975), pp. 309–23; Thomas A. Kselman, *Miracles, and Prophecies in Nineteenth-Century France* (New Brunswick, N.J., 1983). On the Irish, see Sheridan Gilley, "The Roman Catholic Church and the Nineteenth-Century Irish Diaspora," *Journal of Ecclesiastical History* 35 (April 1984):188–207; Emmet Larkin, "The Devotional Revolution in Ireland, 1850–1870," *American Historical Review* 72 (April 1967):625–52; David W. Miller, "Irish Catholicism and the Great Famine," *Journal of Social History* 9 (Fall 1975):81–98; Miller, *Emigrants and Exiles.* For Germany, see Michael J. Phayer, *Sexual Liberation and Religion in Nineteenth Century Europe* (London, 1977); Jonathan Sperber, *Popular Catholicism in Nineteenth Century Germany* (Princeton, N.J., 1984).

17. Cf. Dennis Clark, "The South's Irish Catholics: A Case of Cultural Confinement," in Randall M. Miller and Jon L. Wakelyn, eds., *Catholics in the Old South: Essays on Church and Culture* (Macon, Ga., 1983), pp. 195–209; Dolan, *Catholic Revivalism;* Timothy Smith, "Religion and Ethnicity in America," *American Historical Review* 83 (December 1978):1155–85.

18. Hughes, "The Influence of Christianity upon Civilization," in Kehoe, *Complete Works* 1:357, 364–65.

19. As cited in J. L. Spalding, *Life,* p. 221.

20. M. J. Spalding, "The Charge of Idolatry," p. 410.

21. For a good reflection on the combination, see Alfred C. Rush, C.SS.R., *The Autobiography of St. John Neumann,* Epilogue.

22. Cf. *The Ursuline Manual; or A Collection of Prayers, Spiritual Exercises, etc.,* rev. John Power, (New York, 1844), pp. 135–55, 274–77.

23. Frederick William Faber, *The Blessed Sacrament; or, the Works and Ways of God* (Baltimore, 1855), pp. 14–15, 33, 36. On the importance of Faber, see Ann Taves, *The Household of Faith: Roman Catholic Devotions in Mid-Nineteenth Century America* (Notre Dame, Ind., 1986).

24. For the immigrants, see Dolan, *The Immigrant Church;* on the Sodality

of the Blessed Virgin, see "Sodalities of New York," *Ave Maria* 2 (December 22, 1866):807–809; on confraternities in general, Taves, *Household of Faith.*

25. John Talbot Smith, *The Catholic Church in New York* (New York and Boston, 1905), 1:312–28.

26. Jay P. Dolan, *The American Catholic Experience* (New York, 1985), pp. 213–14.

27. "History of the Sodalities," *Ave Maria* 2 (November 24, 1866):741–42.

28. For an analysis of the post–Civil War developments, see Joseph P. Chinnici, *Devotion to the Holy Spirit in American Catholicism* (New York, 1986), pp. 3–90.

29. *The Golden Book of Confraternities* (New York, 1854), pp. 14–15.

30. Ibid., pp. 13–14. For a contemporary analysis, see Rt. Rev. J. J. Keane, "Catholic Societies," *The Memorial Volume: A History of the Third Plenary Council of Baltimore* (Baltimore, 1885), pp. 190–208.

31. See "Reports of Tabernacle Societies," in *Eucharistic Conferences: The Papers Presented at the First American Eucharistic Congress* (New York, 1896), pp. 196–214.

32. The relationship between devotionalism, feminization of piety, and domesticity has yet to be examined. For significant reflections, see Barbara Welter, *Dimity Convictions: The American Woman in the Nineteenth Century* (Athens, Ohio, 1976), especially pp. 21–41, 83–102; David S. Reynolds, "The Feminization Controversy: Sexual Stereotypes and the Paradoxes of Piety in Nineteenth-Century America," *New England Quarterly* 53 (March 1980):96–106; and most important, Colleen McDannell, *The Christian Home in Victorian America 1840–1900* (Bloomington, Ind., 1986). For support to the interpretation offered here, see Susan Levine, "Labor's True Woman: Domesticity and Equal Rights in the Knights of Labor," *Journal of American History* 70 (September 1983):323–39.

33. The structures of home, school, and parish have been well examined by Dolan in *The American Catholic Experience*, chaps. 6, 7, and 9. For a fine analysis of home devotions, see McDannell, *The Christian Home.*

34. M. J. Spalding, "The Charge of Idolatry," p. 416.

35. John Hughes, "The Communion of Saints," in Kehoe, *Complete Works* 2:779–85.

36. Neumann, *"Spiritual Journal,"* December 1, 1834, April 11, 1835, January 2, 1835, etc.

37. Cf. John Hughes, "Introduction" to *An Inquiry into the Merits of the Reformed Doctrine of "Imputation,"* p. ix; M. J. Spalding, *Evidences,* pp. 201–202, 223–24.

38. "St. Vincent de Paul," *Ave Maria* 1 (July 15, 1865):148.

39. Hughes, "The Communion of Saints," p. 780; M. J. Spalding, "The Charge of Idolatry," p. 416.

40. M. J. Spalding, *Evidences,* p. 217; Hughes, "The Communion of Saints," p. 381. For pertinent reflections on "devotional eschatology," see Thomas E. Wangler, "'Catholic Religious Life in Boston in the Era of Cardinal O'Connell," in Robert E. Sullivan and James M. O'Toole, eds., *Catholic Boston: Studies in Religion and Community, 1870–1970* (Boston, 1985), pp. 239–72, especially pp. 244–51.

41. Cf. *The Ursuline Manual;* Taves, *Household of Faith,* pp. 36–39, *passim;*

J. D. Bryant, *The Immaculate Conception of the Most Blessed Virgin Mary, Mother of God; A Dogma of the Catholic Church* (Boston, 1855), pp. 219–38; *Constitutiones Diocesanae in Synodis Philadelphiensibus, Annis 1832, 1842, 1847, 1853, et 1855, Latae et Promulgatae* (Philadelphia, 1855), p. 31; and James Hennesey, S.J., "The Baltimore Council of 1866: An American Syllabus," for background on the Immaculate Conception.

42. Rt. Rev. Wm. H. Elder, "Devotion to the Blessed Virgin Mary," in *Sermons on Subjects of the Day, Delivered by Distinguished Catholic Prelates and Theologians, at the Second Plenary Council of Baltimore, United States, October 1866* (Dublin, 1868), pp. 126–37, here pp. 127–28.

43. As cited in J. L. Spalding, *Life,* 221; cf. M. J. Spalding, "The Charge of Idolatry," pp. 405–406, and Hughes, "Influence of Christianity upon Civilization," p. 367, for further reflections on Mary.

44. Elder, "Devotion to the Blessed Virgin Mary," p. 132.

45. Neumann's pastoral letter of 1854 as cited in Bryant, *The Immaculate Conception,* p. 233.

46. Elder, "Devotion to the Blessed Virgin Mary," p. 127.

47. Neumann as cited in Bryant, *The Immaculate Conception,* p. 232; Elder, "Devotion to the Blessed Virgin Mary," p. 135; J. L. Spalding, *Life,* pp. 457–58.

48. The differences in Irish and German devotional practices have been well studied. See, for example, Dolan, *The Immigrant Church,* pp. 45–67, 68–86; idem, "Philadelphia and the German Catholic Community," in Randall M. Miller and Thomas D. Marzik, eds., *Immigrants and Religion in Urban America* (Philadelphia, 1977), pp. 69–83; Hugh · McLeod, "Catholicism and the New York Irish 1880–1910," in Jim Obelkevich, Lyndal Roper, and Raphael Samuel, eds., *Disciplines of Faith, Studies in Religion, Politics and Patriarchy* (New York, 1987), pp. 337–50.

49. Cf. Chinnici, *Devotion to the Holy Spirit,* pp. 57–77. For examples, see, for the Italians, Rudolph J. Vecoli, "Cult and Occult in Italian-American Culture: The Persistence of a Religious Heritage," in Miller and Marzik, *Immigrants and Religion,* pp. 25–47; Robert Anthony Orsi, *The Madonna of 115th Street: Faith and Community in Italian Harlem, 1880–1950* (New Haven, Conn., 1985); for the Poles: Joseph John Parot, *Polish Catholics in Chicago, 1850–1970* (Dekalb, Ill., 1981), pp. 215–32; John Bukowczyk, " 'Mary the Messiah': Polish Immigrant Heresy and the Malleable Ideology of the Roman Catholic Church in America 1880–1930," in Obelkevich, Roper, and Samuel, eds., *Disciplines of Faith,* pp. 371–89; for Hispanics: Virgilio Elizondo, *Galilean Journey, The Mexican-American Promise* (Maryknoll, N.Y., 1983), pp. 32–46; Frances M. Campbell, "American Catholicism in Northern New Mexico: A Kaleidoscope of Development, 1840–1885" (Ph.D. diss., Graduate Theological Union, Berkeley, 1986).

Part III   The Spirituality of Americanism, 1866–1900

1. On the commencement address, see Thomas R. Ryan, C.PP.S., *Orestes A. Brownson: A Definitive Biography* (Huntingdon, Ind., 1976), 532–

34. For the education at Saint John's, see Christa Ressmeyer Klein, "The Jesuits and Catholic Boyhood in Nineteenth Century New York City: A Study of St. John's College and the College of St. Francis Xavier, 1846–1912" (Ph.D. diss., University of Pennsylvania, 1976).

2. "Mission of America," in Henry F. Brownson, ed., *The Works of Orestes A. Brownson* (Detroit, Mich., 1885), 2:551–84, reprinted from *Brownson's Quarterly Review* for October 1856.

3. "Mission of America," p. 559. For Hughes's reaction, see Ryan, *Orestes A. Brownson*, p. 534, and Thomas T. McAvoy, C.S.C., "Orestes A. Brownson and Archbishop John Hughes in 1860," *Review of Politics* 24 (January 1962):19–48.

4. Bibliographical information will be furnished as the people are introduced. For background to Americanism, see Philip Gleason, "Coming to Terms with American Catholic History," *Societas—A Review of Social History* 3 (Autumn 1973):282–313; Thomas T. McAvoy, C.S.C., *The Great Crisis in American Catholic History* (Chicago, 1957); Robert Emmett Curran, "Prelude to 'Americanism': The New York Academia and Clerical Radicalism in the Late Nineteenth Century," *Church History* 47 (March 1978):48–65.

Chapter 8   Conversion and the Mission of America

1. Cf. Isaac Hecker, "Dr. Brownson and the Workingman's Party Fifty Years Ago," *Catholic World* 45 (May 1887):200–208. The best general treatment is Edward J. Langlois, C.S.P., "Isaac Hecker's Political Thought," in John Farina, ed., *Hecker Studies, Essays on the Thought of Isaac Hecker* (New York, 1983), pp. 49–86; also David J. O'Brien, "An Evangelical Imperative: Isaac Hecker, Catholicism, and Modern Society," in ibid., pp. 87–132.

2. Isaac Hecker, "Dr. Brownson and Catholicity," *Catholic World* 46 (November 1887):222–35, here 222. Especially helpful on the Transcendental period are John Farina, *An American Experience of God: The Spirituality of Isaac Hecker* (New York, 1981), chaps. 4–6, and Mary E. Lyons, "A Rhetoric for American Catholicism: The transcendental voice of Isaac T. Hecker" (Ph.D. diss., University of California, Berkeley, 1983).

3. Cf. Isaac Hecker to Orestes Brownson, October 16, 1843, in Joseph F. Gower and Richard M. Leliaert, eds., *The Brownson–Hecker Correspondence* (Notre Dame, Ind., 1979), pp. 74–75; "Hecker's Diary," for October 17, 1843, typescript, p. 91, in Paulist Fathers Archives, Saint Paul College, Washington, D.C. For Hecker's ecclesiology, see Dennis J. Dease, "The Theological Influence of Orestes Brownson and Isaac Hecker on John Ireland's Americanist Ecclesiology" (Ph.D. diss., Catholic University of America, 1978); and Margaret Mary Reher, "The Church and the Kingdom of God in America: The Ecclesiology of the Americanists" (Ph.D. diss., Fordham University, 1972).

4. Orestes A. Brownson, "No Church, No Reform," in H. F. Brownson, *Works*, 4:496–512, here 499, reprinted from *Brownson's Quarterly Review* (April 1844). For Brownson's key concept of "life by communion," see Ryan, *Orestes A. Brownson*, pp. 252–57. His early efforts at reform are traced in A. M. Schlesinger, Jr., *Orestes A. Brownson* (Boston, 1939).

5. Brownson, "No Church, No Reform," pp. 500, 509, and "Church Unity and Social Amelioration," in H. F. Brownson, ed., *Works,* 4:512–26, reprinted from *Brownson's Quarterly Review* (July 1844).

6. Taken from *The Paulist Vocation,* printed privately for use by the Paulist community, p. 36. The classic work on Hecker is Walter Elliott, C.S.P., *The Life of Father Hecker* (New York, 1891). Cf. also Joseph McSorley, C.S.P., *Father Hecker and His Friends* (New York, 1953); and John Farina, "Isaac Hecker's Vision for the Paulists: Hopes and Realities," in Farina, *Hecker Studies,* pp. 182–220.

7. Isaac Hecker, *Questions of the Soul* (New York, 1855); *Aspirations of Nature* (New York, 1857); "Riflessioni Sopra il Presente e l'Avvenire del Cattolicismo negli Stati Uniti d'America," *La civiltà cattolica,* 3d ser., 8 (November 6, 19, 1857), 385–402, 513–29. For Hecker's "new apologetic," see Joseph Francis Gower, "The 'New Apologetic' of Isaac Thomas Hecker (1819–1888): Catholicity and American Culture" (Ph.D. diss., Notre Dame University, 1978).

8. This summary is taken from Hecker, "Riflessioni," pp. 517–24, with quotation from p. 521.

9. See Edward Langlois, "Isaac Hecker's Political Thought," in Farina, *Hecker Studies;* and Joseph Gower, "Democracy as a Theological Problem in Isaac Hecker's Apologetic," in Thomas M. McFadden, *America in Theological Perspective* (New York, 1976), pp. 37–55.

10. Hecker, *Aspirations of Nature,* p. 360.

11. "The Future Triumph of the Church," in *Sermons Delivered during the Second Plenary Council of Baltimore* (Baltimore, 1866), pp. 66–86.

12. Isaac Hecker, "Notes on the Holy Spirit," Paulist Fathers Archives, Saint Paul College, Washington, D.C., pp. 3–35, and "The Church in View of the Needs of the Age," in *The Church and the Age: An Exposition of the Catholic Church in View of the Needs and Aspirations of the Present Age* (New York, 1887).

13. Hecker, "Notes on the Holy Spirit," pp. 22, 43, 112, 116–18, for summary of argument.

14. For a general survey of the ideas of these men, see Thomas P. Wangler, "The Birth of Americanism: Westward the Apocalyptic Candlestick," *Harvard Theological Review* 65 (July 1972):415–36. For dependence on Hecker, see Chinnici, *Devotion to the Holy Spirit,* pp. 36–48; Dease, "Theological Influence"; Gerald P. Fogarty, S.J., *The Vatican and the Americanist Crisis: Denis J. O'Connell, American Agent in Rome, 1885–1903* (Rome, 1974).

15. John Joseph Keane, "The Catholic Church and Economics," *Quarterly Journal of Economics* 6 (October 1891):25–46, here 37–38.

Chapter 9   Piety, Asceticism, and Prayer

1. Hecker to Brownson, March 15, 1844, in Gower and Leliaert, *Brownson–Hecker Correspondence,* p. 86; *Questions of the Soul,* chaps. 17–30; Brownson, "Mission of America," pp. 557–59.

2. Orestes A. Brownson, "Rights of the Temporal," *Brownson's Quarterly Review* 22 (October 1860):462–96, with quotations from pp. 464, 466, 467; see also "Civil and Religious Freedom," in H. F. Brownson, *Works* 20:308–42, reprinted from *Brownson's Quarterly Review* (July 1864);

"Recent Events in France," *Brownson's Quarterly Review* 18 (December 1871):481–502.

3. O. A. Brownson, "Rights of the Temporal," pp. 471, 473–74, 489.

4. For Hecker's work, see Mary Ethel Lyons, "A Rhetoric for American Catholicism," and John Farina, "Isaac Hecker's Vision for the Paulists," in *Hecker Studies*.

5. Isaac Hecker, "The Saint of Our Day," in *Paulist Sermons 1863* (New York, 1864), 90–102, quotations from pp. 96–97, 102.

6. Isaac Hecker, "Sermon on St. Patrick's Day," March 17, 1869, Paulist Fathers Archives, Washington, D.C., with quotation from p. 4.

7. For background to this essay, see Hecker, "Notes on the Holy Spirit," pp. 12–13, 72, Ash Wednesday, 1875; "Notes on Interior States while abroad in 1874, '75, ['76]," Paulist Fathers Archives, Washington, D.C.

8. "St. Catherine of Genoa," in *The Church and the Age*, pp. 170–80; "Notes on the Holy Spirit," p. 90; John Farina, "Isaac Hecker's Vision for the Paulists," in Farina, *Hecker Studies*, pp. 204–215.

9. For Keane, see Patrick Henry Ahern, *The Life of John Keane, Educator and Archbishop, 1839–1918* (Milwaukee, Wisc., 1955); Thomas E. Wangler, "Emergence of John J. Keane as a Liberal Catholic and Americanist (1878–1887)," *American Ecclesiastical Review* 166 (September 1972):457–78.

10. For a more thorough treatment, see Chinnici, *Devotion to the Holy Spirit*, pp. 36–48, with specific reference to pp. 12–13 and 41–42.

11. John Joseph Keane, "Inaugural Sermon," *Catholic Mirror* 29 (August 31, 1878):4–5; "Address to the Catholic Young Men's National Union," *Catholic Mirror* 30 (June 28, 1879):1; for his general thinking, see "Catholic Societies," in *The Memorial Volume: A History of the Third Plenary Council of Baltimore*, pp. 190–208.

12. See Chinnici, *Devotion to the Holy Spirit*, pp. 42–48, for complete treatment, and John Joseph Keane, *A Sodality Manual for the Use of the Servants of the Holy Ghost* (Baltimore, 1880).

13. O. A. Brownson, "Church Unity and Social Amelioration," p. 515; long quotation from "American Literature," in H. F. Brownson, *Works*, 4:203–20, here 212, reprinted from *Brownson's Quarterly Review* (July 1847). For further confirmation, see O. A. Brownson, "Catholic Secular Literature," in H. F. Brownson, *Works*, 19:293–308, especially 297–98, reprinted from *Brownson's Quarterly Review* (July 1849).

14. "Renunciation," in *Sermons Preached at the Church of St. Paul the Apostle, New York, During the Year, 1861* (New York, 1861), pp. 158–75, with quotations from pp. 164, 171. A longer analysis is in Lyons, "A Rhetoric for American Catholicism," pp. 56–94.

15. "Self-Denial," ibid., pp. 330–45, with quotation from pp. 336–37.

16. Hecker, *Questions of the Soul*, chap. 17ff; cf. Elliott, *Life*, pp. 315–16, and his chapter, "Father Hecker's Spiritual Doctrine," pp. 302–25.

17. Isaac Hecker, "Spiritual Guidance," *Catholic World* 46 (February 1888):715–16, with quotation from p. 715. Cf. "The Guidance of the Holy Spirit," ibid. 45 (August 1887):710–12; and (September 1887):846–47.

18. John Joseph Keane, *Pastoral Letter* (Richmond, Va., 1883), especially the section entitled "Holiness of Life," pp. 15–22, with quotations from pp. 18, 20.

19. Elliott, *Life*, pp. 305, 303.

234

NOTES TO CHAPTER 10

20. Keane, *Pastoral Letter*, p. 17.
21. As quoted in Elliott, *Life*, p. 188.
22. Hecker to Brownson [November 1, 1845], in Gower and Leliaert, *Brownson–Hecker Correspondence*, pp. 138–41, with quotation from p. 139; for his reading, see Elliott, *Life*, p. 311; and on his mysticism in general, see Farina, *An American Experience of God*.
23. Elliott, *Life*, p. 316.
24. Keane, *Pastoral Letter*, pp. 18–20.
25. For Hecker, see Robert W. Baer, C.S.P., "A Jungian Analysis of Isaac Thomas Hecker," in Farina, *Hecker Studies*, pp. 133–81; for Keane's understanding of "an intelligent Christian life," see *Pastoral Letter*, and for his views on women, see statements collected in Maurice Francis Egan, *Onward and Upward: A Year Book Compiled from the Discourses of Archbishop Keane* (New York, 1902). I do not believe that this issue can be pushed too far, but there seems to be a connection between the Holy Spirit as a principle of communion (the feminine) in the Americanist synthesis, and the general support for the equality of women that pervaded the movement. Further exploration is necessary.

Chapter 10   The Mystery of the Incarnation

1. John Joseph Keane, *Emmanuel* (Philadelphia, 1915), pp. 32–34.
2. On Elliott, see Joseph McSorley, *Father Hecker and His Friends: Studies and Reminiscences* (Saint Louis, Mo., 1953), pp. 237–53. The following interpretation of the Americanist image of Christ is based on Isaac Hecker, "Filial Freedom," and "Christ's Human Side," in *Paulist Sermons, 1864* (New York, 1865), pp. 217–28, 296–309; John Joseph Keane, "The Ultimate Religion," and "The Incarnation Idea in History and in Jesus Christ," in Rev. John Henry Barrows, ed., *The World's Parliament of Religions, The Columbian Exposition of 1893*, 2 vols. (Chicago, 1893), 2:1331–38, 882–88; James Gibbons, "The Needs of Humanity Supplied by the Catholic Religion," ibid., 1:485–93; Walter Elliott, "The Supreme End and Office of Religion," ibid., 1:462–65; A Diocesan Priest [Thomas F. Hopkins], *Novena of Sermons on the Holy Ghost in His Relationship to the World* (New York, Library Association, 1901).
3. Walter Elliott, *The Life of Jesus Christ* (New York, 1901), i–xxv; the quotation beginning "man's capacity" is taken from p. 3.
4. Elliott, *Life*, p. vii.
5. Ibid., p. xxv.
6. Hecker, *Questions of a Soul*, pp. 92–126; "Christ's Human Side," p. 303; Keane, *Emmanuel*, p. 25.
7. Keane, *Emmanuel*, p. 87.
8. Elliott, *Life*, pp. xxi, 438; Hecker, "Notes on the Holy Spirit," p. 24a; John Joseph Keane, "The Conflict of Christianity with Heathenism," *American Catholic Quarterly Review* 5 (July 1880):468–85.
9. Elliott, *Life*, p. 377; Hecker, "Notes on the Holy Spirit," p. 37a; Keane, *Pastoral Letter*, section on "Holiness of Life"; cf. Hecker, "Spiritual Guidance"; "The Church, in View of the Needs of the Age," in *The Church and the Age*.
10. Hecker, *Questions of the Soul*, pp. 231–48; Keane, "Catholic Societies,"

pp. 196–97; Elliott, *Life*, pp. 507, 511, 518. The view contrasted sharply with Rev. John Hennessy, D.D., "The Sanctity of the Church," in *The Memorial Volume: A History of the Third Plenary Council of Baltimore*, pp. 224–44.

11. Elliott, *Life*, p. xxii.
12. Ibid., pp. 423–24; cf. Hecker, "The Things That Make for Unity," *Catholic World* 47 (April 1888).

Chapter 11 The Crisis of Americanism and the Structures of the Catholic Spiritual Life

1. For "Pentecostal fire" cf. John Ireland, "Introduction to the Life of Father Hecker," *Catholic World* 51 (1890):285–93, as cited in Dease, "Theological Influence of Orestes Brownson and Isaac Hecker," p. 29, n. 43; on Preston, see Chinnici, *Devotion to the Holy Spirit*, pp. 48–56; on Elliott, see McSorley, *Father Hecker and His Friends*, pp. 237–53; on the Jesuits, Robert Emmet Curran, ed., *American Jesuit Spirituality, The Maryland Tradition, 1634–1900* (New York, 1988); on mission preaching generally, Dolan, *Catholic Revivalism*; for the citation of the Third Plenary Council of Baltimore, see Joseph Clifford Fenton, "Devotion to the Holy Ghost and Its American Advocates," *American Ecclesiastical Review* 71 (December 1949):486–501; on Frances Xavier Cabrini, see Pietro Di Donato, *Immigrant Saint: The Life of Mother Cabrini* (New York, 1960).
2. The description of Josiah Strong's *Our Country* is taken from Martin E. Marty, *Righteous Empire: The Protestant Experience in America* (New York, 1970), p. 158. The standard work on nativism for the period is John Higham, *Strangers in the Land: Patterns of American Nativism 1860–1925* (Westport, Conn., 1980), reprint; cf. Barbara Welter, "From Maria Monk to Paul Blanshard: A Century of Protestant Anti-Catholicism," in Robert N. Bellah and Frederick E. Greenspahn, eds., *Uncivil Religion: Interreligious Hostility in America* (New York, 1987), pp. 43–71. On the school controversy, see Daniel F. Reilly, *The School Controversy (1891–1893)* (Washington, D.C., 1943). The period is well discussed in Robert Emmet Curran, S.J., *Michael Augustine Corrigan and the Shaping of Conservative Catholicism in America, 1878–1902* (New York, 1978).
3. Preston to Jacobini, January 2, 1890, as cited in Curran, *Michael Augustine Corrigan*, p. 309. Nelson J. Callahan, ed., *The Diary of Richard L. Burtsell, Priest of New York: The Early Years, 1865–1868* (New York, 1978), i–xxvii, has the latest assessment of the "Americanizing" clergy.
4. The standard account is McAvoy, *The Great Crisis in American Catholic History*. For the international context, see Gerald P. Fogarty, *The Vatican and the American Hierarchy from 1870 to 1965* (Stuttgart, 1982). On Elliott's *Life*, see Lawrence V. McDonnell, C.S.P., "Walter Elliott and the Hecker Tradition in the Americanist Era," *U.S. Catholic Historian* 3 (Spring/Summer 1983):129–44, and John Farina, "The Uses of the Early Diary of Isaac Hecker," ibid. 3 (Spring 1984):279–93.
5. Klein, "Catholicisme américain," *Revue française d'Edembourg* (September–October 1897):305–14. Felix Klein had also written a preface to the French edition of Elliott's *Life*.

6. Charles Maignen, *Le Père Hecker: Est-il un saint?* (Rome, 1898); A.-J. Delattre, S.J., *Un Catholicisme américain* (Namur, Belgium, 1898); see also P. L. Pechenard, "The End of 'Americanism' in France," *The North American Review* 170 (March 1900):420–32.

7. The English text is in John Tracy Ellis, ed., *Documents of American Catholic History* (Milwaukee, Wisc., 1955), pp. 553–62; the Latin text is in *Lettres apostoliques de S.S. Léon XIII* (Paris: A. Roger et F. Chernoiz, 1903), 5:182–201.

8. The encyclical letters are printed in Etienne Gilson, ed., *The Church Speaks to the Modern World: The Social Teachings of Leo XIII* (New York, 1954). For background, see John Courtney Murray, S.J., "Leo XIII on Church and State: The General Structure of the Controversy," *Theological Studies* 14 (March 1953):1–30, and the important article interpreting *Testem Benevolentiae* from this perspective, Margaret Mary Reher, "Pope Leo XIII and 'Americanism,' " *Theological Studies* 34 (December 1973):679–89.

9. Leo XIII, "On the Christian Constitution of States," no. 4, in Gilson, *The Church Speaks to the Modern World*, p. 163; "Rights and Duties of Capital and Labor" *(Rerum Novarum)* 32, ibid., p. 222; cf. James P. Scull, S.J., *The Relationship of Institutions of the Natural Law with the Supernatural Order* (Rome, 1966).

10. "On the Christian Constitution of States," no. 10, in Gilson, *The Church Speaks to the Modern World*, pp. 165–66.

11. For reflections on *Satis Cognitum*, see John Courtney Murray, "Freedom, Authority, Community," *America* 115 (December 3, 1966):734–41.

12. For the text of *Divinum Illud*, see John J. Wynne, S.J., ed., *The Great Encyclical Letters of Pope Leo XIII* (New York, 1903), pp. 422–40, quotations from pp. 429–31.

13. For background, see Charles Curran, "The Changing Anthropological Bases of Catholic Social Ethics," *The Thomist* 45 (April 1981):284–318.

14. For a similar view of religious life, see Delattre, *Catholicisme américain*, p. 31, with its reference to the unpromulgated decree *De Ecclesia* of Vatican I. Leo's whole approach should be seen in the light of Vatican Council I. For background, see Patrick Granfield, "The Church as *Societas Perfecta* in the Schemata of Vatican I," *Church History* 48 (December 1979):431–46.

15. For background on the adaptation of preaching in the United States, see Thomas Joseph Jonas, "The Divided Mind: American Catholic Evangelists in the 1890's" (Ph.D. diss., University of Chicago, 1980).

16. For Leo's letter to Keane, see Ahern, *The Life of John J. Keane, Educator and Archbishop 1839–1918*, pp. 285 and 277–89 for reception of encyclical.

17. For information on the piety of Leo XIII, see Hubert Jedin and John Dolan, eds., *The Church in the Industrial Age*, vol. 10 of *History of the Church*, trans. Margit Resch (New York, 1981), pp. 257–69; André Boland, "Léon XIII," in *Dictionnaire de spiritualité* 9:611–15; on Preston and Zardetti, see Chinnici, *Devotion to the Holy Spirit*, pp. 48–56, 64–72. On Modernism, see Michael V. Gannon, "Before and After Modernism: The Intellectual Isolation of the American Priest," in John Tracy Ellis, ed., *The Catholic Priest in the United States: Historical In-*

vestigations (Collegeville, Minn., 1971), pp. 293–383. It is generally considered now that the reaction to Americanism and Modernism were of one piece, and the two need to be considered together. For purposes of convenience, I have focused on *Testem Benevolentiae*, although, as the career of Joseph McSorley indicates, the reaction to Modernism certainly influenced the development of Catholic spiritual life in the United States. Cf. McSorley, "The Church and the Soul," *New York Review* 1 (June–July, 1905):59–68, where he notes the sense of "ecclesiastical limitations" growing keener.

18. Leo XIII, "On the Christian Constitution of States," no. 6, in Gilson, *The Church Speaks to the Modern World*, p. 164. For further confirmation of this interpretation, see Curran, *Michael Augustine Corrigan*, pp. 505–20, on "The Bifurcated Catholic."

19. Ireland's article is "The Genesis of 'Americanism,' " *North American Review* 170 (May 1900):679–93. For background, see Thomas Wangler, "The Americanism of J. St. Clair Etheridge," *Records of the American Catholic Historical Society of Philadelphia* 85 (March–June 1974):88–105; Neil T. Storch, "John Ireland's Americanism after 1899: The Argument from History," *Church History* 51 (December 1982):432–44.

20. Joseph McSorley, "Devotion to the Holy Spirit," *Catholic World* 71 (June 1900):290–304, with long quotation from pp. 298–99. For a fuller analysis, see Chinnici, *Devotion to the Holy Spirit*, pp. 78–84.

21. McSorley, C.S.P., *The Sacrament of Duty and Other Essays* (New York, 1909), "The Sacrament of Duty," pp. 9–27, with long quotation from p. 23. It is interesting to note that the same book contained an essay on Christ as "The Ideal Man," pp. 28–47, which clearly continued the apologetic approach of Hecker.

22. Benjamin J. Keiley, "Devotion to the Sacred Heart," *The Catholic Mirror* (June 1, 1901):3.

23. The best example here is the Irish-Italian conflict. Cf. Rudolph J. Vecoli, "Prelates and Peasants, Italian Immigrants and the Catholic Church," *Journal of Social History* 2 (Spring 1969):217–68, and John V. Tolino, "Solving the Italian Problem," *American Ecclesiastical Review* 99 (September 1938):246–56. Ethnic conflicts also contributed to the tendency to concentrate on ecclesiastical structures.

24. *Longinqua Oceani* can be found in John Tracy Ellis, ed., *Documents of American Catholic History* (Chicago, 1967), 2:499–511, with quotation from p. 502.

Part IV   A Fractured Inheritance, 1900–1930

1. *The Review* (August 8, 1901), p. 301, as quoted in Alfred J. Ede, "The Lay Crusade for a Christian America: A Study of the American Federation of Catholic Societies, 1900–1919" (Ph.D. diss., Graduate Theological Union, Berkeley, 1979), p. 75. On O'Connell, see James M. O'Toole, "Prelates and Politicos: Catholics and Politics in Massachusetts, 1900–1970," in Robert E. Sullivan and James M. O'Toole, eds., *Catholic Boston*, pp. 15–65. For Mundelein and the "new generation of prelates," see Edward R. Kantowicz, "Cardinal Mundelein of Chicago and the Shaping of Twentieth-Century American Catholicism," *Journal of American History* 68 (June 1981):52–68, and Henry B. Leonard, "Ethnic

Tensions, Episcopal Leadership, and the Emergence of the Twentieth-Century American Catholic Church: The Cleveland Experience," *Catholic Historical Review* 71 (July 1985):394–412.

Chapter 12   Spirituality and Social Reform

1. Francis L. Broderick, *Right Reverend New Dealer: John A. Ryan* (New York, 1963), p. 18.
2. John A. Ryan, "Journal," 1892–1898, p. 38, Ba-32, Archives of the Catholic University of America (ACUA).
3. Ryan, "Notes, Moral Theology, History of Moral Theology," 1915, p. 57, Ba-33, ACUA.
4. Ibid., pp. 57–59. On Vatican I, see Roger Aubert, "Le Concile du Vatican et la connaissance naturelle de Dieu," *Lumière et vie* 14 (March 1954):165–96.
5. Ryan, "He Is Risen, He Is Not Here," Sermons, Ref. R–Sm, B2–43, ACUA; "Christmas," ibid.
6. Ryan, "God Is Charity," ibid.; "He Is Risen, He Is Not Here."
7. Ryan, "Journal," 1892–1898, p. 29, ACUA; "Self-Denial," p. 12, Ref. R–Sm, B2–43, ACUA; cf. "Whosoever doth not carry his cross and come after Me, cannot be My disciple," ibid.
8. Ryan, "Notes, Moral Theology, History of Moral Theology," p. 83; "Christmas"; cf. "I Am the Way, the Truth and the Life," Ref. R–Sm, B2–43, ACUA.
9. Ryan, "Journal," p. 39, ACUA; "Compassion on the Multitude," Ref. R–Sm, B2–43; "The Church and the Workingman," *Catholic World* 89 (September 1909):776–82.
10. Ryan, "Duty," Ref. R–Sm, B2–43, ACUA; cf. "The Church and the Workingman."
11. "Is the Modern Spirit Anti-Religious?," *Catholic World* 85 (May 1907):183–93.
12. For Bouquillon and the revival of moral theology, cf. his textbook, *Theologia Moralis Fundamentalis*, 2nd ed. (Bruges, Belgium, and Cincinnati, Ohio, 1890); C. Joseph Nuesse, "Thomas Joseph Bouquillon (1840–1902), Moral Theologian and Precursor of the Social Sciences in the Catholic University of America," *Catholic Historical Review* 72 (October 1986):601–619. For Ryan's views, see "Notes, Moral Theology, Fundamental," Ba-33, and "De Virtute Religionis," Ba-34, 1915, ACUA; "Moral Theology, St. Paul, 1902–1905" Ba-33, ibid.
13. "Notes, Moral Theology, Fundamental," 21–33; "De Legibus," pp. 65ff., Ba-33, ACUA.
14. "Duty"; cf. "Prayer," Ref. R–Sm, B2–43, ACUA; "De Virtutibus Theologicis, De Spe et Caritate," Ba-34, ACUA.
15. "De Legibus," pp. 72, 89.
16. "God Is Charity," Ref. R–Sm, B2–43, ACUA.
17. John A. Ryan and Moorhouse F. X. Millar, S.J., *The State and the Church* (New York, 1922). For background, see Broderick, *Right Reverend New Dealer*, pp. 118–20, and John W. Gouldrick, C.M., "John A. Ryan's Theory of the State" (Ph.D. diss., Catholic University of America, 1979).

Chapter 13   The Eucharist, Symbol of the Church

1. Rev. A. Letellier, S.S.S., "Nocturnal Adoration," in *Third Eucharistic Congress of the United States* (Westchester, N.Y., n.d.), pp. 128–37; Confraternity of Perpetual Adoration activity can be found in *Eucharistic Conferences*, p. 213.
2. John Talbot Smith, *The Catholic Church in New York*, (New York, 1905) p. 316.
3. "The People's Eucharistic League," *Emmanuel* 6 (January 1900):34–41; T. J. O'Brien, "Eucharistic Confraternities and the People's Eucharistic League," in *Third Eucharistic Congress of the United States*, pp. 121–27; Rev. Francis Xavier Lasance, *Visits to Jesus in the Tabernacle: Hours and Half-Hours of Adoration Before the Blessed Sacrament, with a Novena to the Holy Ghost and Devotions for Mass, Holy Communion etc.* (New York, 1898).
4. "Start of the Eucharistic Movement in the United States," *Emmanuel* 51 (February 1945):31–33; "Fifty Years of Eucharistic Service," *Emmanuel* (January 1945):1–3; John J. O'Brien, S.S.S., "Golden Jubilee of Our First National Eucharistic Congress," *Emmanuel* (September 1945):290–96; Joseph F. Rummel, bishop of Omaha, *The Sixth National Eucharistic Congress* (New York, 1931), pp. 215–30.
5. Pope Leo XIII, "The Most Holy Eucharist," in Rev. John J. Wynne, S.J., ed., *The Great Encyclical Letters of Pope Leo XIII* (New York, 1903); Cardinal James Lecaro, "Active Participation: The Basic Principles of the Pastoral-Liturgical Reforms of Pius X," *Worship* 28 (February 1954):120–28; *Third Eucharistic Congress of the United States*, pp. 37–39, for resolutions; cf. similar resolutions in *Eucharistic Conferences*, pp. 183–86.
6. Thomas E. Wangler, "Catholic Religious Life in Boston in the Era of Cardinal O'Connell," in Robert E. Sullivan and James M. O'Tolle, eds., *Catholic Boston: Studies in Religion and Community, 1870–1970* (Boston, 1985), pp. 239–72.
7. "Fifty Years of Service," *Emmanuel* 51 (January 1945):1–3.
8. Chinnici, *Devotion to the Holy Spirit*, pp. 57–77; Rt. Rev. William Stang, *Pastoral Theology* (New York, 1897), p. 310; cf. P. Corrigan, *Episcopal Nominations* (New York: Sullivan & Schaeffer, 1883), chap. 2; Edward McSweeney, "Roman Catholic Priest and the Public," *Catholic World* 47 (September 1888):743–51.
9. Rt. Rev. John Hennessy, "The Sanctity of the Church," in *The Memorial Volume: A History of the Third Plenary Council of Baltimore* (Baltimore, 1885), pp. 224–44; Rt. Rev. William Stang, "The Eucharistic Apostolate," in *Third Eucharistic Congress*, pp. 57–62, here p. 58.
10. For the relationship between Sacred Heart devotion and the Eucharist, see Leo XIII, "The Most Holy Eucharist"; Rev. William O'Brien, "The Relation of Devotion to the Sacred Heart and to the Blessed Sacrament," in *Third Eucharistic Congress*, pp. 165–77, and notes of congress, pp. 39, 90–91.
11. Rev. H. Brinkmeyer, "Priests' Eucharistic League," in *Eucharistic Conferences*, pp. 150–62, here p. 151.
12. See, for example, Brinkmeyer, "Priests' Eucharistic League"; Rev. D. J. McMahon, "The Holy Eucharist and the Personal Life of the Priest," ibid., pp. 60–73; D. F. Feehan, "The Holy Eucharist and the Ministry

of the Priest," ibid., pp. 74–88; Rev. John Price, "Relations of Priest and People," in *Proceedings of the Fourth Eucharistic Congress of the United States of America* (Pittsburgh, Pa., n.d.), pp. 163–70. The quotation is from Rev. Joseph Selinger, "The Holy Sacrifice of the Mass in the Economy of Christ," ibid., pp. 95–99, here p. 95.

13. Brinkmeyer, "Priests' Eucharistic League," p. 153. Cf. W. B. Hannan, "Jesus in the Blessed Sacrament, the Model of the Interior Life," *Emmanuel* 35 (October 1929):261–63, for a later example.

14. To support this interpretation, see Price, "Relations of Priest and People," especially pp. 168–69; Herman Heuser, "The Care of Churches and Sacristies," in *Third Eucharistic Congress,* pp. 156–64; R. Neagle, "Attendance at Mass on Sundays or Week Days," ibid., pp. 63–68; A. A. Lambing, "Our Defects in Saying Mass; Rubricae Praescriptivae et Directivae," in *Proceedings of the Fourth Eucharistic Congress*, pp. 149–60. Concerns for complete purity emerge clearly in the meditations in *Emmanuel* 2 (June 1896):130–36; 3 (March 1897):61–68; (May 1897):105–108; (July 1897):148–51; (December 1897):279–91. The quotation on purity is from *Emmanuel* 2 (June 1896):132. The work of Mary Douglas, *Purity and Danger: An Analysis of the Concepts of Pollution and Taboo* (New York, 1966), provides an interpretive schema.

15. Price, "Relations of Priest and People," p. 163. The promotion of this mystical identification was the whole purpose of the Eucharistic League. Cf. *Emmanuel* 1 (August 1895):119–23; (October 1895):147–49; 2 (January 1896):16–18; (March 1896):60–65; (April 1896):81–87.

16. R. Neagle, "Attendance at Mass on Sundays or Week Days," p. 63.

17. J. F. Foley, "How to Promote Devotion to the Blessed Sacrament among the People," in *Eucharistic Conferences*, pp. 89–114; Walter Elliott, "How the Real Presence Makes Converts," ibid., pp. 163–70. For this interpretation, see Gerald Ellard, S.J., "Pius X and Christocracy, Thirty Years After," *Orate Fratres* 10 (November 1935):8–14.

18. *Emmanuel* 3 (July 1897):148–51.

19. Price, "Relations of Priest and People," p. 169; cf. Joseph W. Printen, C.SS.R., "Woman, Her Dignity and Place in the World, Motherhood—the Ideal," *Sentinel of the Blessed Sacrament* 20 (January 1917):6–8.

20. "Pope Leo XIII on the Work for Poor Churches," *Emmanuel* 2 (July 1896):156–61, here 157.

21. V. F. Kienberger, O.P. "The Nun," *Emmanuel* 35 (November 1929):283–86, here 284–85.

22. "Pope Leo XIII on the Work for Poor Churches," pp. 157–58.

23. Sister of Notre Dame (de Namur), *Rabboni, Heart to Heart Before the Tabernacle* (New York, 1920), 9–10.

24. Gerald Ellard, S.J., "The Liturgical Movement: In and For America," *Thought* 7 (December 1932):474–92, here 479; for Katherine Drexel, see Lou Baldwin, *A Call to Sanctity: The Formation and Life of Mother Katherine Drexel* (Philadelphia: Catholic Standard and Times, 1987).

25. *Third Eucharistic Congress*, p. 117.

26. See Thomas M. Schwertner, O.P., "The Eucharistic Congress and the Holy Name Society," *Emmanuel* 32 (April 1926):110–16; "The International Eucharistic Congresses," *Emmanuel* (March 1926):73–79.

27. Leo XIII; "The Most Holy Eucharist," p. 520.

28. Cf. John J. O'Brien, S.S.S., "Golden Jubilee of Our First National Eu-

charistic Congress," *Emmanuel* 51 (September 1945):290–96, here 294; for unity theme, cf. also "Resolutions Adopted at Priests' Eucharistic Congress," *Eucharistic Conferences*, pp. 183–86.

29. Walter Elliott, "How the Real Presence Makes Converts," *Eucharistic Conferences*, p. 167; Rt. Rev. William Stang, "The Eucharistic Apostolate," *Third Eucharistic Congress*, p. 58; M. P. Boyle, "Significance of the Eucharistic Congress," *Proceedings of the Fourth Eucharistic Congress*, pp. 11–13, here 13.

30. Cf. *Office of the Blessed Sacrament for the Use of the Members of the Nocturnal Adoration* (Baltimore: Foley Brothers, 1884); Lasance, *Visits;* John Price, "Relations of Priest and People," *Proceedings of the Fourth Eucharistic Congress;* H. Brinkmeyer, "Priests' Eucharistic League," *Eucharistic Conferences;* D. J. McMahon, "The Holy Eucharist and the Personal Life of the Priest," ibid.; W. B. Hannan, "Jesus in the Blessed Sacrament, the Model of the Interior Life," *Emmanuel* 35 (October 1929):261–63; some typical pamphlets published by Sentinel Press are *The Real Presence, Eucharistic Directions, One Hour with Him, Our Tryst with Him*, and *Nine Thursdays*.

31. Schwertner, "The International Eucharistic Congress."

32. V. F. Kienberger, O.P., "Permanent Effects of the Eucharistic Congress," *Emmanuel* 33 (January 1927):5–9, here 5, 9; for proceedings of the Chicago congress, see *Twenty-eighth International Eucharistic Congress* (n.d.); for its impact, see *The Eighth National Eucharistic Congress* (1941), p. 5.

33. Cf. the detailed description by V. F. Kienberger, O.P., "The Eucharistic Congress," *Emmanuel* 36 (November 1930):283–94; *The Sixth National Eucharistic Congress.*

34. Gilbert Heuel, O.M. Cap. [sic], "The Holy Eucharist and Catholic Action," *Emmanuel* 42 (February 1936):37–45; William J. Halliwell, "24 × 4 × 7," *Emmanuel* (June 1936):160–63; *The Eighth National Eucharistic Congress; The Ninth National Eucharistic Congress* (Saint Paul, Minn., 1941). For recent interpretations of the period, see Philip Gleason, "In Search of Unity: American Catholic Thought, 1920–1960," *Catholic Historical Review* 65 (April 1979):185–205; William Halsey, *The Survival of American Innocence* (Notre Dame, Ind., 1980).

35. Michael McGoldrick, "The Eucharist as an Antidote for the Evils of the Present Day," *Emmanuel* 33 (July 1927):169–76; Bede Jarrett, O.P., "The Sacrament of Love," *Emmanuel* 36 (May 1930):124–28; Stanley B. James, "The Blessed Sacrament and Our Age," *Emmanuel* 35 (July 1929):188–91, here 191.

36. A Redemptorist Father, "The Social Value of Frequent Communion," *Emmanuel* 34 (September 1928):227–34.

37. V. F. Kienberger, "Permanent Effects of the Eucharistic Congress"; Heuel, "The Holy Eucharist and Catholic Action," p. 40.

38. As quoted from V. F. Kienberger, O.P., "Gleanings of the Eighth National Eucharistic Congress," *Emmanuel* (December 1938):44, 354–73, here 371.

Chapter 14   The Cenacle, Soul of Catholic Action

1. Helen M. Lynch, *In the Shadow of Our Lady of the Cenacle* (New York, 1941); Jude Mead, C.P., "Historical Background of the Lay-Retreat

Movement in the United States," in Thomas C. Hennessy, S.J., ed., *The Inner Crusade: The Closed Retreat in the United States* (Chicago, 1965), pp. 133–60; most helpful are the articles in *Proceedings of the First National Conference of the Laymen's Retreat Movement in the United States of America* (Philadelphia, 1928): Rev. Gerald C. Treacy, S.J., "The Beginning of the Retreat Movement in America," and Joseph L. Durkin, "Organization and Progress of the Retreat Movement in Philadelphia," pp. 13–20, 34–47; B. A. Seymour, "The Retreat Movement in the U.S. up to Now," in *Proceedings of the Third National Conference of the Laymen's Retreat Movement* (Detroit, Mich., 1930).

2. Shealy's address, "Retreats for Laymen," is printed in Gerald C. Treacy, S.J., ed., *Father Shealy—A Tribute* (Fort Wadsworth, N.Y., 1927), pp. 47–59. For McSorley's comments on the century, see "The Common Man," *Catholic World* (October 1956):6–11.

3. Statistics and information compiled from Seymour, "The Retreat Movement in the U.S. up to Now"; *Proceedings of the Fourth National Conference of the Laymen's Retreat Movement* (Pittsburgh, Pa., 1931); *Proceedings of the Fifth National Conference of the Laymen's Retreat Movement* (Washington, D.C., 1934); *Proceedings of the Seventh, Eighth, Ninth and Tenth Conferences, Laymen's Retreat Movement* (Latrobe, Pa., 1944–1945); *Proceedings of the First National Conference, Laywoman's Retreat Movement* (Chicago, 1936); Mead, "Historical Background of the Lay-Retreat Movement in the United States."

4. For the national movement, see the conferences listed above. Gloria L. McEntee, "Report of Historian," for Retreats International, 1974–1977, is very helpful on the women's movement. This was obtained, as were all the proceedings, through the kindness of Rev. Thomas Gedeon, S.J., the director of Retreats International, whose offices are at the University of Notre Dame.

5. For Shealy, see Michael Kenny, S.J., "Reminiscences of Father Shealy," in Michael Earls, S.J., ed., *Father Shealy and Marymount: His Lectures and Conferences* (Worcester, Mass., n.d.), pp. 11–18; Gerald C. Treacy, S.J., "The Pioneer," in Treacy, *Father Shealy—A Tribute.*

6. The address is printed in *The Common Cause* 1 (January 1912):112–14.

7. Terence Shealy, "The Retreat Movement," in Treacy, *Father Shealy—A Tribute,* p. 104.

8. Gerald C. Treacy, S.J., "The Beginning of the Retreat Movement in America," in *Proceedings of the First National Conference.*

9. Thomas F. Woodlock, "Mount Manresa," and John J. Foote, "The School of Social Studies," in Treacy, *Father Shealy—A Tribute,* pp. 8–25, 26–46; George Edwin Rines, "The Magazine with a Mission," *The Common Cause* 1 (January 1912):1–4; Thomas F. Woodlock, "The School for Social Studies," *The Common Cause* 1 (January 1912):83–85.

10. Shealy, "Citizenship in God's Kingdom," in Earls, *Father Shealy and Marymount,* pp. 80–91.

11. Rines, "The Magazine with a Mission," p. 2.

12. Shealy, "Retreats for Laymen," in Treacy, *Father Shealy—A Tribute,* p. 59.

13. Shealy, "Sociology," in Treacy, *Father Shealy—A Tribute,* p. 101.

14. Thomas F. Woodlock, "The School for Social Studies," *The Common Cause* 1 (January 1912):84.

15. Shealy, "The Harvest," in Earls, *Father Shealy and Marymount*, pp. 109–15, with quotations from pp. 111, 113, and 114.
16. Shealy, "The Children of Mary," in ibid., pp. 91–98, with quotation from pp. 95–96.
17. Woodlock, "Mount Manresa," in Treacy, *Father Shealy—A Tribute*, pp. 18, 20, 25.
18. Shealy's conferences and meditation are reported by George F. Roesch, "Notes of the First Retreat," in Treacy, *Father Shealy—A Tribute*, pp. 60–80, with quotation from pp. 76–77.
19. Treacy, "The Beginning of the Retreat Movement in America."
20. The encyclicals can be found in Joseph Husslein, S.J., *Social Wellsprings* (Milwaukee, Wisc., 1942), vol. 2.
21. *Mens Nostra*, in ibid., 8, p. 76.
22. Cf. the encyclicals *Ubi Arcano* and *Quas Primas* in Husslein.
23. The summary is that of Amleto Cicognani as analyzed in Kilian J. Hennrich, O.M. Cap., "The Basis of Catholic Action," *Homiletic and Pastoral Review* 35 (October 1934):20–30, with p. 21 for reference to Cicognani; see also *A Call to Catholic Action* (New York, 1935), for a series of addresses on Catholic Action in the United States.
24. McAllister, "Value of the Retreat Movement to the Lay Apostolate," in *Proceedings of the First National Conference*. For a general description of the impact of Catholic Action on the American laity, see Leo Richard Ward, C.S.C., ed., *The American Apostolate—American Catholics in the Twentieth Century* (Westminster, Md., 1952).
25. See *Proceedings of the First National Conference*, p. 85; Rev. Sigmund Cratz, O.M. Cap., "Catholic Action and Laymen's Retreats," *The Fourth National Conference of the Laymen's Retreat Movement*, pp. 11–15, with quotation from p. 14. This analysis is based on a reading of the national conferences from 1928–1948.
26. Cf. discussion by R. Emmett O'Connell in *Eleventh National Catholic Laymen's Retreat Conference*, 1946 (n.p., n.d.), pp. 31–35, with quotation from pp. 31–32. Especially helpful for this interpretation is the article by Justin McAghon, "Retreats and Catholic Action in Relation to Labor–Management Disputes," and discussion by Rev. L. Chiuminatto, S.J., in ibid., pp. 68–93, where a strong distinction is made between Catholic Action and social action.
27. Cf. Father Paul M. Lackner, "The Retreatant and His Spiritual Life After the Retreat," in *Twelfth National Catholic Laymen's Retreat Conference*, (Saint Louis, Mo., 1948), pp. 109–21; also, the comments in *America* 93 (April 2, 1955):2, on the social accents in Boston's retreats.
28. Logan Bullitt, "Discussion," in *Proceedings of the Sixth National Conference of the Laymen's Retreat League in the United States of America* (Patronage of George Cardinal Mundelein, 1936), p. 87.
29. Cf. the excellent discussion in Rev. Frederick Macdonnell, S.J., "The Format of the Retreat," in *Proceedings of the Third National Conference*, pp. 10–14.
30. Lackner, "The Retreatant and His Spiritual Life After the Retreat," p. 123.
31. John J. Griffin, "The Spiritual Foundations of Catholic Action," *Orate Fratres* 9 (September 1935):464. Cf. H. Carpay, S.J., *L'Action catholique* (Paris: Casterman, 1948), pp. 57–58, in which he argues that Catholic Action breaks down the juridical concept of church and the separation

of two orders of nature and grace. For this reformist interpretation
of the retreat movement I am indebted to some comments by Lucille
Okenfuss, one of the leaders of the women's retreat movement in Saint
Louis, in an oral interview, July 21, 1981. Cf. also Rev. Damien Reid,
C.P., "The Retreatant, Another Christ," in *Proceedings of the Seventh,
Eighth, Ninth and Tenth Conferences, Laymen's Retreat Movement*, pp.
243–49; Thomas J. Molloy, "The Common Priesthood," in *Eleventh
National Catholic Laymen's Retreat Conference*, pp. 146–55.

Part V   Seedbed of Reform, 1930–1965

1. For background to the liturgical movement, see William Busch, "From
   Other Times: A Voice of a Plenary Council," *Orate Fratres* 21 (Sep-
   tember 1941):452–58; Thomas O'Gorman, "From Other Times: Wor-
   ship and Grace in Religion," *Orate Fratres* 20 (October 1946):495–502;
   Alfred Young, "From Other Times: An American Prelude to Pius X:
   On Congregational Singing," *Orate Fratres* 21 (June 1947):356–62;
   Gerald Ellard, S.J., "Pius X and Christocracy, Thirty Years After,"
   Orate Fratres 10 (November 1935):8–14. On the "mystical body," see
   Joseph McSorley, C.S.P., "The Mystical Body," *Catholic World* 81 (June
   1905):307–14; Robert Hugh Benson, *Christ in the Church* (Saint Louis,
   1911). General background can be found in Paul B. Marx, O.S.B., *Virgil
   Michel and the Liturgical Movement* (Collegeville, Minn., 1957), chaps.
   3 and 4.
2. The standard work on Dorothy Day is William D. Miller, *Dorothy Day:
   A Biography* (San Francisco: Harper & Row, 1982). See also her two
   autobiographical works, *The Long Loneliness* (New York, 1952); *From
   Union Square to Rome* (Silver Spring, Md., 1938).
3. See "From Father [Thomas F. Price] Nazareth, N.C.," *The Missionary*
   (Epiphany 1903):124–26; Rev. William Sullivan, "The Non-Catholic
   Missions as an Epoch in the History of Christianity," *The Missionary*
   (Rosary 1912); "The Vital Principles of the Mission Movement," *The
   Missionary* (September 1907):16–19; and the piece mourning Father
   Elliott, *The Missionary* (June 1928):215. Copies of the magazine can
   be found at the Paulist Fathers Archives, Saint Paul College, Wash-
   ington, D.C.
4. Joseph McSorley, "Saint Thérèse, A Child Contemplative," *Catholic
   World* 75 (May 1902):198–214; "The Church and the Soul," *New York
   Review* 1 (June–July 1905):65–66; "The Common Man," *Catholic World*
   184 (October 1956):6–11; "The Cistercians," *Catholic World* 170 (December 1949):198–203; Dom Jean-Baptiste Chautard, O.C.S.O., *The
   Soul of the Apostolate*, translated with an introduction by Thomas
   Merton (New York, 1961 [1946]).

Chapter 15   Virgil Michel: The Priesthood of the Faithful

1. Michel to Father Abbot, August 12, 1918, in Michel, Virgil: Letters,
   1916–1918, Abbot's Papers, Box 99.1, Saint John's Abbey Archives,
   Collegeville, Minn. All further references to Michel's letters, lectures,

and notes will be in this archival collection. For Michel and Orestes Brownson, see Virgil G. Michel, O.S.B., *The Critical Principles of Orestes A. Brownson* (Washington, D.C., 1918); Jeremy Hall, O.S.B., *The Full Stature of Christ: The Ecclesiology of Dom Virgil Michel* (Collegeville, Minn., 1976), pp. 3–9.

2. Michel to Father Abbot, 25/iv, 1925, box 99.1. For Michel's distinctive combination of liturgy and social reform, see Godfrey L. Diekman, "Is There a Distinct American Contribution to the Liturgical Renewal," *Worship* 45 (December 1971):578–87; Hans A. Reinhold, *National Liturgical Week Proceedings* (1947):11. For Beauduin's influence, see Hall, *Full Stature of Christ*, pp. 12–21.

3. Virgil Michel, *My Sacrifice and Yours* (Collegeville, Minn., 1927); Dom Louis Trauffler, O.S.B. and Dom Virgil Michel, O.S.B., *Why Do Catholics Attend Mass?* (Collegeville, Minn., 1928); "Mass: Sacrifice in Christ," Michel Papers, Z-31; "The Life of Christ," ibid.; "Liturgical Prayer," ibid.

4. Michel, *My Sacrifice and Yours*, p. 6; Trauffer and Michel, *Why Do Catholics Attend Mass?*, p. 13; "Liturgical Prayer."

5. H. F. Flock to Rev. Virgil Michel, November 4, 1926, Michel Papers, Z-24.

6. Donald Attwater to Virgil Michel, 15/6/XXVI, Michel Papers, Z-22; Bishop Joseph Schrembs to Fr. Bede Maler, June 21, 1927, as quoted in Colman J. Barry, O.S.B., *Worship and Work* (Collegeville, Minn., 1980 [1956]), p. 274. For the general activities of the liturgical renewal, see Gerald Ellard, S.J., "America Discovers the Liturgy," *The Caecilia* 53 (September 1926):192–93; "The Liturgical Movement: In and For America," *Thought* 7 (December 1932):474–92; "The American Scene, 1926–1951," *Orate Fratres* 25 (October–November 1951):500–508.

7. Virgil Michel, O.S.B., "The True Christian Spirit," *American Ecclesiastical Review* 82 (February 1930):129–42, quotation from p. 130; "Mass: Sacrifice in Christ."

8. Alcuin Deutsch, "The Liturgical Movement as Related to Mass and Sacramental Devotion," *Emmanuel* 33 (October–November 1927): 299–307. For further opinions of Michel, see Marx, *Virgil Michel*, pp. 246–47.

9. Dom Gommaire Laporta, O.S.B., "Eucharistic Piety," *American Ecclesiastical Review* 80 (January 1929):1–13, quotations from pp. 3 and 8.

10. Senex, "Eucharistic Piety," *American Ecclesiastical Review* 80 (June 1929):625–31, quotation from p. 631.

11. William Busch, "The Eucharist as Means and as End," *Orate Fratres* 5 (March 1931):221–28; John LaFarge, "With Scrip and Staff," *America* 42 (March 8, 1930):529–31; ibid. (March 14, 1931):554–55; Howell, "Liturgical Piety," *Worship* 26 (April 1952):229–37; Michel, "Laymen's Retreat," #6, in packet marked "Lay Retreat," Michel Papers, Z-31.

12. As quoted in "Communications," *Orate Fratres* 5 (February 1931):197.

13. Michel to Shuster, February 13, 1929, Michel Papers, Shuster, George, Z-27.

14. Virgil Michel, "The Layman in the Church," *Commonweal* 12 (June 4, 1930):123–25; his "Christian Woman" was published posthumously in *Orate Fratres* (April 13, 1939):248–56. Cf. "A Parish Programme," Michel Papers, packet 3, Z-31, where Michel comments: "Future: ac-

tive and intelligent laity, will do many things re external work, that priest must do because laity have been kept down. Not laity run spirituals, but help run Catholic activities. That their function. Perhaps even minor orders in future?"

15. Michel to Father Gregory, October 6, 1938, Personal File. Cf. "Retreat, St. Benedict's, 1937," Michel Papers, packet 6, Z-31; "Mortal Sin," ibid., Z-31.
16. "Holiness," ibid., Z-31.
17. Michel, "The Layman in the Church," p. 125; "Why Not More Catholic Leaders," Michel Papers, Z-31.
18. "Backgrounds of Liturgical Movement," Michel Papers, packet 9, Z-31; "The Scope of the Liturgical Movement," *Orate Fratres* 10 (October 1936):485–90; "Frequent Communion and Social Regeneration," *Orate Fratres* (March 1936):198–202; "Course in Catholic Background and Current Social Theory," College of Arts and Sciences, Saint John's University, 1937–1938, University Archives, Michel Papers, p. 26. Although Michel broke from the dominant understanding of his period in many ways, he still accepted the theory of church–state relations taught by John A. Ryan. Cf. Dom Virgil Michel, O.S.B., *The Theory of the State* (Saint Paul, Minn., 1936).
19. For Michel's most complete statement, see "Catholic Spiritual Life," *Spiritual Life* 6 (September 1960):218–33, an article first written in 1937.

Chapter 16   Dorothy Day: The Heroic Ideal

1. As quoted in Robert Coles, *Dorothy Day: A Radical Devotion* (Reading, Mass., 1987), p. 11.
2. Dorothy Day, *The Long Loneliness*, p. 189.
3. Dorothy Day, *Loaves and Fishes* (San Francisco, 1983 [1963]), p. 119.
4. For background, see Miller, *Dorothy Day*, chap. 9; Mel Piehl, *Breaking Bread: The Catholic Worker and the Origin of Catholic Radicalism in America* (Philadelphia, 1982), pp. 69ff.
5. *Catholic Worker* 2 (June 1, 1934):1, 5. I am indebted for many of the following references to conversations and help from Brigid Merriman, a doctoral student at the Graduate Theological Union, Berkeley.
6. *Catholic Worker* 3 (December 1935):5, a translation of some of the ideas of Raymond de Becker, one of the editors of Mounier's journal, *L'Esprit*.
7. *Catholic Worker* 8 (June 1941):4.
8. As quoted in Coles, *Dorothy Day*, p. 25.
9. Day, "Obedience," *Ave Maria* (December 17, 1966):20–23, here 21.
10. As quoted in Coles, *Dorothy Day*, pp. 58–59 and p. 66, where Coles notes Day's fondness for Guardini's phrase. The best studies of her social action positions are Piehl, *Breaking Bread*, and William D. Miller, *A Harsh and Dreadful Love: Dorothy Day and the Catholic Worker Movement* (Garden City, N.Y., 1974).
11. As quoted in Coles, *Dorothy Day*, pp. 76–77. For the best presentation of her combination of obedience to hierarchical authority with social protest, see ibid., chap. 4. Cf. also Day, *Loaves and Fishes*, where she states: "The Church is infallible when it deals with truths of the faith such as the dogma of the Immaculate Conception and the Assumption

of the Blessed Virgin Mary. When it comes to concerns of the temporal order—capital vs. labor, for example—on all these matters the Church has not spoken infallibly," p. 118. This ability to combine a sacramental understanding of the church, strict obedience, and freedom in the temporal sphere cannot be understood outside of the historical context. It is similar to that of Jacques Maritain, *Freedom in the Modern World*, trans. Richard O'Sullivan (New York, 1936), which the Catholic Worker people used extensively.

12. Taken from Day's statement on the death of Onesimus Lacouture as cited in John Hugo, *Your Ways Are Not My Ways: The Radical Christianity of the Gospel* (Pittsburgh, Pa., 1986) 1:302–303. For Lacouture, see Jean-Claude Drolet, "Un mouvement de spiritualité sacerdotale au Québec au XXe siècle (1931–1965): Le Lacouturisme," *Canadian Catholic Historical Association* 1973 (Ottawa 1974):55–91. For further comments on Roy, see Day, *Loaves and Fishes*, pp. 124–30; idem, *The Long Loneliness*, pp. 276–84.

13. Day as cited in William D. Miller, *All Is Grace: The Spirituality of Dorothy Day* (Garden City, N.Y., 1987), pp. 58–59. This book, with a long introduction, is an edition of Day's writings on the spiritual life. For Hugo and his advocacy of Lacouture's position, see his *Your Ways Are Not My Ways*, vol. 1. For some general statements on the history of the retreats, see Miller, *A Harsh and Dreadful Love*, chap. 12.

14. For Day's comments, see "What Dream Did They Dream? Utopia or Suffering?" *Catholic Worker* 14 (July–August 1947):1, 4, 6; "Day After Day," *Catholic Worker* 8 (July–August 1941):3; "Called to Be Saints" *Catholic Worker* 12 (January 1946):2; Day, *The Long Loneliness*, pp. 273–94. For different comments on the retreat, see J. C. Fenton, "Nature and Supernatural Life," *American Ecclesiastical Review* 114 (January 26, 1947):97–105; Francis F. Brown, "The Retreat: An Encounter with Silence," *The Priest* 38 (April 1982):38–40. For Furfey, see editorial, "An Uncompromising Christianity," *Catholic World* 143 (September 1936):641–52; Charles E. Curran, "Paul Hanley Furfey, Theorist of American Catholic Radicalism," *American Ecclesiastical Review* 166 (December 1972):651–77.

15. For the 1951 comments, see Hugo, *Your Ways Are Not My Ways* 1:304; "An Interview with Dorothy Day," *National Jesuit News* (May 1972):8–10. Cf. her selections from the retreat in Miller, *All Is Grace*, pp. 53–60, especially Hugo's comments on "rigorism," p. 59.

16. For the content of Hugo's early retreats, see Fr. John J. Hugo, "In the Vineyard: VI.—Positive Christianity," *Catholic Worker* 9 (March 1942):2, and subsequent articles on "Negative Christianity," "The Two Rules," and "The Fundamental Principle of Catholic Action," *Catholic Worker* (April 1942):1–2; (May 1942):1–2; (June 1942):1–2. The full retreat is printed as *Applied Christianity* (New York, 1944), with the imprimatur of Francis J. Spellman; and more recently in Hugo, *Your Ways Are Not My Ways*, vol. 2.

17. Day, *Loaves and Fishes*, p. 128.

18. As cited in Coles, *Dorothy Day*, p. 50.

19. For Day's appreciation of Thérèse de Lisieux, see her book *Thérèse* (Notre Dame, Ind., 1960), and numerous selections from this and other writings in Robert Ellsberg, ed., *By Little and By Little: The Selected Writings of Dorothy Day* (New York, 1983). Day also published parts

of a pamphlet on "Holiness for All," by Archbishop Norbert Robichaud, in *Catholic Worker* 13 (February 1946):4.

Chapter 17   James Keller: To Light One Candle

1. For background, see James Keller, *To Light a Candle: The Autobiography of James Keller, Founder of the Christophers* (Garden City, N.Y., 1963); Richard Armstrong, *Out To Change the World: A Life of Father James Keller of the Christophers* (New York, 1984); John Catoir, "One Person Can Make a Difference," *Maryknoll* 79 (October 1985):55–57; Mary Dorothy Hurley (Sister Mary Felician, I.H.M.), *The History of the Christopher Movement* (M.A. thesis, Saint John's University, Brooklyn, New York, 1952). The quotation is from a letter of Keller's to James E. Walsh as cited in Armstrong, *Out To Change the World*, p. 60.
2. James Keller, "What About the Hundred Million," pamphlet reprint from *American Ecclesiastical Review* (May 1945). I am indebted to Father John Catoir, the present director of the Christophers, for access to their archives and especially to the Keller papers. Unless otherwise indicated, the material for all of the following can be found at the office of the Christophers, New York City.
3. *You Can Be a Christopher*, pamphlet reprint from *Catholic World* (January 1946):23; see also James Keller, *The Priest and a World Vision* (New York, 1946).
4. For statistics on the *News Notes*, see Armstrong, *Out To Change the World*, pp. 81ff.; Catoir, "One Person Can Make a Difference." Keller's major works include *You Can Change the World: The Christopher Approach* (New York, 1948); *Careers That Change Your World: Christopher Guides for Jobs That Make the Future* (Garden City, N.Y., 1950); *Government Is Your Business* (Garden City, N.Y., 1951); *All God's Children: What Your Schools Can Do for Them* (Garden City, N.Y., 1953).
5. The progress and organization of the May Day celebrations can be traced in the Keller papers, "May Day 1947–1951." The quotation is from *News Notes* 7 (May–June 1947):4. For background to the connection between Marian piety and anticommunism, see Thomas A. Kselman and Steven Avella, "Marian Piety and the Cold War in the United States," *Catholic Historical Review* 72 (July 1986):403–24.
6. Cf. Armstrong, *Out To Change the World*, pp. 135–201.
7. *News Notes* 14 (July–August 1948); *Catholic Missions* 9 (Autumn 1934):21.
8. *News Notes* 12 (March–April 1948), as cited in Armstrong, *Out To Change the World*, pp. 85–86.
9. Keller, *To Light a Candle*, p. 117; *News Notes* 12 (March–April 1948):4, citing a Belgian missioner in Beijing.
10. Sister David Miriam Shannon, O.P., to Miss [Carol] Jackson, January 27, 1948, Keller Papers, "Integrity file." Numerous letters in this file indicate that Keller had a large following who supported his missionary method.
11. Keller, *You Can Change the World*, pp. vi–vii, 20.
12. The classmate is Robert E. Sheridan, memo of August 15, 1977, "Keller Responses," Keller Papers. Sheridan gives the citation from Newman; *To Light a Candle*, pp. 50, 87; Keller, *The Priest and a World Vision*, p.

67. I am also grateful for the personal recollections of Florence Levins, Keller's secretary, interview by phone, January 2, 1985.

13. Keller's comment on "efficiency" is cited in Armstrong, *Out To Change the World*, p. 25; compare his comments in *To Light a Candle*, p. 119. For information on his activity in New York, see Armstrong, *Out To Change the World*, pp. 40–47; *Catholic Missions* 14 (October 1935):7, 14. For background, see Richard Wightman Fox and T. Jackson Lears, eds., *The Culture of Consumption: Critical Essays in American History, 1880–1980* (New York, 1983).

14. Keller, *To Light a Candle*, pp. 151–52; Keller, "Memos 1948–1955," Keller Papers. The books in the series were *Three Minutes a Day: Christopher Thoughts for Daily Living* (Garden City, N.Y., 1949); *One Moment Please! Christopher Daily Guides to Better Living* (Garden City, N.Y., 1950); *Just for Today: A Christopher Thought for Each Day of the Year* (Garden City, N.Y., 1952); *Stop, Look and Live: A Story for Each Day of the Year to Bring Out the Power Within You, A New Christopher Book* (Garden City, N.Y., 1954); *A Day at a Time: A Christopher Thought for Each Day of the Year* (Garden City, N.Y., 1957).

15. Keller, *To Light a Candle*, p. 99; *Catholic Missions* 13 (June–July 1936):6–7; "Historical Report # 1," Keller Papers, p. 4; *News Notes* 36 (June 1951); ibid. 35 (May 1951); *News Notes* 14 (July–August 1948):2. For background, see Donald F. Crosby, S.J., *God, Church, and Flag: Senator Joseph R. McCarthy and the Catholic Church, 1950–1957* (Chapel Hill, N.C., 1978).

16. *Catholic Missions* 13 (October 1936):14; cf. Armstrong, *Out To Change the World*, p. 62.

17. Keller, *To Light a Candle*, pp. 70, 112; idem, *You Can Change the World*, pp. v, xii, 49. See for background Halsey, *The Survival of American Innocence*, chaps. 8 and 9.

18. Keller, "What About the Hundred Million?" p. 3; idem, *You Can Change the World*, pp. 21, 28; idem, *Government Is Your Business*, pp. 298, 307; *News Notes* 96 (March 1959); ibid. 12 (March–April 1948):1.

19. Day's criticisms were acknowledged by Florence Levins, interview by phone, January 2, 1985.

20. Peter Michaels, "It Don't Come Naturally," *Integrity* 2 (January 1949):42–44; Feeney's criticism was related in James Keller, "Origins of the Christopher Movement," file "Origins Xers," Keller Papers [1952?]. The inquiry from the Vatican, quoted in Armstrong, *Out To Change the World*, p. 164, mentions the "invitation to all. . . ."

21. Keller's summary statement can be found in ibid., p. 163.

22. Keller to Monsignor Gaffney, March 30, 1959, "Chancery file," Keller Papers; "Origin of the Christopher Movement," in Keller Papers, p. 5.

23. For Keller's subsequent activity, see "The Christophers and Inter-Faith Groups," memo, "Gov't Is Your Business File," Keller Papers; "Report on Spiritual Reactions," September 1, 1954, Keller to Cardinal Spellman; "The Missionary Implications of the Christopher Movement," Keller Papers; *News Notes* for priests and religious throughout the 1950s; Armstrong, *Out To Change the World*, pp. 181–83; *Change the World from Your Parish* (New York, 1960).

24. Keller, *You Can Change the World*, pp. 56–58, 314.

25. Keller, "Christopher Tips for Lay Apostles," *Special Christopher Notes* 16 (c. 1960).

Chapter 18   Thomas Merton: Contemplation for All

1. The standard biographies of Merton are Monica Furlong, *Merton: A Biography* (San Francisco, 1980); Michael Mott, *The Seven Mountains of Thomas Merton* (Boston, 1984). Merton's reflections on his monastic period can be found in "First and Last Thoughts: An Author's Preface," in Thomas P. McDonnell, ed., *A Thomas Merton Reader* (New York, 1962), pp. vii–xii.
2. *The Secular Journal of Thomas Merton* (New York, 1959), pp. 183–84, 190, 193.
3. Ibid., pp. 232–38. For his letters to Catherine de Hueck, see William H. Shannon, ed., *The Hidden Ground of Love: Letters of Thomas Merton on Religious Experience and Social Concerns* (New York, 1985), pp. 3–24, with specific reference to the letter of October 6, 1941.
4. Merton to Catherine de Hueck, December 6, 1941, in Shannon, *Hidden Ground of Love*, pp. 9–11.
5. Thomas Merton, *The Seven Storey Mountain* (New York, 1963 [1948]), pp. 407–408.
6. Ibid., p. 408.
7. *Seeds of Contemplation* (Norfolk, Conn., 1949), pp. 15, 42, 50; *No Man Is An Island* (New York, 1955), p. xxiii; *Life and Holiness* (New York, 1963); *Contemplation in a World of Action* (Garden City, N.Y., 1973), especially the essays "Is the World a Problem?," "Contemplation in a World of Action," and "Final Integration—Toward a 'Monastic Therapy,'" with quotation from p. 171; *The New Man* (New York, 1961), p. 110.
8. See, especially, *Conjectures of a Guilty Bystander* (Garden City, N.Y., 1968), pp. 179–81; Raymond Bailey, *Thomas Merton on Mysticism* (Garden City, N.Y., 1974); John J. Higgins, S.J., *Thomas Merton on Prayer* (Garden City, N.Y., 1973); Gordon Edward Truitt, "A Historical and Theological Analysis of the Main Trends of the Catholic Theology of Prayer in the United States, 1940–1975" (Ph.D. diss., Catholic University of America, 1982); Mott, *The Seven Mountains of Thomas Merton*.

Index

Alcott, Amos Bronson, 91
American Ecclesiastical Review, 182
American Protective Association, 121
American Protestant Association, 40
Anti-Catholic societies, 70
Aquinas, Saint Thomas, 142, 160, 181, 208
Arch-Association of Perpetual Adoration of the Blessed Sacrament and the Work for Poor Churches, 80, 81
Arch-Confraternity of Perpetual Adoration, 151
Arch-Confraternity of the Blessed Sacrament, 68
Arundel, Lady, 1
Arundel, Lord, 1
Ascent to Truth, The (Merton), 205
Ashton, John, 24–25
Aspirations (Hecker), 95
Atonement, Spaulding on, 43–45
Attwater, Donald, 180
Augustine, Saint, 84
Auxiliary Church Building Association, 58
Ave Maria, 79, 82

Badin, Stephen, 29
Baltimore, Lord, 41
Baptism, 184
Baraga, Frederic, 69

Beauduin, Lambert, 178, 179
Bedini, Gaetano, 56
Bellarmine, Robert, 38, 54, 71, 160
Benedict XV, Pope, 75
Benedictines, 178
Benson, Robert Hugh, 173
Berger, Johann, 71
Berington, Joseph, 6–7, 21
Blessed Sacrament, devotion to, 68, 76, 81
Blessed Sacrament, The (Faber), 78
Bonaventure, Saint, 208
Borromeo, Charles, 71, 81
Bouquillon, Thomas, 142
Bourdaloue, Louis, 71
Breckinridge, John, 54
Brent, Anne, 1
Brent, Robert, 1
Breviary, reform of, 174
Brook Farm, 91, 96
Brownson, Orestes, 87–89, 91, 93, 94, 98, 130, 135, 139, 140, 160, 173
  on piety, 101–102, 107
Bruté, Simon Gabriel, 54, 55
Bullitt, Logan, 170
Busch, William, 178, 181, 182

Cabrini, Frances Xavier, 120
Call, The 174
Calvin, John, 60

Calvinism, 96
Canisius, John, 71
Careers That Change Your World
    (Keller), 195
Carey, Matthew, 28
Carnegie, Dale, 201
Carroll, Charles, 2
Carroll, John, 1–34, 36, 38, 40, 56,
    62, 71, 73, 85
  background of, 1–2
  Cathedral of the Assumption and, 2
  on charity, 23–24
  on Christian piety, 26–34
  ecclesiology of, 20–25
  on infidelity, 7, 13
  liturgy and, 16–17, 27–28
  matrimony and, 17–19
  meditation and, 31–33
  moralism of, 29–30
  on priesthood, 24–25
  religious pluralism and, 5–10
  Sacred Heart, devotion to, 30–31
  theological anthropology of, 12–19
*Catechism on the Foundation of Chris-
    tian Faith*, 9, 14
Cathedral of the Assumption, Balti-
    more, 2
Catherine of Genoa, Saint, 103
Catholic Action, 155, 156, 166–71,
    175, 187–89, 201, 202, 203, 207
Catholic Evidence guilds, 167
Catholic Missionary Union, 174
Catholic Missions, 194, 198, 200
Catholic Worker, 187, 201
Catholic World, 100
Catholic Young Men's National Union,
    105
Central Verein, 163
Chabrat, Guy Ignatius, 39
Challoner, Richard, 9–10, 27
Change the World from Your Parish
    (Keller), 203
"Charity" (Carroll), 23–24
Chautard, Jean-Baptiste, 175
Christmas crib, 76
Christopher Awards, 196
Christopher Career Guidance Schools,
    196

Christopher News Notes, 195–97, 203
Christophers, the, 174, 195–204
Church and state, separation of, 56, 57
Church Debt Association, 58
Church Review, 56
Cicognani, Amleto, 202
Clement XIV, Pope, 1
Cold War, 212
Common Cause, The, 161–63, 166
Communion, 100
Communism, 195, 196, 199–201
Confession, 28, 100
Confessions (Teresa of Avila), 71
Confirmation, 184
Confraternity of Christian Doctrine,
    169
Confraternity of Perpetual Adoration,
    146
Confraternity of the Servants of the
    Holy Ghost, 105–106
Congregational singing, 173
Congress of Jerusalem, 152
Conjectures of a Guilty Bystander
    (Merton), 206, 209
Contemplation in a World of Action,
    (Merton), 206
Conwell, Henry, 55
Council of Trent, 13, 182
Counter Reformation, 71, 75, 76
"Critical Principles of Orestes Brown-
    son, The" (Michel), 177
Croiset, Jean, 72

David, John Baptist, 37, 39, 45, 47,
    49, 66
Day, Dorothy, 174, 175, 186–93,
    201, 203, 207, 210–13
De Hueck, Baroness Catherine, 206–
    207
De Sales, Francis, 8, 29, 33, 71–73,
    81
Delattre, A.-J., 122
Deutsch, Alcuin, 178, 181
"Devotion to the Sacred Heart"
    (Keiley), 131-32
Devotional guides, 65, 101
Dichtl, Hermann, 71
Divinum Illud (Leo XIII), 123

Dominican Congregation of Saint Catherine de Ricci, 158
Draft Plan of Clergy Organization, 21
Drexel, Katharine Mary, 152
Dubois, John, 53, 54, 58, 68
"Duties of Parents" (Carroll), 14

E Supremi (Pius X), 136
Elder, William Henry, 83–84
Elliott, Walter, 88, 89, 110, 113, 119, 121, 150, 153, 174
  image of Christ, 114–18
Emerson, Ralph Waldo, 91
Emmanuel (Keane), 115
Emmanuel (periodical), 147, 150–51, 154, 155, 181
Emmerich, Anne Catherine, 71
Enlightenment, 73, 76
Essay Towards Catholic Communion, An, 6
Eucharist, 26, 28, 63, 68, 78, 144
Eucharistia (Kramp), 178
Eucharistic movement, 146–56, 175, 181–84
"Eucharistic Piety" (Laporta), 181
Evidences of Catholicity (Spalding), 39
Extreme unction, 100
Eymard, Pierre Julian, 147

Faber, Frederick William, 78
"Faith and Infidelity" (Carroll), 13
Farrell, Walter, 202
Feasts, 27, 63, 76
Feeney, Leonard, 202, 207
Fénelon, François, 9, 14, 72, 73, 81
Ferrick, John, 157
Field Afar, The, 194
Finlay, Sidney, 161
First National Conference of the Women's Retreat Movement, 159
First National Congress of the Laymen's Retreat League, 159
First Plenary Council, (1852), 70
Fitzgerald, James, 171
Five Sacred Wounds, 68, 76
Flaget, Joseph, 37, 39, 47
Fletcher, John, 7, 13
Flock, H. F., 179

Fordham University Law School, 161
Francis, Saint, of Assisi, 208
Franklin, Benjamin, 2
Free-market capitalism, 54, 58–61
Freemasons, 70
French Revolution, 7, 39, 94
Friendship House, 201, 207
Furfey, Paul Hanley, 191

Garden of the Soul (Challoner), 27
General Regulations (Chabrat), 39
Genesis story, 41–42
Gibbons, James, 104, 122, 127
Gonzaga, Aloysius, 81
Gother, John, 9–10, 27
Goverment Is Your Business (Keller), 195, 201
Gregorian chant, revival of, 173, 174
Guardini, Romano, 190
Guide for Sinners (Louis of Granada), 71

Hecker, Isaac Thomas, 88, 89, 91, 93, 99, 100, 113, 114, 119, 121, 130, 135, 138–41, 177, 189
  asceticism and, 107–109, 112
  on Holy Spirit, 97–98
  image of Christ of, 115–17
  Know-Nothing campaign, interpretation of, 95–96
  on piety, 102–104
  prayer and, 111
  on renunciation, 107–108, 189
  vocation of, 94–95
Hennessy, John, 50
Heuser, H.J., 149
History of the Religion of Jesus Christ (Stolberg), 71
Holocaust, 212
Holy Ghost, doctrine of, 105–106, 112, 117, 124, 130
Holy Name societies, 163, 169
Holy Trinity Church, Philadelphia, 22, 70
Homo Apostolicus (Ligouri), 71
Hoover, Herbert, 154
Hopkins, Thomas F., 50
Howell, Clifford, 182

Huby, Vincent, 10, 32, 73
Hughes, John, 46, 52–67, 69–72, 75–77, 79, 80, 82, 83, 85, 87, 91, 93, 95, 96, 98, 101, 106, 108, 111, 113, 119, 128, 138, 139, 141, 160
background of, 53
critique of emerging social order, 59–62
lay trusteeism and, 54–57
liturgy and, 63
Public School Society and, 56, 60
Saint Patrick's Cathedral and, 52
Hugo, John J., 191–93

Ignatius of Loyola, Saint, 8, 10, 66, 71–73, 102, 130, 160, 165, 166
Imitation of Christ (Kempis), 71
Immaculate Conception, 83, 84
Infidelity, Carroll on, 7, 13
"Influence of Catholicity on Civil Liberty" (Spaulding), 41–42
Institutiones Theologicae (Liebermann), 40
Instructions (Gother), 27
Intermarriage, 18, 55, 56
Introduction to the Devout Life (De Sales), 8, 33, 71, 72
Ireland, John, 98, 104, 121, 128–29, 131, 132, 133, 137, 173

Jackson, Carol, 201–202
Jacobini, Domenico, 121
Jansenist theology, 15
Jefferson School of Social Science, 199
Jesuits, 1, 10, 21, 71, 158
Joseph, Saint, 102–103
Journal (Neumann), 70–73, 81, 83

Keane, John Joseph, 88, 89, 100, 102, 120, 121, 127, 129, 130, 138, 140, 141
asceticism, piety and prayer and, 109–112
Catholic associationism and, 104–105
Confraternity of the Servants of the Holy Ghost, support of, 105–106

image of Christ of, 115–17
social system, principles of, 98–99
Keiley, Benjamin J., 131–33
Keller, James, 174, 175, 194–204, 210–13
Kempis, Thomas à, 10, 71, 81
Kenrick, Francis Patrick, 17, 65, 70
Klein, Felix, 122
Knights of Columbus, 163, 169
Knights of Labor, 98, 104, 105
Know-Nothing campaign, 95–96
Kramp, Joseph, 178

Lacouture, Onesimus, 191, 192
LaFarge, John, 182
Laity's Directory, 10
Laporta, Gommaire, 181, 182
Lasance, Francis Xavier, 147, 154
"Last Judgment, The" (Carroll), 5–6, 12, 15
Latrobe, Benjamin Henry, 2
Lay trusteeism
Hughes and, 54–57
Neumann and, 70
Laymen's League for Retreats and Social Studies, 161
Laymen's Weekend Retreat League, 157
Legion of Decency, 167
Legion of Mary, 201
Leman, Joseph, 152
Leo XIII, Pope, 89, 122–33, 136, 137, 138, 140–44, 147, 151, 153, 156, 161, 162, 166, 174, 178, 182
Lewis, John, 21
Liebermann, Bruno Franz, 40
Life and Holiness (Merton), 206, 209
Life of Father Hecker (Elliott), 88, 121
Life of Jesus Christ (Elliott), 113, 114, 117
Liguori, Alphonsus, 71
Lippmann, Walter, 201
Litanies, 76
Litany of Loretto, 27, 83
Litany of the Holy Name, 76
Liturgical movement, 174, 177–85

Liturgy
  Carroll and, 16–17, 27–28
  Hughes, and, 63
"Live Issue, The," 161
Living Rosary Society, 79
Living Wage, A (Ryan), 137
Loaves and Fishes (Day), 187, 192
Longinqua Oceani (Leo XIII), 133, 136, 144
Loughlin, John, 53
Louis of Granada, 71
Louisville riots, 95

Magna Carta, 41
Maignen, Charles, 122
Manual of Catholic Devotions, A, 63–64
Maréchal, Ambrose, 2
Marian devotions, 83
Maritain, Jacques, 187
Marmion, Columba, 197
Maryknoll, 174, 194, 202
Maryland Constitution, 7
Masses, The, 174
Matrimony, Carroll and, 17–19
Maurin, Peter, 186–89, 191, 192
May devotions, 76, 83
Mazzella, Camillo, 122–23
McAllister, Nilus, 168–69
McSorley, Joseph, 129–33, 158, 173–75
McSorley, Richard T., 157
Meditation, 31–33, 47, 63
Mens Nostra (Pius XI), 166, 167
Merton, Thomas, 175, 205–13
Michel, Virgil George, 174, 175, 177–85, 203, 210–13
Miraculous medals, 76, 83
"Mission of America, The" (Brownson), 100
Missionary movement, 174, 194–204
Missionary Society of Saint Paul (Paulists), 88, 89
Moore, Thomas Verner, 175
Mounier, Emmanuel, 187
Mount Manresa, 161, 163, 166
Mundelein, George, 135
Murray, John Courtney, 201

Mutual aid associations, 104
My Sacrifice and Yours (Michel), 179
Mystics and Zen Masters (Merton), 206

National Eucharistic Congresses, 147
National Labor Union, 104
Native American Party, 40
Nativism, 40–43, 54, 70, 95–96, 121, 127
Nerinckx, Charles, 37
Neumann, John Nepomucene, 46, 68–75, 76, 77, 79, 82, 83, 85, 87, 93, 96, 98, 101, 111, 113, 120, 128
  background of, 69–70
  eucharistic devotions and, 68–69
  Journal of, 70–73, 81, 83
  lay trusteeism and, 70
  on Mary, 84
  perfection, desire for, 72–73
  self-discipline of, 73
  sin, sense of personal, 72
New Deal, 137
New Man, The (Merton), 206, 209
Newman, John Henry, 197–98
No Man Is an Island (Merton), 205, 209
Nocturnal adoration societies, 146, 147, 152
Novenas, 76, 81
Nuns, 151

O'Connell, Denis, 98
O'Connell, William, 135–36
Odd Fellows, 70
Office of the Holy Week, according to the Roman Missal and Breviary, 27
O'Gorman, Thomas, 173
"On Civil Government" (Leo XIII), 123
"On Human Liberty," 123
"On the Christian Constitution of States," 123, 124
Orate Fratres, 178
Our Country (Strong), 121
Oursler, Fulton, 201

Parliament of Religions, 173
Parton, James, 58

Passion of Our Lord Jesus Christ (Emmerich), 71
Passionists, 157, 158
Pastoral Letter of 1883 (Keane), 109, 110
Pastoral Theology (Stang), 148
Paul, Saint, 66, 69
Penance, 28, 108
People's Eucharistic League, 146–47
Père Hecker, Le: Est-il un saint? (Maignen), 122
Philadelphia riots of 1844, 40
Piété de l'église, La (Beauduin), 179, 181
Pious Guide to Prayer and Devotion, The, 31
Pius VI, Pope, 21
Pius X, Pope, 127, 136, 147, 166, 174, 175, 178, 182
Pius XI, Pope, 136, 154, 156, 166–68
Plowden, Charles, 1, 6, 8, 21
Plowden, Robert, 16
Practice of Christian and Religious Perfection, The (Rodríguez), 10
Prayer, 62–66
Prayer books, 77–78, 173
Prayer the Key of Salvation, 65
Preston, Thomas Scott, 50, 119, 121, 127
Price, Thomas F., 174, 197
Priesthood
  Carroll on, 24–25
  eucharistic movement and, 147–50
  Spalding on, 77
Priests' Eucharistic League, 147–48, 154
Propaganda Fide, 146
Protestant Reformation, 59
Protestantism, 9, 79, 81, 121
Public School Society, 56, 60
Purcell, John, 39
Puritanism, 79, 96

Quarterly Review, 101
Quas Primas, 136, 154, 166
Questions of the Soul (Hecker), 95, 100, 109, 115

Red Men, 70
Redemptorist Order, 69–70, 94, 95, 158
Reflections on the Spirit of Religious Controversy (Fletcher), 7, 13
Religious confraternities, 78–80
Religious festivals, 63
Religious of the Cenacle, 158
Religious of the Sacred Heart, 158
Remler, E. J., 65
Renunciation, Hecker on, 107–108, 189
Rerum Novarum (Leo XIII), 137, 141, 161, 174
Retreat movement, 157–71, 174, 175, 191–93
Rheims-Douay version of Bible, 28
Ripley, George, 91
Rodríguez, Alfonso, 10, 29, 30, 33
Rosati, Joseph, 17
Rost, Anton, 71
Roy, Pacifique, 191–93
Ryan, John Augustine, 137–45, 159–62, 164, 174, 184, 188–89
  background of, 137
  Eucharist and, 144
  moral theology and, 142–45
  rationalism and, 138–39, 141
  religious liberalism and, 140–41
  social reform and, 139–40
Ryan, Stephen, 63

Sacred Heart, devotion to, 2, 30–31, 76, 131, 132
Saint Joseph's Church, Rochester, 69–70
Saint Mary's Cathedral, Philadelphia, 55
"Saint of Our Day" (Hecker), 101
Saint Patrick's Cathedral, New York, 52
Saint Paul Hymnal, 173
Saint Paul of the Cross Laymen's Retreat League, 157
Saint Peter's Church, New York, 21, 79
Saint Vincent de Paul Society, 104, 163, 169

Saints, communion of, 81–83
Satis Cognitum (Leo XIII), 123
Schlesinger, Arthur, Jr., 201
Schrembs, Joseph, 180
Scupoli, Lorenzo, 71, 72
Second Plenary Council (1866), 35, 40, 70, 96, 119
Secret societies, 55, 56, 104
Secular Journal (Merton), 209
Seeds of Contemplation (Merton), 205, 208–209
Self-denial, 108
Sentinel of the Blessed Sacrament, The, 146–47, 154, 183
Seton, Mother Elizabeth, 53
Seven Storey Mountain, The (Merton), 205, 207
Shealy, Terence, 158–66, 174, 184
Shuster, George, 183
Sign of Jonas, The (Keller), 205, 209
Sillon, Le, 187
Sisters of Loretto, 46
Sixth Provincial Council of Baltimore (1846), 83
Smith, John Talbot, 79
Smith, Lucy Eaton, 158
Social reform
  Day and, 186–91
  eucharistic movement and, 152–53, 155
  Ryan and, 139–40
Social Reform Press, 161, 163
Socialism, 140, 160, 174, 189
Society for the Propogation of the Faith, 194
Society of Mary Reparatrix, 158
Society of the Divine Word, 158
Sodality of the Blessed Virgin, 79
Sodality of the Holy Angels, 79
Sodality for the Holy Infancy, 79
Sodality of Saint Aloysius, 79
Soul of the Apostolate, The (Chautard), 175
Spalding, Martin John, 37–50, 66, 69, 70–72, 75, 76, 79, 80, 83, 85, 87, 93, 95, 96, 98, 101, 108, 111, 113, 115, 128, 138, 141

on atonement, 43–45
biblical interpretation of immigrant experience of, 41–43
on communion of saints, 81, 82
on corporate and hierarchical nature of social reality, 38–40
image of Christ of, 45–50
on Mary, 84
on priesthood, 77
Spanish Civil War, 207
Spellman, Francis, 202
Spiritual Combat (Scupoli), 71
Spiritual Exercises (Huby), 73
Spiritual Exercises (Ignatius of Loyola), 66, 160, 165
Spiritual Retreat, A (David), 66
Spiritual Retreat (Huby), 10, 32
Stang, William, 148, 153
State and the Church (Ryan), 144
Stations of the cross, 76
Stolberg, Friedrich, 71
Stourton, Charles-Philippe, 1
Stritch, Samuel, 155
Strong, Josiah, 121
Suárez, Francisco, 142, 160
Sullivan, John J., 157
Summorum Pontificem (Pius XI), 166
Supernatural Merit: Your Treasure in Heaven (Remler), 65
Synod of 1791, 18, 27, 28

Tabernacle societies, 146
Temperance unions, 104
Teplotz, Stephan, 71
Teresa of Avila, 71–73
Testem Benevolentiae (Leo XIII), 89, 122–33, 136, 144, 145, 173
Thérèse de Lisieux, Saint, 174, 175, 193, 198
Third Plenary Council (1884), 50, 63, 119–20, 130, 173
Three Minutes a Day—Christopher Thoughts for Daily Living (Heller), 198–99
Thuente, Clement, 152
Transcendentalists, 59
True Piety, 46, 77

Ubi Arcano (Pius XI), 136, 166, 167
Ursuline Manual, 77–78

Vatican I, 121, 138
Vatican II, 173, 174, 213
Vincent de Paul, 82
*Visits to Jesus in the Blessed Sacra-
    ment* (Lasance), 154
*Visits with Jesus in the Most Holy
    Sacrament of the Altar* (Liguori),
    71

Walsh, James Anthony, 174, 194,
    197, 198
Waters of Siloe, The (Merton), 205
Watton, James, 20, 22
Weld, Thomas, 1

"What About the Hundred Million?"
    (Keller), 195
Why do Catholics Attend Mass?
    (Michel), 179
Wilson, Thomas, 29
Women, role of, 150–52, 164–65
Women's retreats, 158, 159
Woodlock, Thomas F., 165

Xavier, Francis, 81

*You Can Change the World: The
    Christopher Approach* (Keller),
    195, 201, 203
Young, Alfred, 173

Zardetti, Otto, 50, 127